CASH IN!

CASH IN!

Funding and Promoting the Arts

ALVIN H. REISS

AN AUTHORS GUILD BACKINPRINT.COM EDITION

AN AUTHORS GUILD BACKINPRINT.COM EDITION

Published by iUniverse.com, Inc.

For information address:
iUniverse.com, Inc.
620 North 48th Street, Suite 201
Lincoln, NE 68504-3467
www.iuniverse.com

Originally published by Theatre Communication Group

ISBN: 0-595-08911-9

Printed in the United States of America

To the three generations in my life, living proof that you're never too old or too young to be creative. To Anne and Abe, Jen and Sam, Ellen and Steve, Bob and Mike. Thanks.

ACKNOWLEDGMENTS

Writing a book in four months is no easy task; in fact, in retrospect, it's a very tough job to do unless you have others contributing to your efforts. I'm very grateful to the many arts administrators throughout the country who answered my urgent questions, even under pressures of their own, and dropped everything frequently to send me the materials I needed when I needed them. In a very large sense this is their book and my hat, as always, is off to them. I'm grateful also to Lindy Zesch of Theatre Communications Group who had the good sense to suggest my undertaking this book at a cocktail party, rather than at a time when we were both perfectly sober. Perhaps most of all I'm deeply indebted to my editor, Robert Holley at TCG, whose on-target suggestions and professionalism played a key role in shaping this book. His encouragement and quiet confidence in me were the greatest factors in helping me to meet my ever-present deadlines. Even when I thought I wouldn't get there on time, Bob knew that I would and there he was, holding the door open for me.

CONTENTS

Contents

PROLOGUE

Who Needs
Money Anyway?

———————————————————————

2   A small snapshot pinned to my bulletin board reminds me of the fragile economic state of the arts. The picture, taken in Durham, N.C. in 1974, shows a smiling conference registrant—me—paying for his luncheon ticket. There's nothing unusual about the scene except for the fact that the keynote speaker at the luncheon for which I was paying was—me.

In the nonprofit arts few things come free. To put it another way, nobody—except top artists—flies first class. In fact, if there was a cheaper fare than super saver, a penury class, arts administrators would find it and use it. Having flown tens of thousands of miles to speak and consult, I'm still waiting for my first first-class ticket.

That the arts need money is readily evident to even the most casual observer of the nonprofit economy. The reason is simple. Because it is a handcrafted product in an automated society, the cost of producing a cultural program increases at a much faster rate than does the cost of producing a mass-produced item. Each performance of a theatre work, an opera or a symphonic concert is a totally new product, and cutting out lines of dialogue from a play, dropping (as was actually suggested by one board member) the second violins from an orchestra—"because it they're not good enough to be first, why do you need them?"—or making a *pas de deux* into a *pas d'un* as economy measures, obviously will not only alter the artistic products so as to make them unrecognizable, but will also make them decidedly inferior to what they were.

In an apparent paradox, many nonprofit arts groups end their seasons in the red even when they have hung out the SRO sign nightly. The reason, however, is understandable. Cultural organizations, in effect, subsidize their products so that they will be available at the lowest possible prices for the audiences they wish to reach. Special efforts, often at considerable sacrifice, are made to reach audiences, students and senior citizens among them, who, because of cost, cannot afford the arts experience.

At the lively Public Theater, the home of the New York Shakespeare Festival, where four or five productions are presented each night, an unusual and highly commendable policy has been in effect for a number of years. Regardless of a production's popularity, up to 25 percent of all available tickets are set aside each evening as discount tickets. Viewed in the light of this kind of cultural altruism, the term deficit seems inappropriate. The gap between income and expenses actually might best be viewed as a needed *repayment for services already rendered.*

Whatever terminology is used, it still comes down to the same thing—a need for money. Perhaps a hypothetical case might best illustrate just how fragile the arts economy is. Envision the following scenario: A theatre company has just completed a successful season with earned income and donations at a record high and, for the first time, no red ink spilling on the page. A time for self-congratulation or complacency? Hardly. The very next season an anticipated government grant might be denied, a sizable foundation award might arrive weeks later than expected, a corporate contributor of substance might move its headquarters to a new city or shift to a new area of interest, single-seat sales might drop substantially when a new production "bombs" or subscribers might be alienated by the season's productions. In other words, no financial cushion is ever too fat for a nonprofit arts group.

The precarious state of the arts economy, especially in the face of stagnant or declining federal support, is evidenced anew each year when national arts service organizations release their annual economic studies. *Theatre Facts 85,* Theatre Communications Group's study of its 217 participating theatres, showed that in 1985 the theatres presented more productions, played to larger audiences, increased their income substantially and still, by season's end, showed a collective operating deficit of more than $4.5 million, the fourth consecutive year that expenses exceeded income. Moreover, a detailed study of a sample group of 37 of the larger theatres showed that although total attendance and subscriptions reached a five-year high and earnings increased by 8 percent, expenses increased by 11 percent, creating a gap between income and expenses 15 percent higher than the previous year.

In other disciplines, the results were the same. Opera America reported in its *Profile Report* that in 1984 the number of companies with deficits grew from 34 to 43 out of the 80 reporting, and the total deficit for all companies showing losses more than doubled to $10.9 million. In the period between 1980 and 1984, the same survey showed that although income increased by 60 percent, expenses increased at a faster rate, 65 percent. In the symphony orchestra field, the same tale of economic woes was repeated with the total deficits of America's 250 professional orchestras spiraling from $500,000 to $10 million between 1974 and 1984.

Given this situation, arts groups have learned to be tenacious in their pursuit of available funds and wildly imaginative and creative in cultivating new sources of income. They have also learned to exercise sound financial judgment, good business sense, top management skills, undaunted optimism in the face of crisis and, above all,

4   a sense of humor when faced with adversity. When Glynn Ross accepted a job as general director of the Arizona Opera Company in 1983, he found himself faced with an accumulated deficit of more than $250,000. He immediately launched a successful "There Is Life After Debt" campaign, along with a sales blitz that sold 81 percent of the house in three weeks. Within a year the deficit was wiped out. Perhaps if Thomas J. Peter were to write a sequel to his best-seller, *In Search of Excellence*, focusing on the nonprofit field, he would find many examples of well-run organizations from among cultural institutions.

The experience of the Old Globe Theatre in San Diego indicates just how sound the financial judgment of an arts organization can be. The theatre suffered an arson-inspired fire in 1978 which destroyed its original structure, and by 1981 its accumulated deficit had risen to $709,000. Instead of launching a public appeal for retirement of the deficit, the theatre's board and staff made the hard decision to direct their total efforts instead toward theatre growth. Relying on sound financial management, they hoped to retire the deficit over a period of years. By the beginning of the 1985-86 season, the annual budget had jumped over 400 percent from $1.5 million in 1981 to $6.5 million, subscriptions had grown to a record 50,000 plus, houses went from 64 percent of capacity to 95 percent and membership from under 200 to 3,400. Moreover, by the end of 1985, the deficit had been reduced to $129,000 and was moving downward.

In the sea of red ink in which arts groups frequently find themselves immersed, size has been no barrier to creative activity. In fact, small groups have sometimes shown that they can be as resourceful and skillful in pursuit of available funds as the most sophisticated university or health organization.

Take the case of the Detroit Community Music School, an operation whose annual budget is only about $870,000. In spite of its relatively small operation, the school has been able to produce an annual funding event that in a single night earns over $125,000, or about 15 percent of its budget. The event is the school's International Wine Auction, an annual fund-raiser held since 1982, which not only helps fill the school's coffers but brings it tremendous local and national attention.

The concept of a wine auction isn't totally new. Few things are. But its success demonstrates that an arts group relying on imagination, hard work and good planning can pull off a funding event of significant proportions. The lesson learned from the Detroit experiences is that arts groups should *adapt*, not *adopt*.

Wine auctions to benefit charitable organizations have been held for some time in the California Napa wine-growing district: the activity is initiated by local vintners to promote their wines while benefitting worthwhile local charities. When a recently relocated Californian joined the music school board in 1982, he recalled the success of the Napa wine auction and suggested that perhaps a similar program might work in Detroit if everyone in the organization got behind it.

They did, and thanks to an all-out effort by board members, volunteers and staff, virtually every wine-oriented business and individual in the Detroit area, from distributors to wholesalers to retailers to private wine collectors, was canvassed to solicit donations of rare and quality wines. The one-on-one campaign extended to California, where leading wineries were approached by mail and by phone to donate to the campaign as a prestigious way of promoting their wines in an area away from their own market place.

The campaign worked and it worked so well that the event—a black tie, $100-per-person affair that includes a wine tasting reception, wine auction and gourmet dinner—has grown in scope, luster and financial reward each succeeding year. Although participation by California vintners was limited initially and most of the donated wine came from the Detroit area, the success of the first year's affair attracted the Californians' attention, and now some of the country's most illustrious wineries participate in what has resulted in a virtual annuity for the school. Net income from the auction has climbed from $40,000 in 1982 to $129,000 in 1985, and a well-organized volunteer structure has been developed to follow through on every step of the campaign.

To indicate the event's status, in addition to its obvious financial success, it now attracts wine connoisseurs who fly in from all over the country to purchase thousands of dollars-worth of wine. Honorary chairmen have included such illustrious wine luminaries as Louis Martini, Robert Mondavi and Brother Timothy of Christian Brothers. Additionally, the school has won new students to its ranks from parents first attracted to the school because of the auction.

Wine may seem alien to the arts funding mix, but it is only one of many seemingly unlikely ingredients used to help funds flow to cultural institutions. For, as arts groups have learned over the past few decades, income from ticket sales and grants from government agencies, corporations and foundations must be supplemented. As long as some basic rules of good taste and propriety are observed, and as long as the cultural product isn't tampered with or changed merely to raise funds, virtually anything goes.

6   That anything ranges from a "Clothes off Your Back Ball" to an opera pub hop to a win-an-orchestra contest to an arts day at the races. From fund-raising dinners held in estate settings to swine balls to musical picnics, little has been left untried in the arts quest for funds—especially if it works. And the real creativity in raising funds and promoting programs isn't solely in coming up with an original idea. Few ideas are totally original. The real talent lies in taking an idea that's already been used, reshaping it to an organization's image or a current situation and then presenting it in a new and different way. In other words, the genius lies in *adapting* rather than *adopting*.

    Some years ago the New York Public Library came up with a "Gifts of Gold" campaign, an idea triggered by the discovery of then board chairman Richard Saloman that he had lost one gold cufflink. Wondering what he might do with the remaining cufflink led to the thought that he, and others in similar situations, could donate their unneeded gold to the library. As a result, the library arranged for a certified goldsmith to be stationed in the library for a period of several weeks to appraise donations of gold—everything from jewelry to gold teeth to coins—and issue evaluation certificates to donors. The campaign worked so well that the library raised $20,000 from donated gold items.

    The library's concept was imaginative enough, but Arena Stage in Washington, D.C. went one step further when it refined the golden idea. Arena arranged a similar campaign, but had it underwritten by the P. Lorillard Company. Lorillard is the maker of Old Gold cigarettes.

    But even that wasn't all. To promote interest in the gold campaign, Arena staged a kick-off and invited such "golden" celebrities as the Treasurer of the United States, and Frances Sternhagen and Tom Aldrich, who were then starring in the Kennedy Center production of *On Golden Pond*.

    But who knows? Perhaps in the future some enterprising arts group might launch the next "Gifts of Gold" campaign in its most fitting locale—Fort Knox. That *would* be a golden opportunity.

CHAPTER 1

Who Are You, What Are You Selling and Why Should Anyone Want to Give You Money?

---

10   Nonprofit arts groups are different from their commercial counterparts, and the difference isn't only in their attitude towards money. Because nonprofits develop their art for its own value and not for its commercial potential—although obviously it's nice to break even—the product is more important than its marketability. While Coca-Cola could introduce a new improved version of the old Coke in the hopes of increasing its market share and tapping new audiences (and in the process discover that the strategy wasn't so sound after all), one doesn't introduce a new improved *Hamlet* with an octogenarian in the title role, or *Don Giovanni* played by a soprano, *merely* because senior citizens or feminists might be lured to the performance. If a change is made in a play, that change should come from an aesthetic concern, and must grow out of a strong, identifiable artistic point of view.

THE ARTISTIC VIEWPOINT

Television shows are geared to winning the biggest audiences on the audiences' terms; the audience, therefore, serves as tastemaker to the medium. The nonprofit arts group, however, plans its programming from an aesthetic viewpoint. It serves as the tastemaker, nurturing and developing an audience on its own artistic terms. Robert Brustein, artistic director of the American Repertory Theatre in Cambridge, Mass., articulated his concern for this kind of identity when he accepted the prestigious Jujamcyn Theatres Award in 1985. "The not-for-profit theatres centered in so many American cities must incessantly try to maintain their identity in the face of mounting pressures to change them," Brustein said. "Only by adhering to our original goals can we continue to provide help for each other and preserve the diversity that becomes a great culture."

Even when a theatre company hits the popular jackpot with one of its productions, it doesn't yank out the rest of a subscription series and replace it with performance after performance of the hit. It might take the production to Broadway or re-introduce it at some later date, but it will seldom if ever change a season for commercial reasons alone. In the few instances where it has happened, the results have proven embarrassing.

THE RIGHT TO FAIL

While remaining true to its audiences and maintaining its artistic integrity, the nonprofit arts group also must have the right to fail.

In the commercial world of entertainment, if you fail, you fail in out-   **11**
of-the-way places on the road (a Broadway bomb is very costly) or
as a summer replacement pilot—and you fail only briefly. Then you
change your product to accommodate the marketplace. If that doesn't
work, you kill the product, although sometimes death is costly and
painful. Remember *Breakfast at Tiffany's*? Remember *Moose
Murders*? Remember Edsel? But in the world of regional theatre,
dance, and opera, failure, at least in the popular sense, may be a vital
part of a group's artistic development. Artistic experimentation, call
it "research and development" in business terms, is a step toward
artistic growth and, at times, box office failure may be the price to
pay for achieving this growth.

Audience trust in an organization's artistic viewpoint is a vital
factor in the organization's fund-raising program. Putting it another
way, organizations with poor artistic products and no discernible artistic policies will have tough times attracting audiences and raising
funds.

If the artistic product is the linchpin in the funding process, there
are other vital ingredients as well. The successful campaign pinpoints
the excellence of the organization and its products and promotes
them, recognizes both the traditional audiences and devises strategies
to reach them, draws upon all the organization's available resources
including its internal audiences or "publics"—staff, board members
and volunteers—and utilizes techniques that get the best results at
the lowest cost. And before it ever attempts to reach out to others,
the organization knows itself, its products, its strengths and its
weaknesses. It has defined its artistic and organizational goals and
it has developed long-range plans to reach them.

PROMOTING THE PRODUCT

But while arts groups may play by a different set of rules from
those of their commercial counterparts, they're neither stuffy nor rigid
in their campaigns to reach their goals. They can't afford to be.
Perhaps one doesn't sell plays and concerts precisely the way one
sells soapsuds, but the same kinds of sales techniques must be used.
At times, in fact, arts groups must sell harder than any used car
salesman does, even if they have a better product to sell. It's no
wonder then that arts campaigns have been funny, provocative, even
sexy. What's wrong with jogging shorts reading "Mostly Mozart's Off
and Running" or a symphony orchestra proclaiming, "We play
around a lot"? While arts groups shouldn't change their products
merely to sell them, they can and should change the wrappings in

12   which they're packaged as frequently as necessary in order to draw audiences and tap the funds needed to keep the program going.

SELLING AN EXPERIENCE

Several years ago, when the Philadelphia Museum of Art was trying to up its attendance and boost membership, it hired a new advertising agency whose most comparable experience was that it had represented an Atlantic City casino, Caesar's Boardwalk Regency. The justification was simple. Marston Myers, marketing vice president of Tyson Ketchum Advertising Agency, said in a *Philadelphia Inquirer* interview, "It seemed to us that selling a museum is selling an experience. And although selling experiences is not all that common, we regard our work for Caesar's as selling an experience."

Those arts administrators who have learned how to market an experience can give a big boost to their programs while also calling attention to themselves. When Glynn Ross was drawing notice to the Seattle Opera with such memorable concepts as promoting *Madame Butterfly* at Union 76 gas stations throughout the state with posters proclaiming "Opera's a Gas" and gas attendants wearing buttons reading "Join the Opera Union," he was approached by a Fortune 500 company interested in hiring him as its corporate promotion director. Perhaps someone in the corporate hierarchy had noticed his Madison Avenue-ish gas station slogan: "Come to the Opera and Bring Ethyl."

EMPHASIZING UNIQUENESS

Assuming that there is an unassailable artistic viewpoint, a worthwhile program and that the rest of house is in order, where does the arts promotional campaign begin? Perhaps the best way to answer that question is to ask a question, one that every organization should ask itself. What is unique about my organization and my program? What sets my program apart from other programs?

Every organization should have some characteristics that set it apart from other groups in the same artistic discipline or the same community. It should have an individuality that can be promoted in the marketplace. In some way or through some activity it should be an "only."

The theatre that can claim to be the only professional theatre in the community has a saleable message. If it is one of several, however, it may have to establish its uniqueness throgh its work or through some aspect of its program. Perhaps it's the only professional theatre that does new works exclusively or that plays in rotating repertory. Perhaps its uniqueness lies in its size (it's the largest) in its scope (it has the longest season with the most plays) in the recognition it has won or in the distinctive kinds of productions it has presented.

Isolating uniqueness is one thing, but communicating uniqueness is another. It takes an awareness of the marketplace, knowledge of the competition and professional communications skills. It takes adaptability as well, since uniqueness, in addition to its importance as an organizational feature, is transitory. Goals can shift and tastes can change and what is emphasized today may be muted tomorrow.

The Brooklyn Academy of Music has been able to overcome mammoth difficulties brought about by its away-from-the-marketplace location and emphasize instead its unique programming concepts. What it has concentrated on communicating is its leadership in the new and the adventurous. What you get in Brooklyn, such as The Next Wave festival of avant-garde performance, you don't get elsewhere, BAM seems to be saying. The deadliness of its formal full name, which conjures up the image of a staid concert hall with stuffy programming—which indeed it once was—has been altered with the new BAM message, and the Brooklyn Academy of Music is now BAM to everyone who knows it.

Several years ago, in fact, to reinforce the BAM name and to generate some earned income at the same time, BAM developed an unusual partnership with a group of America's top comic strip cartoonists through the Newspaper Comics Council. The creators of such famed strips as "Kerry Drake," "Beetle Bailey," "Hagar the Horrible" and "Steve Canyon" designed new limited-edition posters available for purchase at $20 each, featuring their characters promoting BAM and its music, dance and theatre programs. A "Blondie" poster showed Dagwood in the proverbial act of crashing into the mailman. The force of the collision was punctuated by the word, "BAM."

LOGOS

The range of techniques available to help an organization isolate and promote itself and its uniqueness is infinite. Visual identity can be a key. A logo, an organization's visual symbol, is essential, especially if it is so related to the group's image that it can remind viewers of the group without anything else accompanying it. An envelope or

14 letterhead showing the "literary lion" immediately conjures up images of the New York Public Library, while a building design with flags on the top identifies itself to San Diegoans as the calling card of the Old Globe Theatre. In El Paso, the city's arts resources department created a logo that aroused considerable controversy when it was introduced several years ago, but proved so effective a recognition factor and so promotable that it is still being used. The border city highlighted its cultural ties to nearby Mexico with a logo featuring a sombrero-wearing, guitar-strumming Mona Lisa. The relationship was inescapable.

A logo, in fact, can be such a key device that one national organization, Young Audiences, developed an entire publication to instruct its chapters on proper use of its logo. The booklet, *Young Audiences Identity Guidelines*, shows chapters how most effectively to display the readily identifiable logo—a bright sun drawn with childlike simplicity—on stationary, publications, tote bags, posters and calendars.

For groups that do not have memorable logos or that might wish to establish a new image, a logo contest may be the answer. To heighten interest and attention, top local advertising and marketing executives can be asked to be judges, which will serve another purpose as well—it will help tie them to the arts organization and open the door to future relationships. Local banks and department stores might even feature the winning entries and runners-up in their windows.

To promote ACTFEST, Alaska's biennial community theatre festival, administrators sponsored a statewide contest to find a new logo in 1985. Contest rules ensured continuing promotability of the winning entry, for which a $400 prize was offered, by insisting that the ACTFEST name be included as part of the logo; that the design represent the organization and its function; and that the logo be clearly reproducible in black and white and suitable for T-shirts, letterheads and program covers.

THE OUTSIDE ENVELOPE

The logo is a basic tool, but scores of other visual vehicles can remind potential donors and audiences of the arts group and its program. Direct mail is one of the most common ways to reach audiences, and arts groups usually make tremendous efforts to ensure that the material inside the envelope is readable and provocative. But what

about the envelope itself? Any one of a number of factors could deter 15
the recipient from opening it, including machine-generated labels that
cry out "bulk mailing" and "they want my money." The consumer
is so besieged by business junk mail that any envelope that seems
to fit into that category may find a fast path to the wastebasket.

With the advent of computerization, addresses printed on
envelopes with a letter-quality printer can have an individual look.
First-class mail with an attractive postage stamp helps (some dance
companies hoarded dance stamps when they were introduced), but
that can be much more expensive than nonprofit mass mailings. The
envelope itself, however, can be used not only as a prod to get the
reluctant recipient to open it, but can be a sales tool as well. Postage
meter advertising, for example, imprinted on the face of the envelope,
can feature both pictorial and printed messages in a tiny space. Accompanied by an organizational logo, these miniature ads can tell
recipients about a new production or just-launched fund drive, or they
can carry a special message. "Don't Just Applaud Send Money,"
"Utah is Ballet Country," and "Everyone's Going to the Symphony
This Year" are among those that have been used. Arts groups might
even adapt a technique used by some colleges, which list football
schedules on envelope faces, by including a schedule of upcoming
performances near the stamp space. The Cincinnati Opera has used
the space to publicly acknowledge corporate sponsorship, proclaiming on its envelopes, "Cincinnati Opera Thanks Southern Ohio Bank
for sponsoring student matinees."

Some arts groups have used the outside envelope as a dramatic
device to attract attention. An envelope proclaiming that "Hume and
Jessica invite you to join them" may have enticed theatre buffs into
opening an envelope from the Queens Playhouse (the Cronyns tact-
fully explained in the message inside that they would be away on
tour with *The Gin Game*). A "special message from Leontyne Price,
Sherrill Milnes and Hal Prince" in blue ink on the outside of a National Institute for Music Theater envelope attracted the curious
musical buff. When the Connecticut Opera introduced a Pop season
in 1983-84, its envelope featured a red, yellow and blue star with the
word "pop" in the center, followed by the words "goes the opera."
The Paper Bag Players, fittingly, use brown paper bags as their
envelopes. Perhaps the most provocative envelope in recent years was
the handcrafted coffin-shaped one used by the New Hampshire Council on the Arts for its grant announcement. The coffin envelopes
dramatized a Council demand that the state "bury its outdated arts
philosophy" and signaled to legislators the need for more arts funding.

16   *POSTERS*

Although posters are a frequently used visual device, they're often not as effective as they might be, for a simple reason. Although they are visible, they're not always noticeable. Crowded together with other posters proclaiming a range of events, a poster may stand little chance of being noticed unless it's visually arresting or provocative. That's what the Boulder, Colo. Center for the Visual Arts had in mind with its poster promoting the 1983 exhibition, "A Decade of Women's Art." The poster featured 16 women artists either seated with sketchbooks or standing behind easels, drawing the nude model seated on a rug before them—a mustacheoed man clutching an equally naked infant to his chest.

A printed legend may make a poster come alive, as did a promotion piece which showed a plump, beaming Italian mama holding a huge and succulent platter of spaghetti and meatballs. The legend read simply, "Seattle Opera, You'll Eat It Up." In other instances the use of recognizeable figures may help to attract attention. The National Ballet of Canada used soaring ballerina Karen Kain to spread its message, "Join the Air Force."

VISUAL AIDS

The everyday world offers opportunities for visual exploitation, from milk containers printed with a theatre subscription schedule to promotional placemats thoughtfully donated to local coffee shops by symphony orchestras to supermarket checkout tapes with ticket information on the reverse side. Over 40 Safeway Stores in Alberta, Canada stuffed Theatre Network brochures promoting the 1984-85 season into every shopper's grocery bag. The supermarket chain also designed and paid for the 100,000 pieces.

Enterprise and imagination can help arts groups find unique visual props. In Springfield, Ill., 13 arts groups hang over 300 arts banners throughout the downtown area at various times during the year, thanks to local business support. Donated billboards in a number of communities urge drivers to support cultural programs. In Reno, Nev., the Sierra Museum of Art promoted memberships with billboards reading, "M SEUM . . . All that's missing is you." The Seattle Opera went one step further than most groups to make sure that its billboards were noticed, although it may have caused problems for motorists trying to read them as they sped along the roads. The billboards were printed in *mirror image* style to lure the curious to fathom the words, "Opera is Alive and Well in Seattle."

Some years ago, Jack Firestone, then manager of the Louisville Orchestra, happened to look out of his office window and noticed a cement mixer truck going by with a public service message printed on its side. Firestone's reaction was immediate and positive. He contacted the cement company, American Builders Supply, and within weeks the mixers sported Louisville Orchestra logos on one side and a "concrete" message on the other: "Get mixed up with the Louisville Orchestra." As proof that arts groups "adapt" from one another, the Salina, Kan. Arts Commission several years later induced the city to decorate 30 garbage trucks with legends reading, "Salina Overflows with the Arts."

SLOGANS

While a picture or visual image may be worth a thousand words a few well-chosen words used as a promotable slogan can be effective also. To dramatize its fund drive to convert a court house into a museum, the Vancouver Art Gallery used the slogan, "Take the Art Gallery to court. They can't make a move without you." The Cleveland Music School, in a burst of optimism, opted for a double entendre in calling its day-long phone solicitation campaign, "The Perfect Pitch." One dance company may have drawn smiles from supporters with its message, "Eglevsky Ballet, It's Tutu Much," while another may have topped that line with "Tutu is Better Than One."

The best slogans are those that conjure up an immediate identification with the arts group and its product while at the same time conveying a familiar image. When the New York City Opera promoted its star and now general director with the line, "Beverly Sills is a Good High," the image was inescapable. Since then, the opera company has coined a series of punningly clear slogans including, "Once You've Heard Us You'll Change Your Tune," "City Opera is Making Overtures to You" and, in a ploy designed to emphasize both its artistic product and its modest prices, "Come to the Opera for a Song." One of the most effective lines in recent years was one that the Repertory Theatre of St. Louis aimed at television viewers to promote a Shakespearean production. It simply said, "If You Like J.R., You'll Love *Richard III.*"

The slogan or pitch line has been used effectively in ads where the words are meant to titillate or amuse while prompting the reader

18   to take action. The Canadian Opera Company lured tourists to its production of *Lulu* with the enticing message, "Lulu will seduce you in Toronto for only $49.50, hotel included." When *Annie* was romping on Broadway, holiday tourists were wooed with an ad featuring a young girl minus several teeth. The "come-on" read, "All she wants for Christmas is her two front seats." New York's 92nd Street Y appealed to readers by describing an upcoming chamber music program as its "country music series." The "country" aspect was identified below as France (Ravel and Debussy) and Hungary (Kodaly and Bartok).

Humor, then, can be an effective device if it's used gently and if the same message is not repeated ad infinitum. Shock value isn't the same the second time around. Sometimes a light touch can transform an interesting but not particularly innovative sales or promotional event into an exciting moment. The Anchorage Alaska Concert Association, for example, offered an unusual lure, "a free season ticket with every hot dog" to those stopping at its ARTSNIGHT booth. Hot dogs, however, were $35 each. The Dutchess County, N.Y. Arts Council launched its annual weekend arts festival with "The Great Submarine Race," an event presumably featuring submarines racing underwater from the Newburgh-Beacon Bridge to the Mid-Hudson Bridge. Thousands of people were lured to the "finish line" to watch the winning captain emerge in full frogman gear—the (non-existent) submarine was submerged at all times—to accept the winner's trophy and then descend again to the submerged sub.

PROMOTIONAL CAMPAIGN

A tactic often used effectively by arts groups, especially to prepare for an upcoming fund drive, is the promotional campaign, an intensive period of publicity built around a specific theme and designed to focus a good deal of attention on an organization in a short span of time. Promotional campaigns can be clever, funny, hard-hitting or inspirational, but they should feature a definite peg, a clear tie between the promotion and the arts group.

Springboard, the Springfield, Ill. arts council, told audiences to "Go Ape for the Arts." The unusual promotional theme was unveiled for the first time at a major event in Springfield, the opening parade of the Illinois State Fair. Council supporters marched down the town's main street in T-shirts sporting a picture of a banana-eating ape and the slogan "Go Ape for the Arts," while other marchers held a large banner aloft bearing the same message. Along the parade route, surprised onlookers were handed hundreds of bananas. The promotion didn't end there, however. Within weeks, some 18,000 fliers were mailed inviting recipients to join the council. Each featured a picture of a banana-eating ape and asked the pointed question, "What does this gorilla have in common with Shakespeare?" The answer inside was, "He's gone ape for the arts! What about you?"

The Saint Louis Symphony Orchestra initiated a "Symphomania" promotional campaign during the 1984-85 season featuring buttons, bumper stickers, T-shirts and print and broadcast ads. The orchestra defined "symphomania" as "the symptoms induced by the Saint Louis Symphony," and used a "psychiatrist" in a TV commercial to tell audiences to enjoy their symptoms and attend symphony performances.

In Atlanta, the Alliance Theatre Company/Atlanta Children's Theatre built its 1985 promotional campaign around a series of six 30-second public service spots featuring some of Georgia's best-known celebrities. All appeared briefly in dramatic scenes and performed, according to design, poorly. Atlanta Mayor Andrew Young portrayed the Music Man, baseball great Hank Aaron appeared as Hamlet, Georgia football coach Vince Dooley was a witch from Macbeth and Jimmy Carter portrayed Mark Antony. The punch line for each of the commercials was that Atlanta relies on the Alliance Theatre for excellent performance, and the alternative "is to depend on this kind of talent."

Local business and utilities offer good opportunities for arts promotion. The Alabama Shakespeare Festival benefitted from a year's free exposure on the front cover of its city's most widely used publication, the Anniston telephone directory. Promotion pieces inserted with phone or electric bills can help recipients remember the cultural program, or even get them to shell out a few bucks. A small flier with a return membership form from the New York Zoological Society, sent along with Con Edison's electric bill in November 1985, for example, urged recipients to join the society.

In San Diego County several years ago, local arts groups and their financial needs were given tremendous exposure thanks to an insert in an unlikely, yet potent, mailing piece. Thanks to the initiative of a county supervisor, nearly a million property owners received leaflets along with their tax bills, asking them to make tax-deductible contributions to four local arts groups. A notation on the face of the tax bill reminded recipients to "please read the enclosed tax-deductible contribution leaflet." The promotional value of the flier was more than

20 supplemented by its pragmatic value. Donations of over $55,000 from 3,500 contributors resulted.

Tangible give-aways, especially of items that are useable and have an easy-to-remember arts message, also have been helpful in attracting attention. To remind legislators that their support was needed, members of the California Confederation of the Arts personally presented every elected state official with an "Arts Day" gift: a ruler on which was written, "The arts are a measure of a civilized society." The following year, legislators received silk roses with ribbons reading, "The arts are essential to life in a civilized society." In Florida, over 7,000 contributed white styrofoam coffee cups were distributed to state legislators in the opening days of the 1985 legislative session, a peak coffee drinking time. The message imprinted on the cups read, "Florida, State of the Arts." A less practical but more unusual item greeted recipients of an announcement promoting the opening of the Pineapple Dance Center in New York City. Inside a small white box, tied with a pink ribbon bearing the Dance Center's label, was a pair of pink ballet slippers only a few inches long.

BY PROCLAMATION

Many successful promotional campaigns have been tied to specially proclaimed days, weeks or months, such as Manitoba Theatre Week and San Francisco Opera "Ring" Month or, if relating to wider audiences, such occasions as National Dance Week and International Museum Day.

Proponents of such events have been careful to observe several key strategies, beginning with the event's introduction to its audiences. They have learned to make the opening of the day, week or month dramatic and attention-getting, and to sustain the period of time being celebrated with an appropriate number of special events. When the Manitoba Theatre Center in Winnipeg, Canada celebrated its 15th anniversary with a special week some years ago, the mayor of Winnipeg donned his ermine robes of office (hardly everyday attire) to sign the official proclamation in a well-attended public ceremony at the theatre. Simultaneously, thousands of balloons, a number of them containing ticket vouchers, were launched from the theatre roof. Throughout the week, volunteers and staff members led visitors on free guided tours, which included slide showings of past productions and displays of props and costumes. Visitors, including 3,000 people who were not on the theatre's mailing list previously, filled out information forms while they sipped free coffee and tea.

To initiate Oklahoma Community Arts Council Month in 1981, 25 banks in the state stuffed their monthly statements with 140,000 fliers promoting local arts councils. Also, 38 communities throughout the state flooded their audiences with 5,000 bookmarks, 2,000 buttons, 2,000 posters and 2,600 restaurant table tents featuring messages promoting the arts.

Sustaining the momentum of a specially proclaimed period is essential and, as organizations have learned, this means finding specific events throughout its duration to call attention to the promotion. Young Audiences, which has celebrated a national Young Audiences Week since 1971, is a master at this, as are its 37 chapters. In addition to local proclamations initiating the week, chapters have developed such events as exhibits of children's art inspired by Young Audiences concerts held in prestigious business building lobbies, demonstration programs in schools, department store windows featuring the Y/A program and public service announcements. The designation of honorary chairpersons—Leonard Bernstein, Isaac Stern, Marian Anderson, Victor Borge and Beverly Sills among them—has helped to promote the event. During the 1985 week, for example, the New York chapter worked with the special events coordinator of Macy's to have the Y/A dance, instrumental and vocal programs featured on the store's fifth floor. Macy's also ran a full-page *New York Times* ad promoting the week. Each of San Francisco's six Bay Area Emporium-Capwell stores ran special Y/A events during the week as well.

ANNIVERSARIES

The designation of a specially proclaimed period is easier to justify if it's related to some birthday or anniversary, but as arts groups have learned, it's relatively easy to find an appropriate date to celebrate if you look hard enough. Although it's nice to commemorate the 15th or 25th anniversary of a theatre (nobody seems to celebrate 14 or 24), a company whose first performance was 14 years ago needn't wait. It could celebrate its 15th year *in business* (which is different from 15 years in business) or the 15th anniversary since its incorporation or founding. One arts center, hard-pressed to find the right anniversary when it needed it most, settled on the anniversary of its groundbreaking.

Arts anniversaries have ranged from lavish to sedate, but in nearly every instance of note, the promotional benefits have been exceptional or, at the least, unusual. The Montreal Symphony was honored on its 50th anniversary in 1984 with the issuance of a 32-cent stamp

22 by the Canadian government. The Pennsylvania Ballet basked in the glory of its 21st birthday in 1985, not only with a special honorary week proclaimed by Mayor Goode, but with a more earthy honor— the Frog Restaurant created a new drink, the "Pink Slipper," to celebrate the troupe.

Frequently, anniversary celebrations have raised a good deal of money or provided a major boost to an upcoming or ongoing fund drive. One of the more glittering examples was the Lyric Opera of Chicago's 25th anniversary in 1979, which featured a year-long series of events (as did the Metropolitan Opera's 100th birthday in 1984) including an evening which featured an onstage tribute to the Lyric by a once-in-a-lifetime group of past and current opera stars, Pavarotti, Gobbi, de Stefano, Price and Schwarzkopf among them, and which sold $150,000-worth of tickets. Less showy but promotionally effective was the Joffrey Ballet's 25th anniversary "Dancin' in the Street" party (a more elegant in-theatre party also was held) which featured an open-to-the-public afternoon of performances, food, special booths and the distribution of "birthday bucks," anniversary coupons redeemable at a dollar off the purchase price of a ballet ticket. In another ticket ploy, the New York City Opera called attention to its 40th anniversary in 1984 by offering all opening night performance tickets at the same price as in 1944, $2.40 each.

Even in the absence of anniversary dates, special periods can be celebated if there's a peg to hang them on. Because of business sponsorship, the Cincinnati Symphony has been able to offer free concerts downtown and free bus rides to and from the concerts as a hook for Cincinnati Symphony Week, which also features a downtown booth manned by volunteers selling subscriptions and distributing calendars. Not to be outdone, another arts group in the same city, the Cincinnati Ballet Company, initiated its first annual Nutcracker Week in December 1985, immediately preceding the opening of its holiday production of *The Nutcracker*. Launched by a mayoral proclamation, the week included a downtown Nutcracker Parade, a "Nut Hunt" for children at the Cincinnati Zoo, "Nutcracker Sweets" cooking classes and a lavish "Nutcracker Fantasy Ball" at $100 a person with dinner, dancing, orchestra concert and ballet excerpts.

HOLIDAY AND BUSINESS CELEBRATIONS

When anniversaries aren't available, some arts groups focus on holidays celebrated by everyone. In Humble, Tex., the Area Council for the Arts celebrates an annual spring festival, "Mother's Day with the Arts," which has attracted as many as 4,000 people. In San Francisco, the Ticket Box Office (STBS) used Valentine's Day 1985 to send a love letter to theatre audiences by unveiling its "STBS Wall of Fame," a permanent display of theatrical autographs, and by awarding donated boxes of candy and gift certificates to ticket buyers at random times during the day.

Some arts groups are even imaginative enough to hang their celebrations on someone else's birthday, especially if it's the birthday of a local business. Corporations look to birthday celebrations as unique promotional opportunities, especially if they're celebrating 100 years or more in business. In fact, as a September 1985 article in *American Way* magazine indicated, a small group of consultants makes its living from developing promotional programs built around significant corporate anniversaries. When the McKesson Corporation celebrated its 150th birthday in October 1983, it found an artful party partner. At a special benefit concert performed by and for the San Francisco Symphony, the orchestra introduced "Overture 150—A Celebration." The concert also served as a kick-off for a transcontinental orchestra tour underwritten, not incidentally, by McKesson.

San Diego's Great American First Savings Bank opened its centennial celebration in 1985 by sponsoring all eight evening performances of the San Diego Symphony's Holiday Pops winter series. The bank also pledged $100,000 to help renovate the Fox Theatre into Symphony Hall. As bank chairman and chief executive officer, Gordon C. Luce said at the time, "We wanted not only to celebrate Great American's 100th birthday, but to honor the organizations who have made such a valuable contribution to the city's cultural growth. It is fitting that while we are celebrating our own history, we can help preserve the Fox Theatre, an historical landmark in its own right."

In San Antonio, Margaret Stanley, director of the San Antonio Performing Arts Association, put together 25 and 25 to come up with a unique funding ploy. She convinced the San Antonio office of Peat, Marwick, Mitchell & Company to celebrate its 25th anniversary by sponsoring two San Antonio performances of *The Taming of the Shrew*, presented by another silver anniversary celebrant, the Joffrey Ballet.

Sometimes an unusual kind of business celebration can be a happy event for other groups in the community. For its 20th anniversary in 1985, *Washingtonian* magazine decided to host a low-key affair in its offices instead of spending the estimated $100,000 that it would have cost to throw a big anniversary party. It took the money it saved and donated $5,000 to each of 20 local nonprofit organiza-

24 tions, including such cultural institutions as the Center for Talented Youth and the Capitol Children's Museum.

In the absence of specific celebrations, arts groups have had no difficulty in promoting themselves, both to their present audiences and to a larger community as well. Increasingly, enterprising groups find ways to win recognition for their programs by winning recognition for their leaders, in spheres outside the arts. In recent years, Russell Patterson, artistic director of the Kansas City Symphony, was named executive of the year by *Corporate Report* magazine in Kansas City, Mo., and Sunna Rasch, founder of Periwinkle Productions, was named Woman of the Year by the Liberty-Monticello, N.Y. branch of the Association of University Women.

When presented with a potent promotional possibility, arts groups have risen to the occasion, even when a bridge between strange bedfellows stands in the way. The University Museum of Archaeology/Anthropology of the University of Pennsylvania in Philadelphia had just such an occasion when a production of the Broadway hit *Cats* came to the Forrest Theatre—although it took some creative thinking to make the connection. Phoebe Resnick, the museum's alert public information officer, was able to link the show's characters with their ancient counterparts—the Egyptian cats in the museum's collection who were then being spotlighted in an exhibition, "Man and Animals." The result was that the Forrest Theatre manager allowed 100,000 museum fliers, paid for by the Mellon Bank, to be stuffed in his programs. The Shubert Organization also agreed to allow two costumed *Cats* cast members to visit their Egyptian ancestors at the museum exhibit. The photo call turned out to be a field day for the press and tremendous publicity for the exhibition.

Who says that arts institutions have to be stuffy?

CHAPTER 2

It's an Inside Job

28   Not too long ago, a well-known arts consultant uttered words to the recently hired executive director and board of an old theatre that the board wanted to hear—but never should have. Although the theatre was about to be renovated into an arts center at some expense, the consultant advised the board, "Put your $20,000 in the bank. You don't have to do any fund-raising for operations." About a year-and-a-half later, when the center was $150,000 in the red, the same consultant was brought back and asked his advice. "You're not doing anything wrong," he told the board and a new executive director. "You wouldn't have bothered to save the building if I told you that you had to raise funds for operations."

Many facts are kept from arts boards for fear that if they were told what their responsibilities really were, they might be scared away before they ever got started. And yet, when vital information is hidden from the board, both the board members and their organizations are done an injustice. The relationship, which should be built on mutual trust and an acceptance of responsibility, may be doomed before it ever really begins.

Some years ago, when I served as an officer of a national arts service organization, we polled our member companies to find out what they viewed as their major non-artistic problems. The advance expectation among the officers and executive director was that funding and audience development would occupy the top two slots. We were surprised. When the results were tabulated, standing alone as the number one problem was—the board of directors. And yet, when we thought about it more carefully, we realized that the result shouldn't have been totally unexpected. For it is the board of directors, a group of volunteers, that holds the key to financial stability. All too frequently, however, its members are reluctant to turn that key in the right door.

INTERNAL PUBLICS

The board may hold the key. Still, it is only one of several internal audiences or publics, albeit a critical one, that an arts group must involve in its activities if it is to achieve financial stability and growth. And in the most ideal situation, the board members and officers will come out of an organization's other inner audiences. To illustrate this, we might draw a large circle to represent a cultural organization and a series of concentric circles within it, with each of these smaller circles representing a particular inner audience or public of the organization. The audience closest to the center obviously is the one most

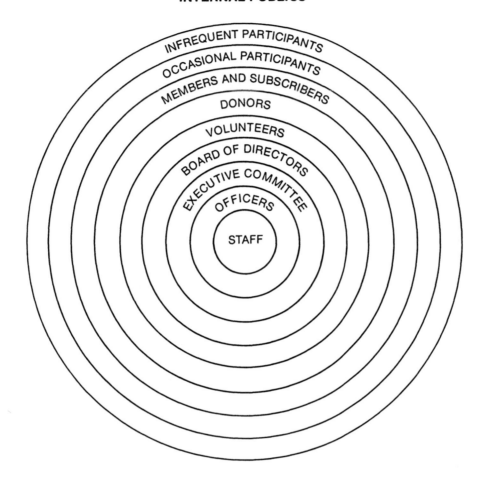

deeply involved with the day-to-day operations of the organization. It is the professional staff.

Moving out from the center, the next closest circle would represent the organization's officers. In succession, with some slight variations according to organizational differences, each circle—which would be slightly larger than the one preceding it because it comprises more people—would represent: executive committee; board of directors; volunteers; donors; members and subscribers; occasional organizational participants and infrequent participants. In the vast expanse outside the circle would be the largest group by far, the non-involved and the never-attenders. In the best-managed organizations, information would flow in a continuing stream from public to public, so that each specific audience would help educate and involve the audience behind it. As members of more distant publics became more

30　closely involved with the organization, they would move closer to the center.

If this ideal kind of development were followed to its ultimate conclusion, arts support would grow organically and logically. The organizational leaders of tomorrow would be the occasional participants of today. The officers and board, instead of being never-nevers arbitrarily leapfrogged ahead into positions of leadership because of prestige or wealth, would be those people who have grown with the organization and experienced its development as well as its problems from a range of levels.

Unfortunately, the ideal progression is not a well-blazed trail in the arts, because the exigencies of day-to-day operations prevent many groups from devoting all the attention they should to each of their internal publics. But it can happen more often than it does. An approach I devised, "The AIR Factor," has been useful to a number of organizations. AIR, which stands for AROUSE, INFORM/INVOLVE and REWARD, connotes the kinds of activity that an organization should direct to each of its internal audiences, with the intensity of activity correspondingly greater for those publics closest to the organization's center.

Even the newcomer to the organization, the occasional participant, must be aroused by the organization, not only through its artistic program but through activities and mailings. The excitement of the organization's potential must be conveyed. The information program should flow to each level, with the heaviest concentration reserved for the three internal publics closest to the center. Ways should be devised to actively involve participants at each level of the organization, and whenever possible, special skills of audience members should be identified and utilized. Well remembered is the former retired newspaper syndicate executive from New York who found herself in Durham, N.C. when her husband was transferred there. When she happened to drop in at the local arts council looking for something to do, a staff member discovered her special organizational skills and wisely turned her loose. Inside of several months, she had organized and was running a large and well-oiled volunteer program—as a volunteer.

Getting audiences to move from aroused and informed participants to involved participants is perhaps the key aspect of any successful program. Some arts groups have done it by identifying the interests of particular target groups and combining them with areas of organizational interest. Theatre companies such as San Diego's Old Globe Theatre have won the active involvement of young professionals in the community by providing a common meeting ground and the opportunity to develop rewarding as well as socially stimulating projects in behalf of the group. The Old Globe's Players, a group of some 20 young professionals, sold over $100,000 in subscriptions during one recent season and, organized into two competing teams, had a lot of fun doing it.

New York City's New Museum of Contemporary Art, seeking to strengthen its ties to one of its key audiences—collectors—organized an Art Quest program in 1981, limited to 50 members paying $1,250 each. In return for the money, the members, all sophisticated art collectors, were invited to see top private collections, visit the studios of unaffiliated artists and meet with critics and other art experts. Not only have several Art Quest members since joined the board, but virtually all of them have become enthusiastic museum volunteers. "They've given us extraordinary support," claims museum development director Virginia Strull. "They've become deeply involved in our annual benefit, gotten their friends to buy tickets and promoted our activities. They've also purchased works at our auction, donated art to us and helped us build a bridge to other collectors."

Many arts organizations that have successfully involved participants in their programs have learned to reward them for their contributions. Recognition is an inexpensive item to offer, and newsletters, printed programs, meetings and even recognition nights all serve to refuel a flagging spirit that may need a pat on the back. Lack of recognition, on the other hand, can stifle a volunteer's willingness to contribute and can diminish the status of that volunteer in the eyes of his or her friends and spouse.

THE BOARD OF DIRECTORS

Arts groups have employed a range of tactics to effectively attract and mobilize their volunteer forces, and some have been quite successful. The board, which one knowledgeable observer once defined as "long, narrow and wooden," has been a special area of concern, beginning with its recruitment. The prospective member who is asked to join the board solely because his name is needed on the stationery will turn out to be quite *stationary* indeed. In fact, he may never move a muscle to help the organization.

The Delaware Symphony hasn't been afraid to ask for more than a name on its letterhead. In fact, the Symphony has taken its case for active board members public by printing an article in its newsletter

32 outlining the duties and responsibilities of board membership. The article was appropriately headlined, "No 'Figureheads' or 'Dead Wood.' "

Perhaps the problem has been that arts groups, fearful of losing a prospect by asking the potential board member to give too much, seldom emphasize the reverse side of the coin—what a board member will get from his involvement with the organization. Yet, if really analyzed, arts board members are well compensated, just as corporate board members are. The only difference is that in the arts the compensation isn't money.

WHAT A BOARD MEMBER GETS

Although the list is far from exhaustive, the following constitutes just some of the compensation given to arts board members:

—An identification with excellence
—An opportunity to play a leadership role in a significant organization
—An involvement with a growing concern, and the opportunity to help it grow larger
—A tremendous learning experience (One businessman-arts board member had his salesmen help sell symphony tickets. "If they can learn to sell symphony tickets," he reasoned, "they can learn to sell anything.")
—Personal prestige
—Social contact at a peer level with other community leaders serving on the board
—The excitement of a challenge
—The opportunity to provide a key service to the community.

WHAT A BOARD MEMBER GIVES

Given these rewards, what must a board member give back in return? The list might include:

—Taking pride in the organization and promoting its accomplishments to its many communities of involvement
—Helping to expand the reach of the organization into many segments of the community by opening the door to new relationships

—Providing support for the organization's continuing quest for **33** artistic excellence
—Recognizing the seriousness of the task and acknowledging fully all the responsibilities of board membership including financial
—Helping others recognize that the organization is not seeking a dole or a handout, but a repayment for services already rendered
—Studying the organization and its needs, and studying the cultural discipline of which it is a part.

Some arts organizations that are demanding in what they ask of board members have learned that they receive a great deal in return. Robert Joffrey, head of the Joffrey Ballet, insists that his board members be people who enjoy ballet. "They go to rehearsals," he says, "and they take pride in our work."

Perhaps one of the reasons that some organizations have difficulty in putting together a working board is that what they want instead of a working board is a "smorgasbord." Instead of recruiting members for their individual accomplishments, their interest and prior involvement in the organization and their ability to contribute something of significance, they recruit by types. Working on the concept that it's important to have every base covered, they seek to represent virtually every profession or activity of significance—one lawyer, one educator, one religious leader etc.—on the mistaken impression that the person recruited will represent that area. In reality, few people ever really represent anything other than themselves, and the individual is far more important than his or her field of activity. Certainly many people can help to open doors to a particular field, but they can't deliver that field on a silver platter.

It's rewarding to a group when someone with a particular skill or attribute can be brought onto its board and contribute something. However, for most groups, among other attributes, what they would welcome most is money. This concern led the Chamber Ballet USA in 1982 to place an unusual ad in *The Wall Street Journal*. It read, "Support dancers, not institutions. Contribute $10,000 cash (minimum) for salary support exclusively, and become a trustee of New York's new gem of a company." It worked to the extent that the $300 ad brought in responses from five executives, one of whom joined the board.

While large organizations, to the chagrin of many smaller groups, seem to attract the most prestigious board members, some organizations of relatively smaller size have done well in the board member

34 sweepstakes because they are able to convey a sense of excitement about their activities. In October 1985, for example, the Philharmonia Virtuosi issued a press release to announce the addition of four new members to its board including the distinguished anchor of ABC's *World News Tonight*, Peter Jennings. Joining Jennings on the board were the president of a New York marketing and public relations firm, the chairman of a real estate leasing and consulting operation and the head of a leading fund-raising firm. Continuing board members included, among others, the managing director of a securities firm, an attorney and political leader, a real estate developer, a banker and the vice president of a Fortune 500 company.

The board's role in fund-raising has been written about ad infinitum, but the classic three G's of "give, get or get off," are still the time-honored modus operandi for many organizations, along with the three W's sought of every board member, "wealth, wisdom or work." What really motivates boards to raise funds? Getting them to do what they like to do may be one answer. "If I have a board member who only likes to give parties," claims Theodore Kesselman, a member of three arts boards and president of one, "and the parties are big moneymakers, I'll keep him on the board." Some organizations are fortunate in having board members who contribute money themselves, and don't mind asking their friends or associates for funds. One such organization circulates printouts to its board members of everyone who buys tickets to its galas, and asks them to call on those whom they know for donations. Veteran fund-raiser Maurice Gurin suggests to board members that they use the "wince" test when soliciting donations from their peers. "If they don't wince when you mention a figure, then ask them for more."

Because the board is a critical public, it also can be used to draw the involvement of other internal publics into greater participation. Although it isn't done as often as it might be, the addition of members, subscribers or volunteers to committees chaired by board members can help to increase their involvement at a significant level and groom them for board membership. Of course, this implies that board members actually serve on committees, perhaps even chair them. Not enough do. Groups are learning that in order to have an effective board, committee service is essential, because it involves members between meetings of the board. Some groups, such as the aforementioned Delaware Symphony, insist that board members actively serve on two committees.

When a board becomes bored, the meeting is often the culprit. What happens all too frequently is that the board members, top decision-makers in their business lives, become petty bureaucrats on an arts board. They get bogged down in considering minutiae and spend precious minutes or even hours debating such weighty subjects as what color would be best for a benefit invitation. Tighter meetings, structured to consider matters of policy and drawing upon the special abilities of members (the day-to-day exigencies can be left to staff or the executive committee), can help increase involvement in the organization. A focus on issues which make the case larger than the organization can help also. The mailing of pertinent materials on such matters as how nonprofit organizations in fields other than the arts are finding exciting new ways to generate earned income might pique the interest of a board member. Frequently, the participation of an outside guest, invited because of his or her expertise in some broad matter that concerns the board—i.e., the impact of videocassettes on live entertainment—can spark new interest. And the "R" in the AIR factor is critical when it comes to the board. Profiling a member in each or every other issue of an organizational newsletter, as many groups do, or sending out press releases on new honors or achievements accorded members in their business lives, might benefit the arts organization as much as it does the board member.

RECRUITING MEMBERS AND DONORS

Although most organizations invite their audiences to become members, in many instances "member" is merely a euphemism for donor. The terms are frequently so intertwined that it is difficult to tell whether an organization really is recruiting members who vote at the annual meeting and have other privileges, especially since the donor ranks are swollen also with "privileged" individuals. What is most interesting perhaps is the terminology used to define various categories of member, donor or friend and the benefits offered.

To tie in with its artistic product, the New York Gilbert and Sullivan Players established membership ranks going from "Merchant Seamen" at $25 to $74 to "Bobbies and Brigands" at $75 to $199 all the way up through "Dragoons" and "Gondolier Godfathers" to "Fairy Godmothers" at $1,000 or more. Leaders of the Des Moines Symphony, during one recent year, must have used a thesaurus to find and name 10 categories of donor without using the term donor. They were: Giver, Friend, Contributor, Supporter, Patron, Benefactor, Guarantor, Pacesetter, Sponsor and Leader. An especially fitting nomenclature was devised by the arts group that named its three categories Friend, Good Friend and Best of Friends.

When different categories are established at different contribu-

36 tion levels, arts groups have learned that there must be some differentiation among them in the way of benefits. Many public television stations have given away commercial premiums—books, records, umbrellas and tote bags among them—to entice members to higher levels of donation. Most performing and visual arts groups, on the other hand, have generally tied their increasing benefits to their program or artistic product. Some organizations have combined both, as New York's Public TV Channel 13 did with booklets containing coupons good for free and discount admissions to city museums added to the consumer items. The offering proved to be mutually beneficial for both the TV channel, which had important new premiums to offer to members, and the museums, which won both print and on-air publicity.

Norfolk's Chrysler Museum tied in premiums to its artistic concerns one year by offering contributors to its Art Reference Library Fund a single item in various sizes—bags that were "ideal for carrying books." Utility bags were given for $8.50 donations, tote bags for $10 donations, duffle bags for $12 donations and better duffle bags for $15 gifts. Carnegie Hall listed 10 categories of Friends in one of its brochures, going from a low of $35 to a high of $10,000 with the standard "all of the above benefits plus" terminology at each new level. Included at lower levels were such cultural standbys as free admission passes to dress rehearsals and a subscription to a Friends newsletter. Added at succeeding levels, in addition to more free passes, invitations to luncheons and screenings and behind-the-scenes tours, were discounts on rental cars and classical records.

Although consumer items keep cropping up among the benefits offered to arts contributors, at least one cultural group has gone on record as firmly opposing the concept. On the cover of its flier several years ago, the Emelin Theater in Mamaroneck, N.Y. emblazoned in big red letters the words "Say No" while in an inside fold the words "No to commericial premiums" appeared. The remaining panels, all marked "yes," outlined such theatre-related benefits offered to new members as ticket discounts and a calendar of events.

At times, small gifts without great monetary value, but either useful or reflective of the organization's activity, have been effective membership awards. The Art Institute of Chicago some years ago offered members wallet-sized plastic card cases with its crest embossed on the outside. In the pockets inside, the museum included a membership card and another card listing the Institute's hours and the hours that the member's room was open. The Chicago Symphony, which has offered its members such on-target benefits as visits to nearby musical instrument factories, gave out a bonus recording by the orchestra one year, with a special attachment included for those "who feel moved to conduct when listening to great records." The extra bonus was an imprinted Chicago Symphony Society baton.

When an arts group shoots for the top, attempting to attract donors at the highest echelons, the rewards offered are usually very personal and confer a unique kind of recognition—or at least they should. The Alliance Theatre campaign to attract "Top Billing" individual donors at $1,000, $3,000 and $5,000 levels was promoted in a red, white and black brochure headlined, "See Your Name in Lights," although obviously much of the effort was a one-on-one, behind-the-scenes approach. As the brochure indicated, all of the donors in those categories received program listings in a special Top Billing Marquee, listings on a Top Billing plaque in the theatre and their names on a theatre seat for a year, as well as invitations to special events. Only those in the $5,000-plus category, however, were given the most special VIP ticket service, featuring a "direct number to the Arts Alliance Box Office for all your ticket service needs."

To recruit members when membership is merely a jumping off point for additional donations, many organizations have used unique events as a come-on. Museums with blockbuster exhibitions have recruited thousands of new members by promising guaranteed entry to a "can't afford not to be seen at" event. When the Minneapolis Society of Fine Arts was planning for the U.S. premiere of the exhibition, "Dutch and Flemish Masters: Paintings from the Vienna Academy of Fine Arts," it used the occasion to launch a special mailing to prospective members. Recipients were given the opportunity to attend the "Opening Night with the Masters" preview and reception a day prior to the official opening at a special reduced rate if they became members.

SAMPLER PROGRAMS

Other institutions have used sampler programs as a recruitment device, offering audiences the opportunity to sample the benefits regularly enjoyed by members. The Queens Museum set aside December 8, 1985 as a day to introduce prospective members to the museum. Events included museum tours, demonstrations of papier mâché reliefs, music and refreshments. A mailing describing the event included information on member benefits and a response envelope urging recipients to join, but as it indicated, "If you're not sure about becoming a member now, check the box that says MAYBE and try us out on December 8." Several years earlier, New York's Museum

38 of Modern Art offered visitors paying the regular admission fee a card which read, "Your next visit to the Museum of Modern Art can be free as a Member for a Day." Recipients, after filling out a registration card, were entitled to return to the museum on any day within a three-month period and, on that day, enjoy all the privileges of membership including use of the members' dining room and the members' 25 percent discount on purchases at the museum's gift shop.

ATTRACTING VOLUNTEERS

Volunteerism connotes willful involvement, and anytime an arts group can move subscribers, donors or members into the volunteer category it is a major plus. Volunteer groups sell subscriptions, participate in fund campaigns, organize benefits and undertake such special projects as the sales boutique operated at performances of the Indianapolis Ballet Theatre by the Night Wing, a branch of its volunteer arm, the Wing. The Night Wing is a group of professional women who are unable to meet during the day. Many arts groups have been able to expand their volunteer force by organizing chapters in nearby areas. Others have created high-level volunteer groups devoted to a specific area or need, such as the Metropolitan Museum of Art's Real Estate Council, established to organize the real estate interests of New York City in a support program for the museum.

The Metropolitan Opera's volunteer arm, the Metropolitan Opera Guild, has raised over $28 million for the Met since it was organized in the early '30s through benefits, travel programs and the sale of hundreds of items—scarves, dolls and music boxes—with opera-related themes. The New York Philharmonic's Friends raise over $3 million annually, or about one-fifth of the orchestra's budget. In a *New York Times* interview, Friends chairman, Phyliss J. Mills, said of the group, "The Philharmonic involves its volunteers in every aspect of the organization except playing. Once volunteers, they're hooked forever."

Arts groups have used a range of techniques to draw audiences into the volunteer ranks, and special programs such as Business Volunteers for the Arts have been a major help. Additionally, many corporations have specific programs headed by executives and designed to inform their employees of volunteer opportunities. But, in the long run, many groups discover that their best volunteers come from a group that is already connected to them—their audiences—if they can learn how to tap them. Getting out the word is essential.

Allied Arts of Seattle has reached out successfully for volunteers with   **39**
a simple mechanism, an annual article in its newsletter which includes a paragraph on each of its committees looking for help, and a response box. The paragraphs outline each committee's area of concern and past accomplishments, and list the kinds of skills needed. The Corvallis, Ore. Arts Center has taken a somewhat "laid back" approach to recruitment through a mailing which emphasizes the fun and informality of belonging to its volunteer force, and gives prospects the opportunity of checking off on a questionnaire the specific activities in which they would like to become involved.

One of the more successful recruitment devices, which appealed to the adventurousness of theatre-loving New Yorkers through a "Personals" approach familiar to many singles, attracted over 800 active volunteers in its first two years of use. In a brochure distributed to its audiences, the Second Stage in New York City proclaimed, "Young, attractive Upper West Side theatre seeks adventuresome New Yorkers looking for an intimate relationship. We offer great looks and terrific quality. No cheap thrills, but plenty of thrilling theatre cheap. Good sense of humor and quick mind a must. No experience necessary."

Considering all the publics an arts group has to thank, its board, members, donors and subscribers among them, the recognition aspect of the AIR factor can be a major one. Two audiences that should never be ignored but are frequently overlooked are—the organization's artists and the organization itself. Although it may seem like the height of self-aggrandizement for an arts group to pat itself on the back for the good things it has done, it's essential to its well-being and its continued support to do so. When an organization has won awards, balanced its budget or topped its fund goal, it should let those achievements be known. The headlines of three press releases, all issued within weeks of one another late in 1985, effectively demonstrate the achievements of three different groups: "Old Globe Theatre Releases 1985 Attendance Figures. Earned Income Tops 1984 Record," read one. A second said, "Cincinnati Opera Announces Banner Year of Sales," while a third began, "For Minnesota Orchestra, Artistic Achievements Complement Balanced Budget in 1985."

RECOGNIZING ARTISTS

When arts groups give recognition to their actors, singers and dancers, they are recognizing themselves at the same time. They are also boosting the morale of their most essential public. Some arts groups' efforts on behalf of their performers have been not only quite

40 imaginative, but productive as well. The Kansas City Philharmonic's "Profiles" advertisements of orchestra players (described in Chapter 5), brought new business supporters into the orchestra's orbit. The Feld Ballet, in a much imitated promotion, issued baseball-style cards during the 1984 season. The front of each card showed an action picture of a company dancer along with Feld "team insignia," and featured his or her vital statistics on the back. The cards, perforated so that they could be easily removed, were printed on a self-mailer which also included subscription information and an order form. The ballet company reinforced the obvious relationship to baseball cards with copy that read, "It's spring! Your heart is melting and the Feld leaps into the Joyce for a Five Week Home Run!" In addition to issuing six cards with the subscription brochure, the company packaged the cards into a complete deck of 26—21 company dancers and five visiting dancers—and sold them for $2 each.

The Orchestra of Illinois promoted its musicians and raised money at the same time in 1984, by allowing audience members to "adopt a musician" of their choice. Each new "parent" received certificates of adoption as well as a letter from each adopted musician listing essential information about his or her background and career, and the promise of a spring reception at which musicians and parents would meet. Adoptions, offered at rates from $250 to $1,000 (the highest price was for the conductor), were inspired both by the well-known Cabbage Patch dolls, and zoos that have introduced successful "adopt an animal" programs.

THANKING DONORS AND SUBSCRIBERS

Arts groups have also been imaginative in finding ways to thank and recognize subscribers and donors. In addition to the usual letters and program listings, some groups have held special performances and programs for their supporters, or have sent them small gifts. To acknowledge the contributions of major donors to its newly opened concert hall, Somerset County College in New Jersey gave them specially made brass ticket stubs complete with seat numbers. The Frederick, Okla. Arts and Humanities Council, in the middle of renovating its theatre, didn't wait until it was finished to thank its key donors. In an auditorium filled with lumber and no seats, it held a special reception for them. In Fort Wayne, Ind., the Philharmonic found a good way not only to thank renewing subscribers but to alert non-renewers that they still had time to sign up. The orchestra notified its audience that a season-end concert was designated as "Carnation

Night," with "thank-you" carnations pinned to the backs of the seats
of all renewers. The notices also had a pitch to non-renewers: "If you
haven't renewed, we'll be happy to accept your order on May 3 and
one of our Women's Committee members will reward you with a carnation and a springtimer smile."

When Seattle's A Contemporary Theatre celebrated its 20th anniversary in 1984, it found a nice way to recognize its long-term supporters. The theatre dedicated the first production on its mainstage
to all the donors who had supported ACT for at least 10 of the previous
20 years, regardless of the amount they had contributed. Each of the
238 donors was sent a special packet whose cover announced the
special dedication, along with a letter of thanks and a badge saluting
their contribution. The packet cover was used as the program cover
on opening night, and was displayed in the theatre lobby throughout
the run of the production.

When the San Diego Symphony wanted to reward its patrons,
especially its largest donors, for their support, it turned to a concept
used by some governments. It named its group sales manager to the
additional post of ombudsman. Although the ombudsman responded to requests for information and took complaints from a range of
orchestra supporters, his main efforts were directed to those who had
contributed $1,000 or more to the orchestra. A pre-season letter sent
to these large donors informed them of the post, and told them that
they could get personal help, including extra concert tickets to meet
a sudden emergency, or special assistance in arranging for attendance
at musical events in other cities.

In coming years, there is no doubt that arts groups will find new
ways to recognize and reward their audiences for their support.
Although nobody has ever accused them of it, perhaps arts organizations, or at least some aspect of their activities, might be viewed as
social services. That might even be of help in raising funds.

CHAPTER 3

Whose Public
Is This, Anyway?

———————————————————

44   Potential audiences are everywhere, and in their efforts to reach and tap them, arts supporters and promoters have said some unusual and unexpected things. According to the folklore of the arts, a leading presenter of classical music concerts attempting to recruit the non-involved to his programs asserted, "Good music isn't as bad as it sounds." The famed impresario, Sol Hurok, is reported to have said, somewhat less optimistically, "If they don't want to come you can't stop them."

Although arts administrators frequently talk about the need for reaching "them," or the public, basically there is no single arts public to reach. Every cultural program and organization relates not to a single audience but to many different external publics, each having its own interests and needs, its special likes and dislikes, its own leadership and its individual relationship to the arts group. (A public in this instance is defined as any group of people, whether formally organized or not, whose constituents bear a similar relationship to one another and usually, a similar relationship to the arts organization.) The successful audience program not only shows an understanding of these publics and recognizes the differences between them, but attempts to discover their objections, if any, to the arts product and what needs they may have that can be met through the cultural program. Most important, it finds ways, without arbitrarily changing the arts product, to influence that public in its favor.

Clearly, arts groups can't have a single message or promotional technique to apply to all of their audiences. As so many cultural institutions have learned over the years, no single message, no matter how well it is articulated, reaches every public the same way. Different publics react differently according to their own needs and interests. The need for different messages hit home to me in a rather curious way while I was in a hotel elevator on my way to speak at an arts conference. On the wall to my right as I entered was a message written in virtually every language known to man. It read (in English), "In case of emergency press red button." The hotel staff must have thought that they didn't miss anyone with the message because of the wide range of languages in which it was written. They were almost right. They reached everyone except me and others like me who are—color weak.

EXTERNAL PUBLICS

The list of external publics is endless, including everyone from children to senior citizens, the educational community to blue-collar workers, "Yuppies" to movie aficionados. Obviously, not every arts group can or should try to reach every public. Some are more significant than others, and some which are relatively insignificant at most times could become very important if a particular program or event were in their major area of interest. Although a theatre may have sports fans far down on its list of audience priorities, a production of *That Championship Season*, a play about the reunion of a coach with his old high school team, may make them a target audience.

When the Michigan Opera Theatre presented a rare production of a Polish opera, *The Haunted Castle*, in 1982, it turned to a key public that it had never before tapped, the Polish community. Boosted by an honorary committee of well-known Polish-Americans including the Archbishop of Detroit and the head of the Polish National Alliance, the company's working committee of eight couples, several of Polish extraction, initiated a promotional and funding campaign designed to involve the Polish community of Detroit. Activities including a polka party, a lecture by a Polish musical authority and a dinner party and tour of an old Polish church in the city involved hundreds of Polish-Americans. Moreover, several Polish organizations held fund-raisers for the opera company while others lent Polish costumes and even *Haunted Castle* scores. The result of all this activity was $60,000 raised for production of the opera, and large audiences of Polish Americans at its six performances. A year earlier, the same opera company, which seeks out rarely produced works, raised $40,000 from the Armenian community when it produced the Armenian opera, *Anoush*.

When an arts group seeks to reach an external public that it has identified as a priority target, it invariably discovers that members of that public, and even perhaps some of its leaders, are within its internal publics. And just as information flows from internal public to internal public, it can flow from internal public to external public.

Convenience, price, appropriateness of program, place and time of presentation are all questions of concern to members of specific audiences. For example, a performance held in a downtown theatre at night might not be as attractive to senior citizens as it would be to young couples who could remain downtown after work and dine out before attending the show. Ticket prices that are reasonable for professionals may be high for students or older people on fixed incomes.

While the artistic product should never be at the mercy of a particular public, the way in which it's wrapped can be changed to meet the needs of a target audience. To make it more appealing to workers, a concert could be moved to a union hall or in-plant auditorium.

EXTERNAL PUBLICS

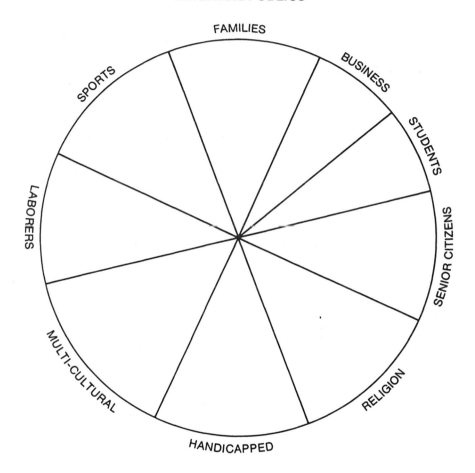

Special bus transportation might be arranged if a key audience had difficulty in reaching an inconvenient location. For a number of years, the Brooklyn Academy of Music, across the river from Manhattan, has operated the BAM bus before and after every performance.

Sometimes, an audience never before identified becomes a target not only because of the theme or nature of the work, but because of its time of presentation. The Yale Repertory Theatre's low-priced weekly series some seasons ago found an unusual on-target audience precisely because it was being presented on Monday evenings during the fall. The series was promoted as "Salvation for Football Widows," and the results proved the point. Some 70 percent of the subscribers were women, presumably escaping from television's Monday night National Football League Game of the Week.

Sometimes, it is a special need of an audience that might otherwise go unnoticed that prompts the alert arts administrator to target a program for that audience. So it was with "donut holes" and the Boston Symphony. Dinah Daniels, now the publicity head of the Los Angeles Philharmonic, tells of the time she asked her elderly grandmother why she never went to performances of the organization that Daniels then worked for, the Boston Symphony. Daniels knew that her grandmother liked good music and that the concert hall was convenient to her home. "I get hungry when I go to concerts," her grandmother replied, "and so do other old people. If there was something to eat, like donut holes, it could make a difference." And so was born the Boston Symphony's midday series for older people, including with the music, coffee and donut holes.

COLLEGE STUDENTS

Knowledge of what a public doesn't like or want may be just as important as knowing what appeals to it. This was clearly evidenced in what has now become one of the classic arts examples of audience reach. In this instance the arts group isolated a public it wished to outreach, analyzed its attitudes towards the artistic product, pinpointed some specific needs which its product might meet, found ways to answer many objections and then developed a peer-speaks-to-peer approach to selling. The organization was the Seattle Opera. The target audience was University of Washington students. The product was opera performances.

From the start, the opera company knew that, although the potential audience was a large one, its list of objections as a public was monumental. To begin with, many college students held the somewhat stereotypical view that opera was an alien art form, highly stylized and formal in its presentation. Compounding the problem was the fact that it was presented in a foreign language in unfamiliar surroundings and was costly to attend. Because the opera company was planning to present a low-priced, opera-in-English series, it could answer several of the objections, but to effectively respond to the more serious negative reactions—one student had termed opera "booooooring"—required a considerable effort of near herculean proportions.

The opera company chose to let peer speak to peer, to allow students to respond to students. They took an ad in the University of Washington newspaper to recruit "Whiz Kid" students to sell opera

48 in a language that other students could understand. The results of that effort were historic. Bumper stickers reading "Bravo Opera" were distributed, along with buttons proclaiming "Opera Lives." Posters were placed in strategic campus spots. Ads written by the five students selected from the more than 60 that responded, answered the question, "What is *Bohème?*" by describing it as the story of "four old-time hippies in an attic." In another ad, *Samson et Delila* was termed "the original Middle-East crisis" complete with "orgies, dancing girls, a feast of passion and lust." Every student who had ever struggled with English lit courses could relate to their peers' description of *Il Travatore*, which was said to have "a plot so involved that it makes *Finnegan's Wake* seem easy."

The effort didn't end there. Several hundred free opera tickets were distributed to student residence leaders, followed by letters with more information on the new subscription series which they were told "surpasses the popular light show as a galactic happening." And, the letter added, "the cost per evening is only slightly more than a movie." The opera company also sponsored a junk sculpture as its main exhibit at the Seattle Teen Spectacular, to strengthen its ties to young people and to show that opera was living and dynamic and that those involved in it had a sense of humor. The tone of the successful campaign was perhaps best symbolized by a series of light-hearted newspaper ads done in cartoon style in which a co-ed, voicing her disbelief that her "jock" boyfriend had never been to the opera, answered many of his presumed objections to the ticket cost, the language barrier and the need for interesting weekend entertainment. Her last words, voiced with a confident smile on her face, were, "I think I'll wear my red dress."

As the Seattle Opera campaign of long ago and the more recent Michigan Opera program targeted at the Polish community demonstrate, peer involvement can be a key to a successful campaign aimed at a particular audience. There is no doubt that the most effective selling can be done on a peer-to-peer basis, and recognized leaders can sell programs better to their audiences than the most eloquent arts leaders can—if they can be persuaded to do the selling.

Selling classical ballet to "pop" audiences is a case in point. Most ballet companies would have a difficult time trying to reach those audiences on their own, but with the help of a recognized figure in that world they might have a chance, as the Joffrey Ballet did, when it used Bette Midler and Joan Rivers as their spokespersons in fun commercials aired on Pop stations. The Pennsylvania Ballet, aiming to reach the same audience some years ago, found unexpected help from one of Philadelphia's most popular "deejays," Tom Brown, who "adopted" the dance company in a personal campaign to interest listeners in attending its performances. Brown publicized the ballet on his show, promoted raffles with free tickets to performances and promoted listener excursions to attend ballet company programs in New York City and at a suburban music festival.

More recently, the Old Globe Theatre was in the process of selling a promotion designed to reach an even younger audience, 14- to 24-year-olds. The theatre's program was designed to tie in a San Diego area "now" station to an offering of reduced-rate tickets for station listeners, including before and after picnics for ticket buyers, hosted by the radio station. A key to the promotion, which was about to be wrapped up at the time of this writing, was a month-long series of humorous commercials designed to answer rock-oriented youngsters' objections to theatre, paid for by local merchants who tied in also with special gift offers.

Many groups have learned that they may have good "salesmen" in unexpected places, like taxicabs, especially if they want to reach visitors to a city. When the Kimball Art Museum opened in Fort Worth, Tex. in the '70s, it included among its preview events a special party and tour for cab drivers and for construction workers who helped build the museum. The Arts and Culture Committee of the Greater Philadelphia Chamber of Commerce has hosted "Taxi Driver Appreciation Days," with cabbies and their families feted at local cultural institutions with free admission, souvenirs and refreshments. Lincoln Center found an even more unlikely salesman one year, when it was presenting its "Out-of-Doors" festival. A local postman who happened to drop in during its opening program became so excited about what he saw that he scooped up a pile of fliers sitting near the fountain and stuffed mailboxes along his route with them. The next day, he returned to see the performances and asked a Center official if he could have hundreds of additional fliers to distribute. Perhaps one of these days some enterprising arts organization will tap a word-spreading public that Hollywood has regularly invited to its previews over the years—hairdressers.

FAMILIES

Families are also a somewhat overlooked audience. Groups that find a way to reach them, however, may find it easier to reach parents

50 and children separately when they are promoting future target events to them. The Kentucky Opera hosts regular Family Nights with sponsorship from Brown-Forman, and also has included among its subscription offerings a "Free Granny Offer," allowing grandmothers a free subscription if they are accompanied by two children 15 years or younger who have purchased subscriptions. In rural Tifton, Ga., where background in the arts is not the norm, an arts council called the Arts Experiment Station has offered a low-priced family subscription series for several years. An entire immediate family can attend each event for a set price, regardless of the number of members it has. The concept, supported with funding, has paid off in increasing local interest in cultural programs.

One of the more imaginative family-oriented programs was devised by the concert manager of a conservatory some years ago in an effort to win new audiences for low-priced student performances, and not incidentally, favorably change the image of the institution. Aware that many non-attenders viewed conservatories as forbidding places, Ruth Glazer of the Eastman School of Music set out to develop a special event that could present the institution as a warm and friendly place and attract family groups interested in inexpensive quality entertainment presented in a relaxed atmosphere. The result was a highly successful late afternoon-to-evening event intentionally and aptly named "A Musical Picnic." The light-hearted "picnic" concept was carried out in every aspect of the event, from fliers and promotional materials featuring whimsical child-like drawings printed on brightly colored stock, to the actual program. Recipients were encouraged to bring the entire family, and children's playrooms were set aside for the very young. Free parking, a concert hall program and box suppers were included in the $3 and $4 ticket price. Children's tickets were only $2.

The actual program featured volunteer hosts and hostesses in opera costumes to greet 5:30 p.m. arrivals for a dance program and Imagination Playroom, where Eastman students entertained youngsters. At 6:30, the overflow audience of 3,300, including 2,000 children, assembled in the concert hall for the box suppers and a program featuring a film about the escapades of two children accidentally locked in a concert hall. An orchestra concert included a musical roulette wheel from which children selected the order of the works, a narrated "Carnival of the Animals" with an artist sketching the animals on stage and a concluding march with the audience encouraged to clap and whistle.

Holidays such as Mother's Day and Father's Day have afforded arts groups opportunities to reach family audiences. It is not completely clear, however, what audiences the Bronx Arts Ensemble Orchestra intended to reach in its 1985 and 1986 Mother's Day concerts. The programs were presented at Woodlawn Cemetery.

CHILDREN

Children represent not only audiences for the arts but a possible access to funds—through their own volunteer services and through their parents and relatives. At the Boulder, Colo. Center for Visual Arts, children attending a school art show were invited to bring in pennies to the gallery and lay them end to end in the hopes of laying a trail one mile long. Although the hoped-for mile wasn't reached, the children brought in more than 50,000 pennies. The result was tremendous publicity for the gallery and $500 in its pocket. In Lansing, Mich., students donated their art works, which had been exhibited at the Impression 5 Museum, to the cultural institution, which then sold them to local businesses for display. In Princeton, N.J., a unique cooperative arrangement between the Princeton Chamber Orchestra and the local Multiple Sclerosis drive utilizing teenage girls as a volunteer ticket sales force resulted in a highly successful season subscription campaign for the orchestra. The girls, who had worked as volunteers for a previous M.S. drive, were loaned to the orchestra in an effort to reach new subscribers, especially newcomers to the community, not reached in the past. Under the arrangement, the girls sold orchestra subscriptions, over $5,000 worth, and the orchestra in turn contributed 10 percent of the revenues raised to M.S.

Some groups have devised everything from distributing coloring books to organizing treasure hunts to relate youngsters to their programs. In an effort to interest youngsters in Shakespeare, a Wantagh, N.Y. high school teacher assigned her students to research, write and publish their own newspaper, *The Elsinore Echo.* The paper, which thoroughly involved an entire class, was devoted to the activities of Hamlet and his friends and featured gossip columns, tongue-in-cheek advertisements and editorial and advice columns including one letter signed, "Melancholy in Denmark." A mental health report advised readers, "To be or not be be? If this is your question, call the suicide hotline." At the Community Music School of the University of Redlands, very young children are successfully enticed into an involvement with music through a "Petting Zoo" of musical instruments, part of the school's annual open house. The school marks off a "string pen," a "percussion pen," a "brass pen" and a "wood-wind pen" on the lawn, and faculty members and students bring their

52   musical instruments and sit in the appropriate pen. Children are free to roam from pen to pen and, with the assistance of the teachers, to try out any of the instruments.

THE OFFICE AND BLUE-COLLAR WORKER

While children are tapped frequently, office and blue-collar workers are publics seldom solicited by arts organizations. The reasons aren't difficult to fathom. As a public, workers have had little opportunity to experience arts programs, and their interests have been known to lie in more popular forms of entertainment. Still, there are circumstances where the effort to reach them may be worth it, especially if easy ways can be found to win their interest. To tap into the huge number of employees working in New York's financial district, the Soho Repertory Theatre published redeemable half-price tickets for Thursday evenings only in the newsletter of the Lower Manhattan Cultural Council. The Seattle Opera was able to reach out to Boeing workers through lunch hour mini-previews of each new production, featuring several singers and a pianist, arranged by a Boeing executive who moonlighted as an opera chorus member. The promotional events attracted audiences averaging 250 workers. Perhaps even more important, the giant company, with a local work force in the thousands, placed opera posters throughout its plant, featured announcements about opera performances over the employee intercom and featured articles on the arts group in the *Boeing News*.

The Battery Dance Company, based in Lower Manhattan's financial district, has been able to draw workers to its audience through an aggressive all-out effort designed to reach them at a time they can be reached, the lunch hour, and at places they can be reached, their office buildings or outdoor plazas. Free programs at the renovated offices of Citibank on Wall Street, at Continental Insurance headquarters and at the Battery's own outdoor Downtown Dance Festival held at such sites as the World Trade Center Plaza and Chase Manhattan Plaza, have, according to artistic director Jonathan Hollander, "boosted our paying audience tremendously. From each of our festivals alone, we add about 500 interested people to our mailing list."

Several years ago, on a consulting visit to Syracuse, I learned about one of the more rewarding relationships with blue-collar workers that any arts group has ever experienced. It involved the Syracuse Symphony, an orchestra which was noted for programs presented throughout the area, not only by the full orchestra, but by

its components broken down into such smaller units as brass quintets,
string quartets and even a rock ensemble. As part of a funding pitch
to a major local corporation, the symphony was also soliciting the
company's worker's committee, which had its own discretionary contributions committee. After making an impassioned plea to the
workers for a grant, orchestra administrators were startled when one
of the workers suddenly exclaimed, "Damn it. I feel cheated." The
room was suddenly hushed as everyone turned to look at him. "All
those programs you do are great," he said. "My kid told me about
the concerts and he really liked them. But when I was a kid we didn't
have programs like that. I was cheated." The workers voted a major
contribution to the orchestra.

DOCTORS

One of the best circumstances for a relationship of mutual interest between a cultural organization and a sought-after public is
when need meets need, when involvement with the arts helps a non-
arts group to achieve certain objectives. This was well demonstrated
in Youngstown, Ohio, when the Mahoning County Medical Society
was looking for an appropriate way to celebrate its 100th anniversary in November 1972. Along with such ideas as a history of
medicine exhibit at a county fair, the planning committee of doctors
also came up with the concept of a "meeting of the century" to
celebrate 100 years of service. And since the doctors were celebrating
their birthday, they thought it might be especially meaningful if they
turned things around and gave a birthday gift to the community.

Fortunately for the arts, one of the doctors planning the event
had been involved with several local cultural organizations. He proposed that the recipients of the birthday gift be Youngstown's four
leading arts institutions, as a way of thanking them for their contributions to the community. Every society member was urged to contribute $100 towards the birthday gift, one dollar for each year, and
the "meeting" was turned into a well-publicized, giant, black-tie community celebration to honor both the doctors and the four cultural
institutions—the Youngstown Playhouse, Youngstown Ballet Guild,
Butler Institute of American Art and and Youngstown Symphony.
Both the Symphony and the Playhouse performed briefly at the
celebration.

When the celebration ended, the four arts recipients divided a
$31,000 donation from the doctors' group. Moreover, they benefit-

54   ted greatly from the publicity the program generated over a period of several months, and developed a new and close relationship with a key public. But there was a quid pro quo for the doctors as well. For choosing to use their centennial to honor others instead of patting themselves on the back, the medical society received thanks and recognition from the arts groups—the Butler Institute held a "Medicine in Art" exhibit during the celebration month—and from the community at large. And that, perhaps, was a key goal of the centennial program.

YOUNG PROFESSIONALS

In recent years, the young, upwardly mobile professional has emerged as one of the target audiences of the arts. It's easy to understand why. As a public, the young professionals have all the attributes sought after in arts audience members, a high level of education, a good income, money to spend on entertainment, an interest in social involvement, a spirit of adventure, a need for the new and, for many, both a familiarity with and an interest in the arts. That many of today's young professionals will be tomorrow's top executives provides still another powerful reason for groups to find ways to involve them in their activities. And they have.

Special singles nights have become part of the subscription offerings of groups in every area of the performing arts. At A Contemporary Theatre in Seattle, singles nights have included pre-performance light suppers at which to meet and mingle, and such after-performance events as free disco admissions. Other groups have sponsored special events to draw singles into their orbit. Studio Arena Theatre has had a "curtain raiser," featuring a talk by the artistic director, theater tour, hors d'oeuvres and cocktails, while the Ohio Ballet has hosted TGIF parties at a local shopping center and a special singles night which included a performance and post-performance party with company dancers. Thanks to an insert in Cleveland's "Finest Singles Calendar of Events," and partial sponsorship from *Cleveland Magazine* including a free ad, the latter program turned out to be the dance company's most successful special event of the 1983-84 season. Indicative of the efforts arts groups make to reach affluent singles was the San Diego Pops Orchestra's pre-Christmas performance and party for singles in December 1985. The evening included a no-host reception, dinner and concert, with the audience seated cabaret style, all for $15 a person.

When the arts interest within an audience is matched by a business interest in the same market, and that audience is made up of young professionals, some good things can happen. Carnegie Hall, for example, which has long been interested in attracting young professionals not part of the regular concert scene to its audience, benefitted from the concern of Dewar's "White Label." Dewar's, whose "Profiles" ad campaign is aimed at successful young professionals, sponsored two series of free, hour-long "Highlight" lecture-demonstrations for young professionals at Carnegie Recital Hall during the 1983-84 season, one in classical music and one in jazz. The programs, conducted by such notables as Michael Tilson Thomas, Gunther Schuller and Billy Taylor, were followed by informal cocktail receptions featuring both the evening's artist and complimentary drinks and hors d'oeuvres from Dewar's. Guest lists were compiled by a public relations firm, which contacted major New York companies to uncover young employees who might be interested in attending.

SPORTS FANS

Sports fans are among the most overlooked of potential publics for the arts. In fact, some people refuse to admit that anyone who enjoys sports could possibly like the arts. This kind of either/or attitude carried to an extreme sets up an adversary relationship between the arts and sports that precludes the possibility of mutual involvement. Several years ago, in fact, the National Endowment for the Arts unwittingly carried the "like them or us" proposition to an entire nation with a public service television commercial whose key message was that "we've got more fans than you do." The unlikely carrier of this message was the oft-deposed and oft-reinstated manager of the New York Yankees, Billy Martin, who was shown clumping through the Metropolitan Museum of art in his full baseball regalia, including spike shoes, while telling viewers that the arts had more fans than the three local sports teams, the Yankees, Knicks and Nets, had.

If, indeed, many people who go to football games also go to theatre and the opera—and at least some of the hundred million people who watch the Super Bowl must be in the arts audience as well—cultural groups are missing a good bet if they don't try to tap in to this market and utilize as their salesmen top athletes who are also arts supporters and attenders. Those groups that have, happily, have found success. Those that haven't should be encouraged to try.

56   In an interview that appeared in the sports pages of *The New York Times*, hockey goalie Dan Bouchard was asked about the then recent move of his team, the Flames, from Atlanta to Calgary. Speaking of Calgary, Bouchard said, "There's too little culture here. I need a life outside of hockey so I can relax when the game is over. So do the players' wives. But you can't see a play, the ballet or a concert the way you could in Atlanta." It's not known if anyone from a Calgary cultural organization pounced immediately on Bouchard to invite him to its programs. If not, they missed a good bet.

Prominent athletes make news. The pages of our daily papers devote much more attention to sports than they do to the arts, but instead of lamenting the situation and crying about a "jock mentality," arts groups might be better served if they took advantage of the promotional and fund-raising potential of top sports figures and put them to work. The Dallas Symphony, for example, featured former star quarterback Roger Staubach as the cover boy on one of its subscription fliers. Dressed as Mozart, Staubach urged audiences to "compose yourself—everybody's doing it." The Eglevsky Ballet used local hockey stars Bobby Nystrom and Garry Howatt of the New York Islanders and football star Richard Todd as in-person drawing cards for its cocktail party promoting the company's upcoming fund benefit. Basketball coach and former player Tom Heinsohn lauded the virtues of Boston's museums in a full-page newspaper ad. The late football coach Paul "Bear" Bryant, Alabama's most popular figure, contributed radio spots promoting the arts in Alabama, and also made spots for a national campaign on behalf of the National Assembly of Community Arts Agencies. Baseball great Steve Garvey has been an avid supporter of the arts in San Diego on may occasions, and recently posed for the Old Globe Theatre's 50th anniversary poster along with San Diego Padres teammate Tony Gwynn.

In addition to promoting cultural programs, sports figures have also been helpful in raising funds and, interestingly, in serving on arts boards (although not too many have been asked). Footballer Lynn Swann was on the board of the Pittsburgh Ballet and baseball star Ted Simmons served on the board of the St. Louis Arts Museum—before being traded to Milwaukee, where he became an active arts volunteer and spokesman for the Performing Arts Center Impresarios. During the 1983 season, Steve Garvey helped promote "Steve Garvey's RBI for the Arts Club," which asked fans to pledge donations for every run he batted in to COMBO, San Diego's arts and education fund. Garvey, the honorary chairman of COMBO's annual fund campaign, also made television spots to promote the campaign and personally pledged $10 for each of his runs batted in. Broadcasters and former football heroes Frank Gifford and Don Meredith gave several benefit performances of *The Odd Couple* during the 1985 season for the Santa Fe Festival Theatre. Basketball star Alvin Robertson of the San Antonio Spurs was one of the guest conductors at the "Battle of Conductors," an event held at Trinity University to raise funds for the San Antonio Symphony. Athletes have made personal contributions to arts groups also. Basketball greats Kareem Abdul-Jabbar and Ralph Sampson donated the land under a hotel they owned in Birmingham to the Alabama Symphony, a gift worth $50,000 a year in rental fees to the orchestra.

Tennis champion John McEnroe, a contributor to the matching fund campaign of the Queens Museum and a noted resident of Queens, N.Y., also allowed the museum to use him as the focus for its fund drive. McEnroe's picture appeared on the cover of the campaign brochure, along with a teaser line that read, "The Queens Museum Challenges John McEnroe to a Match." Inside the brochure, both the museum and McEnroe were identified as winners of the match because "John McEnroe's tax-deductible contribution helped release matching federal dollars."McEnroe was also a prominent part of a fund-raising sales drive by the museum. His silhouetted picture, along with the words, "Meet the Challenge," appeared on the front of T-shirts selling for $8 each. The back of each shirt read, "The Queens Museum Challenge Match, 1980-1984."

Top professional sports teams have been among arts boosters and contributors for years. It is understandable when the link between a major league team and a major cultural institution is considered, for both are among the essential amenities that make a city "big league." One year, the Utah Stars, a professional basketball team, contributed $2,500 to a dance company, Ballet West, as its unique way of thanking its own fans for their support. "It is our pleasure," said a team spokesman, "to give this recognition to another Utah-based professional company that has received international acclaim for the excellence of their performance—Ballet West." Ballard Smith, president of the San Diego Padres baseball team and chairman of the San Diego Symphony's Capital Campaign to renovate the local Fox Theatre into a new symphony hall, indicated that he took on the fund campaign chairmanship because, "A truly first-class city needs the best of everything from baseball to classical music."

Other recent links between the arts and professional sports have

58 included the sponsorship by Atlanta's High Museum's Members Guild of a Community Night at an Atlanta Braves baseball game, with museum director Gudmond Vigtel throwing out the first ball, and a pre-game concert by the Indianapolis Symphony at a National Basketball Association game. In Philadelphia, the local chapter of Young Audiences reached both sports and arts fans with an illuminated message flashed every 60 seconds for a week on a screen outside Veterans' Stadium reading, "Champion of the Arts, Young Audiences . . . In School Performances . . . Call 732-8369." The Cincinnati Ballet hosted an unusual fund-raiser at the downtown Shillito Rikes store in October 1985, aimed at both sports and dance fans. By donating $25 to the dance company, fans qualified to participate in an exercise class led by the Ballet along with members of the Cincinnati Bengals football team as special guests.

The imagination and creativity demonstrated by some arts groups have prompted them to use the sports metaphor and reap tremendous publicity benefits from it. To promote its performance of works from the Cleveland Guild of Composers, the Pittsburgh New Music Ensemble decided to emphasize the fact that the concert would be held several hours before the Super Bowl. Fliers showing a football attached to a musical staff read, "Pittsburgh Plays Cleveland, Super Sunday, 1:30 pm Before the Super Bowl." When Chicago was overtaken by a collective mania during the 1985 football season, as the Chicago Bears moved towards the Super Bowl, the Art Institute of Chicago decided to cash in on the media interest in the Bears and at the same time help dispel its image as a stuffy institution. The museum had several of its sculpture instructors make two oversized Bears helmets. Placed atop the statues of the two lions at the museum's entrance, the helmets attracted tremendous attention and became a major newsmaker. The stunt even turned into a national media event when one of the helmets was stolen and later retrieved. The museum then moved the helmets inside its doors, where they served as an audience draw.

The Reno Philharmonic has turned a sports tie-in into an annual funding event. The orchestra's Monday Night Football Party, held each fall, draws large crowds at $20 a person for a big-screen television broadcast of the football game, food, prizes and betting pools. Local interest in sports gave the Cincinnati Symphony the opportunity to organize several all-day CSO Sports Classics, events held in parks that drew several thousand participants to a range of professional and amateur athletic competitions and celebrity events during the two years it was held. Promoted through local Y's and swim, tennis and

running clubs, the day featured everything from roller-skatathons to 59
paddleboat competitions to celebrity fun relays to a softball game with
orchestra members as players. Admission charges and entry fees for
races helped raise nearly $20,000 from each of the Classics.

Corporate interest in professional sporting events has also proved
a boon to some arts groups. Aware of the fact that many large companies purchase season tickets from the local professional baseball,
football and hockey teams to give to customers and employees, the
Minnesota Orchestra decided to tap the market and become an additional business benefit item. In the first year alone, over 200 companies responded positively to the orchestra message, "If you own
Vikings, Twins and North Stars seats, why not the Minnesota Orchestra?" and purchased $60,000-worth of tickets.

GOVERNMENT OFFICIALS

If the sports public is often overlooked, then government is a
public at the opposite end of the spectrum. Although it is virtually
impossible to overlook government, because that's where a good deal
of the money is, involvement with it is too often viewed only as a relationship of supplicant to funder. Arts leaders have done a superb job
in organizing state and national advocacy groups into effective lob-
bying forces, and over the years the arts have been fortunate in the
development of organized groups of elected officials at every level of
government, banded together specifically to focus on arts needs. At
last count, the Congressional Arts Caucus had over 200 members,
while such groups as the U.S. Conference of Mayors and the Arts,
Tourism and Cultural Resources Committee of the National Conference of State Legislatures have a range of specific programs,
publications and support mechanisms for the arts. Yet, the one-on-
one relationship between arts groups and their local legislators, and
the use of legislators and other government officials in the marketing
and promotional programs of individual arts groups, have not been
developed to their fullest potential.

When crunch time comes and government funding becomes so
tight that priorities determine who gets what, the arts must stand
in line with the many other areas seeking support, such as education, health and welfare and social concerns. Legislators who now
support arts funding guests may be hard pressed to vote for additional funds when questions of the poor and the sick must also command their attention. However, as a number of arts groups have

60 already discovered, the symbolic support of their legislators and other government officials as an avenue to other funds may be extremely useful. An appearance of a key official at a funding event, an appropriate message sent at the appropriate time, or the services of a top legislator as chairman or honorary chairman of a major benefit or drive can be extremely useful to cultural organizations.

When Washington, D.C.'s Phillips Collection draws a table of such top government officials as Chief Justice Warren E. Burger, Defense Secretary Caspar W. Weinberger, FBI chief William H. Webster and CIA head William J. Casey to a dinner honoring major corporate contributors, as it did in April 1985, then it's not too difficult to draw other paying guests. When the Queens Museum sends its supporters a letter from Governor Mario M. Cuomo in which he identifies himself as a long-time resident of the area and indicates his belief in "supporting one's local institutions—especially those which directly improve the quality and character of our lives," it doesn't hurt the funding cause—particularly when the governor "encourages you to do the same."

As many groups have discovered, the direct involvement of political people in their programs may be a way to tap their services later, especially if the political leaders receive good exposure from the experience. Arts groups have been adept at using their programs and activities as a stage for key officials, and the officials have been more than willing to participate. To open its 1985-86 season, the Albany Symphony featured at its first concert Albany's Mayor Thomas M. Whalen, III narrating Copeland's "Lincoln Portrait." To announce its newest ensemble, a symphony chorus, the Jacksonville Symphony had a press conference at which Mayor Jake Godbold and several other leading citizens sang the "Hallelujah Chorus." In Etobicoke, a Toronto borough, the mayor hosted a well-attended luncheon for corporations to promote the community arts council and its member groups, while Congressman and Mrs. James H. Scheuer hosted a garden party at their Queens home for the Queens Symphony.

Honoring legislators, both as a group and individually, is one way to involve them. The Bronx Council on the Arts had a good idea some years ago when it honored *all* of its local legislators—seven councilmen and two councilmen-at-large—at a cocktail party held to laud their support of the arts, even though not all of them were known as avid arts supporters. More recently, another Bronx institution, the Bronx Museum of the Arts, picked up on the idea and honored all its state legislators, five state senators and 10 state assemblymen, at its annual benefit. In North Carolina, the Charlotte Symphony didn't forget that Governor James G. Martin once was its principal tuba player. In 1985, it endowed its principal tuba chair in perpetuity as the Governor James G. Martin Chair. The governor and his wife, incidentally, served as honorary chairmen of the symphony's annual ball that season.

Even if they can't attend, legislators like to be invited to the programs they support with their dollars. As arts groups have discovered, it can't hurt the cause. In 1982, all of North Carolina's 12 outdoor theatres joined in presenting each of the state's General Assembly members with free season passes so they could attend programs funded with state dollars. While remembering legislators and government officials is an absolute must, forgetting them when they're no longer in the same positions may be a terrible faux pas that could come back to haunt groups later. With some puzzlement, William J. Bennett, the former chairman of the National Endowment for the Humanities, wondered why he no longer received invitations to openings and social events from the museums, art galleries and other cultural institutions he regularly heard from—and helped fund—before he became the Secretary of Education in 1985. "The relationship between education and culture apparently has not yet been established in their minds," he commented in a newspaper interview.

If politics is a game, as it has often been called, arts groups must learn to be good players and call in their chits when they need calling, or even be a little devious if it helps the cause. Sometimes a circuitous route can turn into a straight line, as when an organization honors a good friend of a high official to ensure that the official attends a special event. The Joffrey Ballet won tremendous recognition and attracted some extra support when Nancy Reagan attended the dance company's glittering Los Angeles benefit in September 1985. But as David Murdock, Joffrey board co-chairman confided to the *Los Angeles Times*, Mrs. Reagan's attendance was merely a case in which he called in his chits. Some four years earlier, Murdock had become involved with the dance company because "the First Lady phoned and asked me to help." He said that he would, but only on condition that Nancy Reagan would be there if he needed her help. He did and she was.

CHARTING PUBLICS

The list of publics available to the arts is endless and not every one of them could or should be reached. But learning to identify

REISS-SOURCE CHART
SAMPLE LISTING OF A TARGET AUDIENCE BUSINESS

(The listing below is purely hypothetical)

Public needs/objections	Identifiable leader(s)	Relationship to concept/precedent	Audience reach	Special projects
•Chamber of Commerce	J. Smith, chamber exec. v.p., husband of arts board member	History of promoting community arts. No financial support	Monthly mtg. Monthly mag. Annual rpt.	Centennial Celebration upcoming Special Downtown Day
Needs • Attract business to community • Promote community	Sam Jones, former board member, is now arts council board			
Objections • Arts of little community interest • Arts not economically significant		*Precedents* • New national study shows chambers support arts		
Response to objections • New economic impact study shows arts make major contribution		• Nearby chamber used arts to help recruit industry with success		

publics and then finding ways to reach key ones is an urgent necessity for every arts organization. A concept of charting publics that I developed several years ago and have since introduced to scores of arts groups has made the task easier. My chart is simply a visual way to keep everything I already know and will learn about an arts group in the future in front of me. The various boxes can be filled in anytime by anyone in an organization, whenever new information is learned.

The series of boxes (see illustration) begins on the far left with a listing of the public, its needs, its objections (if any) to the arts program, and the arts institution's possible responses to these objections. The second box lists the identifiable leader of that public, a key individual in it who has the closest relationship to the arts organization or program. The third and critical box asks the user to list both how that public has related to its program or programs like it in the past, or how it currently relates to it. It also asks what precedents there are elsewhere to show how other groups in that public have related to an arts program. The next box seeks to identify how that particular public reaches its own audiences through meetings, publications or special programs, and the last box is used to indicate any special upcoming events or programs relating to that public that might be useful to the relationship. For example, if the particular public is local business and the chamber of commerce is celebrating its 50th anniversary during the following year, these facts are worth noting on the chart, since a special anniversary event may be put together that links the chamber to the arts group.

The box concept isn't foolproof certainly, since without detailed input, it doesn't serve much of a purpose. But if new information is added whenever it becomes known, administrators will find it a simple and worthwhile visual tool that keeps their key publics in the public eye. The only problem is that if arts groups have too many publics to chart, they may run out of wall space. But then, that isn't as bad as running out of money.

Whatever the public is, the creative administrator can invariably find a new approach to it or find new ways to relate members of that public to its own programs. Congressmen, for example, can insert favorable comments about a local arts group into the *Congressional Record*, which makes an impressive promotional mailing piece, or they can host a reception for a constituent group when that group appears in Washington, D.C. When the Philadelphia Theatre Caravan was appearing at the Kennedy Center early in 1986, Congressman William H. Gray, III of Philadelphia was co-host for a reception in the group's honor.

CASH IN!

64   In dealing with publics, imagination and common sense are an arts group's best allies. Those faculties were certainly in evidence when the University of Delaware was presenting a production of *Dracula* some years ago. It found a new public, an unlikely yet logical one, which was looking for a way to reach its own audiences. The result was a joint promotion linking the theatre with the Blood Bank of Delaware. In a promotional letter, Count Dracula invited recipients to join the Blood Bank—with all the publicity about the play, he had more blood than he could use—and see the new production about his life.

CHAPTER 4

Whose Business
Do You Want?

---

68   Why do arts groups seek funding from business? Probably for the same reason that Willie Sutton tapped into banks: "Because that's where the money is." Not only does business have lots of money, but it will spend that money if the return is good enough. Without demeaning corporations and their considerable contributions to the arts, it is realistic to assume that business, like most individuals, is not totally altruistic. That earthy American philosopher—Mae West—could have been referring to corporate support of the arts when she uttered her immortal words, "Goodness has nothing to do with it."

In recent years, the arts have become a commodity of some importance, not only to the corporate sector but to government as well. A *New York Times* article (June 13, 1985) indicated that a mixture of art and tourism was not unique, and that it "typifies a common practice today, the governmental use of art as a business and diplomatic tool." The article pointed also to federal cultural exchange programs which "use art to blaze paths of communication between governments and people, to promote new national 'images' abroad, and even to lay the groundwork for specific business ventures and political campaigns."

For business, the return from arts support can be just as pragmatic, ranging from an identification with excellence, image enhancement and boosting relations with customers and clients, to the more commercial rewards of identifying new markets, promoting specific products and increasing sales. In addition to the cultural institutions, the audiences of the institutions have become a drawing card for corporate support as they have become recognized as a market of great significance, with high standards of living and money to spend on entertainment and consumer goods, including luxury items. In fact, although a good deal of business support comes in the form of donations from the corporations themselves or from their foundations, there has been a strong increase in business expense giving, with the money coming from public relations and advertising budgets. The cause-related marketing concept, introduced to the arts in the '80s by American Express, who tied donations to cultural groups to the use of American Express cards, is a sound business practice but it is hardly philanthropy.

Because of their continuing economic needs, few arts groups can afford to look gift horses in the mouth and, as a consequence, not enough arts groups recognize the inherent value that they and their audiences have to business. The result is that arts groups may sell their names and their products much too cheaply.

Those savvy arts groups that recognize their worth to business,

however, have learned to knock on many doors at the same corporation to win support. Frequently, they've discovered that the best way
to win corporate funding is not to ask for funding—at least initially.
They may ask for many other things, however—promotional help,
the use of mailing lists, technical assistance, free equipment or the
purchase of tickets—knowing very well that the key to future support may be the involvement of a top business leader now. Referring
to his business counterparts, one corporate arts supporter once said,
"Get them to do something for you now and they're in your debt
forever." Forever may be too long a time to hope for, but when it
comes to business support there is no doubt that familiarity breeds
content.

Aside from donating money, what are some of the things that
business can do for arts groups? Whenever a business is on the verge
of moving to a new facility, it may decide to get rid of much of its
furniture, and there's no reason that the beneficiaries of this largesse
can't be arts organizations. When Exxon refurnished its New York
City offices in the early '70s, it donated a good deal of furniture and
office equipment to some 40 arts groups.

Companies that may not be ready to provide financial support
will frequently be more than willing to lend their space, free of charge,
to cultural groups, or to lend the services of their employees. When
Philadelphia's Gallery Salon was looking for space to present weekend
performances and exhibitions, it was able to get free use of an unused portion of a construction site from Abbotts Square Apartments.
Businesses may also provide promotional help: a laundry in Hunts-
ville, Ala. allowed the local arts council to use its illuminated revolv-
ing sign for announcements; and Pike's Limited, a transport company, donated the roof of its hangar at Newfoundland International
Airport to the Newfoundland Festival for free advertising.

Advertising agencies and public relations firms frequently have
done pro bono work for arts clients, and sometimes the results have
been impressive. Ogilvy & Mather, which has donated its services to
the American Museum of Natural History, has created some
memorable radio ads, including one used to open the museum's hall
of gems featuring Carol Channing singing "Diamonds are a Girl's Best
Friend." Another, opening with music from the old-time television
series "Bonanza," was followed by the voice of Bonanza star Lorne
Greene inviting audiences to attend the new exhibiton at the museum,
"Masterpieces of the American West." Greene told his listeners to
"mosey on down to the museum" because "it's more than just an
art show. Why you could say it's a regular bonanza."

70   *THE DONT'S OF CORPORATE SOLICITATION*

Although many arts groups know what to do in seeking business involvement, it may be just as important to know what not to do. One thing, certainly, is to be sure not to bite the hand that feeds you. According to the folklore of the arts, one Connecticut arts group, a recipient of support from United Technologies, produced a cabaret skit that was all about the Gray boys, Zane, Dorian and Harry. Harry, the chairman and chief executive officer of United Technologies, was reported not to have been the least bit amused.

Another tactical "don't" is, never offer a corporation a project which is not in the image of its image. When the Whitney Museum was looking for a corporation to sponsor its major Jasper Johns retrospective, it reportedly brought some of Johns' works to a meeting of the corporate contributions committee of a major company. Some of the businessmen were disturbed at Johns' portrayals of one of his favorite motifs—the American flag—which didn't look like the flag they were accustomed to seeing. They turned down the proposal. Presumably, in visits to other companies, Whitney officials referred to the patriotic themes in Johns' works rather than showing the actual paintings.

Leonard Fleischer, Exxon's accessible senior arts advisor, recalls the morning when three separate callers each demonstrated one of the "no-nos" of corporate support solicitation. The first caller asked for Robert Kingsley, Fleischer's predecessor, who had died several years earlier. A second caller asked Fleischer if it was worth applying again, since his company had been turned down twice already. A third caller asked Fleischer where Exxon was located now, although the company hadn't moved in several years.

WHAT TO ASK FOR

For the arts group wishing to tap into corporations, a good first thing to ask for in lieu of money might be advice. Many companies want their executives to become involved in community service, and they may be flattered to think that their advice is being solicited. One arts groups, Hospital Audiences, decided one year that instead of asking a leading corporation for a grant, which it had reasonable expectations of receiving, it would ask that corporation for the loaned services of one of its executives for a year, to help develop an organizational marketing plan. Another group, Seattle Opera, saw one of its offices turned into a "war room," complete with huge charts and graphs, courtesy of a team of management volunteers from Boeing who worked with the opera company in formulating long-range plans. Now, national programs such as Business Volunteers for the Arts exist to help tap and train people skilled in business to work with arts groups. But any enterprising arts organization anywhere, in the absence of such programs in its community, can find its own business volunteers. And while arts groups are looking, they might also cast an eye on recently retired executives. A 1985 study by Russell Reynolds Associates showed that within six months of their retirement, some 75 percent of top executives serve as volunteers for non-profit organizations.

Another thing to shoot for which is much easier to win than a direct outlay of cash—although it has great monetary value—is the business-sponsored social/funding event. In fact, any time a new hotel, restaurant or store is opening in a community, the right words can convince its proprietors that they can make a splashy debut and reach the kinds of people they want to reach by making their official opening a benefit for an arts group. Posh franchises are especially susceptible to this message because established arts groups have just the kinds of audiences they wish to attract. In fact, it is the practice of all Gucci franchises to select a local organization to benefit from their openings, as the Baltimore Opera happily learned in 1985. The new Pucci franchise in the Atlanta area, which opened some months earlier, not only selected the Atlanta College of Art as its beneficiary, but also auctioned off Emilio Pucci's own hand-painted, framed designs to benefit the college. After Gucci and Pucci support, will elegant sushi franchises be next? If so, one hopes arts groups will be the first to knock at their doors.

HOTEL SUPPORT

New hotels and motels seeking to promote their presence in the community have been especially generous to the arts. The Ramada Inn in Poughkeepsie, N.Y. celebrated its opening by inviting guests to pay for an evening of dancing and entertainment, with all proceeds going to the Duchess County Arts Council. When the Adams Hotel opened in Phoenix, it celebrated the occasion by hosting the Phoenix Symphony's annual ball, a dinner and cocktail reception for 2,500 people, and picking up the $35,000 party tab.

In Houston, where they do things in a big way, the Lancaster Hotel (renovated from the former Auditorium Hotel) tied its opening, and in fact its pre-opening, to the arts. During its renovation period,

72   the hotel, located across the street from the Alley Theatre and Jones Hall for the Performing Arts, donated and maintained space for the promotion of local arts groups on an eight-foot-high fence around its building site. After opening, the hotel donated rooms and suites to local arts groups on an open-ended basis for use for fund-raising events and meetings. The Four Seasons Hotel in the same city donated a one-bedroom condominium, worth an estimated $96,000, to the Cultural Arts Council for use by visiting artists and guests of the Council's 11 member institutions.

Even long after their openings, hotels have found reasons to tie in to the arts. To promote the publication of a new *Best of Charlotte* guide to the city's restaurants, night life, entertainment and shopping, Guest Quarters of Charlotte, N.C., an all-suite hotel and the book's publisher, threw a fund-raising party. The result was a $21,000 windfall for the party beneficiary, the Charlotte Opera. Governor House Hotel in Montgomery, Ala. doesn't even need a new reason to help the arts. Every year, the hotel gives the "Governor House Arts Award" to a local cultural group. The prize is an all-expense-paid dinner at the hotel for 300 people which the recipient group can use, if it wishes, as a fund-raiser. Most assuredly, many do.

DEPARTMENT STORES

Department stores, which, along with banks, may be the most accessible local businesses for the arts, offer promotional and funding possibilities not only when they first open but long afterwards. Why are stores and banks such good targets? There are two key reasons. First, both banks and department stores are people businesses, dependent on traffic and people movement into their facilities. Involvement with the arts can help to bring them those people. Second, most stores—those in the same price range—and banks look a lot like their competitors. Significant promotions and activities on behalf of the arts can help them to express individuality and project a desired image. Is it any accident that Bloomingdale's, billed in one press release as "America's trend-setting fashion store," sponsors so many arts-supportive events in its New York City flagship location, or that Bloomie stores in other cities get on the arts bandwagon? Or is it any accident that Bloomingdale events are innovative, creative and attention-getting, terms which could be applied to many arts undertakings?

When Bloomingdale's in Dallas decided to help boost area theatre audiences in 1985, nothing less than "The Ultimate Cast Party" to benefit 10 nonprofit local theatres would do. The store saluted the theatres for 10 days with displays and live performances in its Valley View location, and promoted the program with widespread newspaper advertising. It then followed up with the party, a $50-per-person, in-store benefit. The funds raised, about $9,000, were placed into an umbrella fund to be used to help increase the theatre's visibility in the community. According to Kelly Moncrieff, then Bloomingdale's director of public relations, the promotion helped all the participants. "Bloomingdale's is in North Dallas, away from the downtown area and away from the areas where the theatres are located. We wanted to give both the theatres and the store greatly increased visibility." The store also distributed 30,000 discount theatre coupons along with purchases at the store, as a sales promotion tool.

For the opening of its new store at a shopping mall in Melbourne, Fla., Jordan Marsh was looking for a special way to introduce the Jordan Marsh name to the community. The vehicle was a spectacular "Forties Fun Night" for the benefit of the Brevard Symphony. The special atmosphere of a '40s nightclub was created just outside the store's entrance, with dancing, buffet, drinks and entertainment all paid for by the store. Similarly, when Frederick & Nelson wanted to open its first store in downtown Portland, Ore.—it already had two stores in the suburbs—it wanted to stage a major local event and attract as much attention as possible. For that reason, the prestigious Oregon Museum of Science and Industry was selected as the beneficiary of an event billed, "Focus on Oregon, a Benefit for the Museum." It raised $20,000 for the cultural institution. Saks Fifth Avenue previewed the opening of a store in a suburban shopping mall outside of Detroit, and scored something of a coup at the same time by bringing together two of Detroit's leading cultural institutions— the Detroit Symphony and the Institute of Arts—to share in a fund-raising benefit for the first time.

New department stores don't open every day in every community, but existing stores can be counted on to find ways to help the arts, especially if a tie to an arts group's audience or to the group itself, as a symbol of excellence and community pride, is important to them. When Filene's introduced its spring fashion campaign through a benefit for the Metropolitan Center, and when another Boston store, Jordan Marsh, launched its own fashion promotion by hosting the Massachusetts Cultural Alliance's annual Cultural Times Ball, one of Madison Avenue's key publications, *Advertising Age* noted, "The upscale audiences attracted by cultural organizations seem to be exactly what this area's leading department stores are looking to attract." It is no wonder, then, that enterprising arts groups can help local stores find promotional themes that benefit both the stores and the arts. These have included "We love the theatre" campaigns, week-long salutes to arts groups and the underwriting of productions, such as Maas Brothers Florida chain has done for the Asolo State Theater. And if a party idea happens to be particularly good and ties in to a store's promotional concept, then anything can happen.

Some year ago, when the Nelson Gallery of Art in Kansas City, Mo. was seeking to promote an upcoming Van Gogh exhibit, it benefitted from the fashion awareness of one of its supporters. She recognized that yellow would be a key fashion color that season and that yellow was featured prominently in the artist's work. The result was a promotional bonanza: a leading local department store, Harzfeld's, introduced a new high fashion color to its customers, "Van Gogh Yellow," as part of its major fashion promotion. Both the fashions and the upcoming art exhibit were promoted prominently in store windows and in half-page color advertisements in the local press, which featured a Van Gogh farm scene in yellow. The enterprising museum benefitted further when another business, a local movie house, reissued the film *Lust for Life*, a fictionalized biography of Vincent Van Gogh.

A BUSINESS MARKETING TOOL

While the museum profited greatly from the exposure it received, the department store and movie theatre reaped equal benefit. What may not be recognized often enough by cultural administrators is the fact that they are in a unique position to help businesses market their names and products. The rewards they receive in return, money or promotional help, can then be viewed as a form of repayment for the services they've provided. The experience of the East New York Savings Bank is a case in point. Some years ago, when the bank was planning to open a new branch on West 42nd Street in New York City, its marketing vice president came up with a novel way to promote the branch opening and location. He would identify it with a neighborhood landmark. The landmark selected by the bank was the New York Public Library, right across the street, which was about to launch a campaign of its own to match a $500,000 grant from the National Endowment for the Humanities.

The bank's promotion linked its opening with the library's drive, utilizing several full-page ads each week in each of New York's daily newspapers plus a heavy barrage of radio commercials. The bank's message was so unusual that it immediately attracted tremendous attention. Instead of just offering new depositors the traditional lure of bankdom—free gifts for opening a new account—it gave them an option. In lieu of taking the free gift, they could donate the cost of that gift to the New York Public Library by instructing the bank to send an equal amount directly to the library. The concept of the choice was heightened by the print ads, which showed all of the free gifts along with a picture of bank chairman John P. McGrath standing behind a table on which they were placed. The caption read, "East New York Savings Bank has a gift for you, but we'd rather you didn't take it."

When the dust settled, virtue had triumphed. Riding the wave of tremendous publicity occasioned by the bank ads, and boosted by the funds contributed by both bank depositors and the bank, the library campaign attracted triple the support it had projected. Even before the funding deadline, the library was able to announce that it had topped its goal by $200,000. Incredibly, in spite of the acquisitive nature we tend to ascribe to the American public, a full 20 percent of new depositors waived their free gifts in order to contribute to the library. Moreover, some *non-depositors* sent donations for the library to the bank, along with effusive thank you notes. What is more, corporations were spurred into contributing because of the bank's action.

What was probably the most interesting and lucrative result of the campaign was its effectiveness as a marketing tool for the bank. The tie to a cultural institution helped the business as much as it helped the cultural group. The bank experienced the most successful branch opening in its history, with both the number of new accounts and the amount of money deposited far exceeding all expectations. The bank also received tremendous publicity and recognition for the public service it had performed, and hundreds of congratulatory messages. Proving the adage, mentioned earlier, that once business does something for you they're in your debt, the bank became a staunch supporter of cultural programs in the years following. In fact, several years later, the bank *adapted* its earlier promotion and instead of offering free gifts to new Christmas Club accounts, donated the cost of the gifts, $15,000, to Hospital Audiences. Interestingly, the bank equalled the amount of the previous year's new Christmas Club deposits, in spite of the withdrawal of the free gift offer, and had no negative feedback from its customers.

The radio and television comedian Fred Allen once said, "Imitation is the sincerest form of television." If you substitute the word "business" for "television," the line might refer to innovative business support mechanisms for the arts. Few companies want to be the first

76 on the block to try something new, but once it's been tried and it works, then others will surely follow. In fact, when I was lecturing on business support of the arts to a group of businessmen in Tucson and mentioned the "turn your gift into a donation" concept, it didn't take long for a local banker to contact the East New York Bank and initiate a similar campaign in his own city. The "adapt not adopt" adage can apply to business as well as to the arts, and arts groups are wise to look for a second corporate sponsor once there's been a precedent established.

One of the positive aspects of an arts group's developing a relationship with a local business is that the relationship can be reinforced every year. In Akron, O'Neils, a leading department store, has sponsored an "Emerald Isle Ball" on behalf of the Akron Symphony every St. Patrick's Day since the mid-'70s. In Amarillo, Tex., the annual "Christmas Roundup," a merchant's market on behalf of the local Arts Alliance and the Symphony Guild, has become something of a local holiday tradition. A fund event that nets close to $50,000 each year is a nice tradition to have.

PROFITS-SHARING

A nice tradition to initiate—it's even good as a one-time venture—is getting local businesses to pledge a portion of their receipts to the arts. It might almost be termed a profit-sharing idea. In New Orleans, the Maison Blanche department store sponsored a day in honor of the New Orleans Symphony for several years (until the store changed ownership), and while promoting the orchestra in the store throughout the day, also turned over 10 percent of its proceeds to it. With a precedent established, the orchestra was then able to find another department store sponsor, and in recent years the Godchaux Department Store has had a New Orleans Symphony Day, turning over 10 percent of its gross receipts to the orchestra. In Oklahoma City, a group of merchants ushered in the 1985 Christmas shopping season by closing store doors at 6:00 p.m. on a Thursday night and then reopening them an hour later, not only to launch the holiday season, but also to contribute a percentage of their sales to the Oklahoma Ballet. In nearby Tulsa, Stein Mart, an off-price department store, started its holiday season a week earlier, the Friday following Thanksgiving, by featuring mini-performances by members of the Tulsa Philharmonic throughout the day, and then donating 10 percent of its sales to the Philharmonic.

Arts groups elsewhere have also benefitted from donations of a percentage of business receipts, and sometimes the concepts have been interesting and adaptable. The San Diego Repertory Theatre received a donation of $10 for every student enrolled one fall by a local school, while the Jenkintown, Pa. Music School has been given 1 percent of the total of all supermarket checkout tapes it collects— keeping parents and friends very busy—from a local market. Stockbroker Jack White, head of a discount brokerage firm in San Diego, was concerned with the funding problems faced by local arts groups in 1981, so he pledged a donation of 50 cents from the sale of every listed stock or bond transaction made by his firm for a year. Even smaller businesses can find their own ways to make contributions. Leatherby's, an ice cream parlor in Reno, Nev., issues coupons that give holders a 10 percent discount on purchases, while also rewarding the Sierra Arts Foundation with a 50-cent donation for every purchase of $2 or more.

THE BUSINESS-SPONSORED PARTY

One activity that many businesses feel comfortable with, that can be a boon to an arts group in financial need, is the business-sponsored party, often held at a corporation's headquarters. At this kind of event, the guests, executives of other companies, are seldom solicited directly for funds, although they are certain to be asked for their support at some later date. Many companies donate facilities, food and drink for this kind of pump-priming, and often help to find the potential corporate funders to invite. Cocktail parties and luncheons are the most common settings, although some businesses prefer breakfasts. Atmosphere and tone are very important, and the message of the arts organization, usually articulated through the artistic or executive director, is very clear indeed.

When the reincarnated Lincoln Center Theater Company was launching its first season in fall 1985, after an absence of several years, the New York Times Company Foundation hosted a luncheon in its honor, and invited some nine corporate representatives to break bread with, meet and listen to Gregory Mosher, the company's director, Bernard Gersten, its executive producer, and John Lindsay, former mayor of New York City and the reorganized company's board chairman. Fred Hechinger, long-time *Times* columnist and president of the foundation, greeted the corporate guests.

Equitable Life in New York City has hosted many parties in honor of arts groups, and Exxon's luncheons and cocktail receptions have brought corporate funders into close contact with such organizations

78   as the Paul Taylor Dance Company, the Young Playwrights Festival
of the Dramatists Guild and the American Music Theater Festival,
on whose behalf it held two cocktail receptions for some 20 corporate
guests. As arts groups and their business sponsors have learned,
glamour helps sell, and the addition of a noted celebrity to say a few
words on behalf of the arts group—the indefatigable Celeste Holm
has enlivened many such programs—can touch even the most jad-
ed corporate executive. The appearances of producer Harold Prince,
composer Philip Glass and writer Sheldon Harnick at the American
Music Theater Festival soirées certainly didn't hurt the cause.

   The experience of the Trisha Brown Dance Company demonstrates just how much a corporation's involvement as sponsor of
a social event can mean to an arts group. When Morgan Guaranty
Trust Company of New York hosted a luncheon for the company at
its New York offices in 1984 and invited both corporate and foundation executives, it represented a turning point for the dance troupe,
according to its managing director, John Killacky. "Morgan was able
to attract the higher echelon companies, the kind we couldn't ordinarily draw," he said. "It gave us a new validity and impetus." The Dance
Theatre Workshop, another Morgan Guaranty beneficiary, received
some three or four new grants within months of the business reception on its behalf.

INVITATIONS TO EXECUTIVES

   If arts groups are too small or lack the clout to sell a corporation
on sponsoring an executive event on their behalf, they might find that
joining forces and presenting a movable feast can make a difference.
That's what happened when the Lower Manhattan Cultural Council
was able to get Con Edison to underwrite a bus tour to seven cultural
institutions in downtown New York City. The five-hour afternoon tour
by some 40 corporate executives, which included mini-performances,
exhibits and discussions with the arts groups' leaders, ended with
a reception—and, presumably, some enlightened executives.

   When arts groups themselves have organized special programs
to lure corporate supporters to their ranks, they have done so with
verve and imagination. The Scottsdale, Ariz. Arts Center Association
has used the stage of the city's theatre for an annual luncheon held
specifically for corporate executives. Poshness has been the rule in
food, service and ambiance, with soft lights and a background pianist
helping to set the mood for the pitch for support which has won scores

of new corporate members yearly, as well as donations and in-kind services.

The Oregon Shakespearean Festival, aware that 90 percent of its audience comes from outside its home in Ashland, has—with the help of a plane donated by Alaska Airlines and additional transportation expenses picked up by other corporations—flown in more than 70 presidents and chief executive officers of Washington State companies in a single season to attend performances. When New York City's Playwrights Horizons wanted to explain the inner workings of its operation to corporate executives as a prelude to funding pitches, staff members wrote and presented a 45-minute skit about different aspects of the organization, and presented it as a lunch hour sampler for businessmen.

CORPORATE MEMBERSHIP AND SPONSORSHIP

The George Street Playhouse in New Brunswick, N.J. makes no bones about its interest in winning corporate support, and promotes its annual Corporate Evening at the Theatre with articles in its newsletter headed "We Want Your Company." The event, designed to entice corporate members into the GSP Corporate Club, has featured a wine-tasting, a brief discussion about the theatre program by the producing director and a complimentary performance. But while many arts groups have corporate membership programs, offering special benefits to companies who pay for their privileges, GSP also tries to involve influential corporate figures who seldom win recognition—the secretaries. In addition to its corporate night, the theatre sponsors a yearly Secretaries Night, complete with a reception and free performance, to honor those employees who could be helpful in giving their bosses a nudge in the right direction.

The rewards of corporate membership vary from arts group to arts group, with the size, stature and budget of the group all factors in determining what that group can ask for as membership fees. George Street, for example, offers a three-tiered membership: $100 for associate status, $250 for full membership and $500 for executive producer. The third level, in addition to affording a listing in programs and free tickets to productions, enables a corporation to be listed as sponsor of one mainstage performance of its choice, with acknowledgement in both the playbill and theatre lobby.

The meaning of corporate sponsorship varies among arts groups, and many view it as a special asset not to be given away lightly. The

80   Alliance Theatre Company/Atlanta Children's Theatre, for example, has developed an elaborate and carefully structured program of corporate sponsorship relating to each production. Sponsorship begins at $5,000 for the lunchtime theatre program of five productions, or for the Umbrella Players school tour program of two productions, and goes all the way up to a "dream" investment of a minimum of $25,000 for a special program to bring world-class theatre talent to Atlanta. Sponsorship of a mainstage Alliance production is $15,000. The theatre also offers such other non-production sponsorship opportunities as subsidizing six issues of its newsletter at $10,000, and back-of-ticket messages at $5,000.

Inherent in the Alliance concept is the careful delineation of the benefits offered in return for sponsorship. Mainstage production sponsorship, for example, includes 18 separate benefits ranging from corporate credit wherever the name of the production appears to credit in all ads, press releases and lobby literature on the production to complimentary tickets and employee discounts. Additionally, corporate sponsors are treated to 20 opening night tickets and an opening night party.

The question of sponsorship is critical to many arts groups because they have something significant to sell and they may have a number of potential buyers. Since the early '80s, in fact, one company, Merrill Lynch, Pierce, Fenner and Smith, has developed an aggressive marketing program, with the aid of a sports promotion firm, to buy marketing packages from arts groups. These might include such benefits as renaming an existing series for Merrill Lynch, or having the Merrill Lynch name listed on the backs of tickets. Packages have brought from $5,000 up to $50,000 or more into the treasuries of prestigious arts groups.

Corporate interest in sponsorship has been growing at a rapid rate in recent years, as the arts have joined sports as a sought-after area of business opportunity. In fact, a bi-weekly newsletter focusing on sponsorship of special events, *Special Events Report*, published by International Events Group in Chicago, has increased its focus on the arts, and a number of its articles have captured the corporate viewpoint toward sponsorship of arts events. And, as many arts groups have learned, sponsorship is not patronage. As Bill Kallaway, managing director of Kallaway Limited in London, said in an article in the newsletter referring to sponsorship, "Its principal purpose is the creation of a favorable climate in which to trade. Sponsorship without a motive is patronage, and has no place in the marketing mix . . . Over the next decade, sponsorship must become synonymous with the word leisure and incorporate the arts." Tom Sawyer, vice presi-

dent and marketing director of Baton Rouge's City National Bank, **81**
explained why his bank increased its arts sponsorship funding from
$25,000 to $100,000 in a year this way: "We targeted the arts because
corporate sponsorship of arts events in Baton Rouge is new. Of course
we wanted to be good corporate citizens but let's face it—we're a
business. We looked at the kinds of people the arts attract and found
that these people are our best potential customers."

Corporate sponsorship is big game, with the potential for some
very lucrative returns. As arts groups become more and more
desirable to companies seeking sponsor relationships, they will have
to be careful to establish their own guidelines as to what they will
and will not do. In addition to questioning the quid pro quo aspects
of any relationship—will we get as much as we're giving?—an arts
organization must be concerned that whatever project is undertaken
is in good taste and will not be harmful to its image. And in spite of
the guidelines established, there are so many gray areas that each
new proposal must be judged individually.

When business sponsorship works, and it usually does, the
returns for the arts can be substantial. For the Van Cliburn International Piano Competition in 1985, a major event in the music world,
a whole group of sponsors was lined up including such companies
as Mobil Oil, Tandy/Radio Shack and Sony, with the last company
contributing electronic equipment and video and audio stock for use
in screening Competition auditions both in Europe and the United
States. In return, Sony received the right to use photographs of the
auditions in its promotional materials, and to publicize the use of its
tape and equipment in the competition. Another sponsor, American
Airlines, was designated the official carrier in return for providing a
range of benefits to the Competition. These included printing 30,000
promotional brochures and staffing a public relations center for the
two-week run of the Competition in Fort Worth; discounting air fares
for attendees; an article on the Competition in its in-flight magazine;
and playing tapes of previous winners on its in-flight channel. Most
important, the airline provided a year's free travel on American
Airlines routes so that the Competition Gold Medalist could perform
in some 40 cities.

There are times, however, when the sponsorship arrangement
might be questioned, especially if the commercial aspect seems too
blatant. Arts groups must ask not only if they are getting as much
as they are giving, but if the resulting promotion projects the desired
image. When Ford of Canada helped underwrite a production of *A
Midsummer Night's Dream* by the Manitoba Theatre Centre, it received, in return, the right to place two of its then-new 1979 cars in

82   the theatre lobby for the entire run of the play. Not only did thousands of playgoers see the cars, but one person even took one for a test drive and bought it. Another sponsor, Procter & Gamble's Secret deodorant, funded the School of American Ballet's National Audition Program in 32 cities as well as New York, and then proclaimed its munificence in advertisements. "Secret," read one such ad, "interested in sponsoring a dance program because of the natural link between the rigors of dance performance and the use of Secret deodorant, searched for a full year before selecting the School of American Ballet."

LOGICAL TIE-INS

The best business-arts ties are those that are the most logical and bring benefits to both partners. In a variation on an old funding theme—the "non-event" for which guests are asked to send checks for the privilege of not attending—the Edmonton Opera sought out and found a logical business sponsor. For its February 1986 "Unlunch," the opera company won support from the Uncola people, the local bottler of Seven-Up. Gray Beverages underwrote the printing costs for the fund mailing and for coupons good for free bottles of Seven-Up for paying non-attendees. In the process, the bottler reaped widespread publicity.

When the Palace Theatre in Cleveland's Playhouse Square presented *Pump Boys and Dinettes*, it led to a natural wedding between Sohio gas stations and the theatre. Sohio sponsored the production, and its gas stations promoted the play by offering customers coupons worth $1 off their admission. The theatre, in turn, offered its patrons coupons worth $1 off full-serve fill-ups at the gas station. Similarly, when the Winter Construction Company in Atlanta gave a $20,000 grant to the Atlanta Symphony to underwrite the Winter Pops Concert series in 1984, it also initiated a campaign to focus attention on its industry and bring some additional cash into the symphony coffers. The result was solicitation of the building industry through a "Hard Hats for the Atlanta Symphony Orchestra" campaign. Winter kicked off the campaign with a reception attended by over 800 building executives, and followed up by offering all contributors to the orchestra specially designed hard hats with symphony orchestra logos. The campaign worked so well that the orchestra established a Hard Hats division in its membership program.

In Madison, Wisc., another business theme helped to tie a local company to the arts. Through an association with the Elaine Powers Figure Salon, which helped to underwrite it, the Madison Symphony

Orchestra League launched a "Shape Up with the Symphony" campaign, designed to help spur volunteers to push orchestra ticket sales. The kick-off luncheon was held at the figure salon, with coordinators wearing exercise clothing. Attendees received tote bags filled with literature about the orchestra's "musical fitness" and received a pep talk from the conductor on the same subject.

The alert arts administrator can often flag a corporation logically suited to sponsor a particular project. When Walter S. Poleshuck, then development director at the American Federation of the Arts, was looking for a corporate sponsor to underwrite a touring exhibition of Maori art from New Zealand collections, he approached Mobil Corporation. He knew that the oil company was involved with the New Zealand government in lengthy negotiations over oil drilling rights, and wouldn't hurt its case by offering to sponsor the showing of native art. He was right. And what could have been a more logical marriage than the Metropolitan Museum of Art's exhibition, "Man and the Horse," and the sponsorship of fashion designer Ralph Lauren's company, Polo. The exhibition focused on the role played by the horse in the development of style in fashion, and included men's and women's costumes used for riding, hunting, racing and for playing *polo.*

Many years earlier, I was able to help a museum find a sponsor for an exhibition it wanted to create by matching the museum with a business that had its own need to meet. The company was Travelers Insurance, which was looking for a way to promote its exhibit at the New York World's Fair during its second season. The cultural institution was the Brooklyn Children's Museum, which was looking for a way to build an exhibition around the work of children in its art and photography classes. The result was that, prior to the opening of the Fair, a busload of youngsters from the museum toured the Travelers exhibit, "Great Moments in Mankind," and sketched, photographed and articulated their impressions of it. Some time later, the exhibition opened at the museum to some fanfare. "A Child's View of the World's Fair: By Children and for Children" featured the drawings, photographs and voices of the youngsters from the museum. Everyone was happy. The museum had an exhibiton paid for by Travelers, featuring the work of its students; and Travelers, a company deeply interested in children because of its commerce in life insurance policies, had sponsored a program that demonstrated its concern for youngsters.

The opportunities for business support and involvement are virtually endless, and it is no accident that the best relationships are those that equally benefit both business and the arts. Carnegie Hall,

84   for one, has reaped rewards from its use as a "benefit" in business customer relations programs. For example, Banker's Trust sponsored a Houston Symphony concert at the hall, and flew up some of its key customers from Houston to attend the concert. When the United States Trust Company wanted to introduce its clients to its new offices in Manhattan, it feted them at a cocktail reception in its new quarters and then bused them to a Carnegie Hall concert by the Academy of St. Martin-in-the-Fields, which it sponsored specifically to tie in to its office opening party.

AIRLINES

Airlines are looking to promote themselves and the routes they fly both through program sponsorship and through designation as official carriers of arts groups that fly from their key cities. The returns to the arts are significant. The Pittsburgh Opera, one of several opera companies that have designated US Air as their official carrier, received $20,000 in complimentary tickets from the airline for the 1985-86 season, for use in artist transportation or staff travel to opera-related functions. The Dallas Symphony benefitted when American Airlines, as a way of promoting its new Dallas-to-London route, awarded it $5 for each passenger who flew that route over a six-month period.

The Jackson, Miss. Symphony League even found an airline receptive to its use as a volunteer "perk," and as a willing vehicle for launching a promotion drive. In addition to offering a free round trip for two to San Francisco to the symphony volunteer with the highest season ticket sales for the 1983-84 season, Delta Airlines played a key role in the "Flying High with the Jackson Symphony" campaign. In fact, the campaign began at the Jackson Municipal Airport where committee chairmen, captains and division leaders gathered in January 1983 to board "Delta Flight 1983-84." On board, the volunteers were welcomed by Delta's marketing manager, told about the San Francisco attractions that awaited the winner, were pumped up for the campaign and served snacks and drinks, before deplaning an hour later without ever having left the ground. Later, at a kickoff party for the nearly 300 volunteers who would be involved in the campaign, in a room decorated with airplane cutouts and posters from San Francisco, Delta donated carrying bags for use as volunteer information kits and filled them with calendars, luggage tags and pens. The "Flying High" theme was subsequently featured in all the subscription campaign materials including brochures, banners and billboards. Happily, subscription sales flew as high as the campaign did, netting the orchestra a record $136,000.

TIE-IN OPPORTUNITIES

The roster of imaginative business-arts tie-ins involves companies in every area of business activity, from small shops and restaurants to giant conglomerates, including some seemingly unlikely partners. Fat Eddie's Bar and Grill was one of the key participants in a business alliance organized to help support the Southwest Theatre Center in Las Cruces, N.M. Edmonton, Alberta rancher Don Cormie was the donor of a yearling bull for auction by the Northern Light Theater, and in Detroit, rock radio station WWWW-FM donated $3,300 to the Detroit Symphony from its sale of a station-produced record album featuring local bands. In Westbank, British Columbia, Mission Hill Vineyards created new wine labels to benefit nearby arts groups and to promote its product at the same time: the labels bore the logos of both the arts groups and the winery. Profits from the sale of such "new wines" as Opus One and Entre' Act Reserve returned hard cash to the Okanagan Symphony and Sunshine Theatre in Kelowna. The winery also helped the Vancouver Symphony Orchestra organize a VSO Wine Club and win benefits of from $10 to $20 for each case of white and red VSO Reserve sold.

A key wedge into the corporation, one that wins not only financial support but individual participation as well, is its employees. Many corporations today have matching gifts and matching membership programs which meet amounts contributed by their employees to arts organizations and other nonprofit groups. A Business Committee for the Arts directory of programs benefitting the arts, published in 1985, lists 255 different entries. Some companies interested in involving their employees in worthwhile outside activities have gone a step further. Metropolitan Life, for example, has published a newsletter for employees about arts organizations funded by the company.

ACKNOWLEDGING CORPORATE SUPPORT

Whatever kind of relationship an arts group develops with a business supporter, either local or national, that group must remember to recognize, whenever possible, that support. Years ago, the media was reluctant to identify those businesses that sponsored

86 arts events or supported programs. Today it is considerably less so, especially since many of those corporate supporters themselves are no longer reluctant to call attention to their good deeds wherever possible. In fact, they frequently place ads to call attention to their support in the very media that once ignored their largesse. It is generally acknowledged that, as a rule of thumb, major corporate supporters of the arts will spend as much on promoting a project they are sponsoring as on the project itself. It is rare indeed *not* to see several advertisements from a corporate sponsor, and obviously, this kind of additional exposure benefits the arts recipient. Certainly no one at the Alvin Ailey American Dance Theater could have had any objections to the frequent ads placed by the Philip Morris Company, the donor of a $300,000 grant to the company in 1985, showing company dancers in action, to promote the Ailey season at the City Center in New York. Headlined, "Meet the Real Movers and Shakers," the ad included at the bottom the Philip Morris name, logo, a list of its companies—Marlboro and Lite Beer among them—and the familiar Philip Morris slogan, "It takes art to make a company great."

Aware of the quid pro quo, arts groups in recent years have made major efforts to acknowledge the support they receive, going beyond the acknowledgement commitments they have made in advance to sponsors. This has included listings of corporate supporters in newsletters, full-page newspaper ads listing business benefactors, special lobby exhibits and profiles of different sponsors each month in printed programs. One arts group, the Albright-Knox Art Gallery in Buffalo, N.Y., even issued a special press release several years ago to tell people that the support received from a corporation for the current exhibition was "absolutely essential." The release went on to request of news media that "when reviewing or mentioning this exhibition, you would make note of this vital support." Other arts groups have publicly noted the contribution of a very special corporate donor by honoring that donor at one of their benefit programs, as the Vineyard Theatre did in May 1985 when it presented its first annual Vineyard Theatre Award for Distinguished Service to the Arts to the American Savings Bank.

At times, giving added corporate recognition may even bring additional benefits to the arts giver. When Young Audiences, Inc. decided to honor Mobil board chairman Rawleigh Warner for his support of the arts at its annual benefit dinner, it had no idea of the extra boost it would receive. However, because Warner was being honored, the public relations staff at Mobil wanted to promote the dinner as effectively as possible. Thus, Young Audiences found itself the subject of

a major Mobil advertisement on the "Op Ed" page of the *New York* **87**
Times, which described the Y/A program and invited other corporations to support it.

In coming years, as government support becomes an increasingly competitive funding arena, arts groups will look to business for
its help and involvement. The kinds of relationships that develop may
take on many new forms. Whatever happens, however, there is no
doubt that the business-arts relationship is here to stay. Why not?
The arts may need business as much as business needs the arts.

CHAPTER 5

It Pays to Advertise, Especially If Someone Else Pays

————————————————————

90   America's advertising industry has embraced the arts. With growing regularity, our finest magazines include ads which use arts settings, employ arts terminology, feature prominent artists and even promote products with names "stolen" from the arts. Perfume ads are set in museums, telephone ads are placed in dance studios, rental cars are teamed with symphonic conductors and quality gin embraces the accoutrements of a concert hall. With relative ease, artists are converted into pitchmen. Violinist Pinchas Zukerman promotes Smirnoff Vodka, ballerina Heather Watts sells Flintstone Vitamins and Cynthia Gregory has never left home without her American Express card. Seated in front of a computer monitor, a tone-deaf hacker may find Jazz to his liking, perform with Symphony or Ensemble, or perhaps look for Encore before he has even begun his work. There is no doubt that computer software has a musical lilt.

The watch we wear may be visual, if it's a Movado Museum watch, or musical, if it's an Amadeus, or "the architect of time," if it's an Ebel. And today's woman may be magically transformed into a Diva if she wears the right scent, forcing her admirers to discover that "many listen but her heart sings only for one." She may find that her mirror reflects La Scala when she looks into it, if she is wearing Stendahl's Harmonique, "a grand symphony of colors for the face and nails all in glorious operatic bloom."

Advertising's love affair with the arts has proved highly beneficial to the cultural field and can continue to be so, if arts groups recognize that in their everyday activities they have a resource of unusual worth. Many arts groups reap income from the rental of their facilities, both interior and exterior, for use as advertising settings, while some of the same groups and others attract pro bono support from local ad agencies and the advertising and public relations departments of large corporations. But perhaps the greatest opportunities for the arts lie in the unusual benefits that await them from within the advertising and promotional budgets of business.

PUBLIC SERVICE CAMPAIGNS

Major national public service ad campaigns have supported the arts as an area of interest since 1970, when, at the behest of myself and others, and Advertising Council initiated its first campaign built around the arts. This kind of support has been invaluable, as have many subsequent national and regional campaigns in behalf of the arts. Well remembered is the television commercial used to promote the arts in Montgomery, Ala. featuring the personality who, arguably, was that state's best known individual, football coach Paul "Bear" Bryant. In what subsequently became one of Alabama's most-watched spots, Bryant told viewers that all of the state's talent wasn't on the football field, it was in the arts, too.

But, as many arts groups have learned, it is possible to win not only institutional advertising support for the arts in general, but time and space promoting a very specific arts product or event. Outdoor advertising companies who sell billboard space are among those who have been generous to the arts, and it's not unusual to drive into cities in Georgia or North Carolina, states that seem to have won a good deal of support, and see billboards promoting a local cultural event. In the upper Midwest, a company called Newman Signs sponsored a program in which 15 artists from the Fargo, N.D.-Moorehead, Minn. area painted poster displays for billboards to promote local theatre, opera and symphony programs as well as arts fund-raising events. In Athens, Ga., local advertising agencies, interested in convincing their potential customers that good advertising is an art, used the city's office of cultural affairs to prove their point by initiating a free billboard campaign to promote local arts groups, utilizing 50 donated billboards in a 24-county area. In one of the more spectacular examples of outdoor business advertising for the arts, Winnipeg's Westin Hotel lit its facade with a 21-story treble clef design to honor the December 1982 debut of conductor Kazuhiro Koizumi with the Winnipeg Symphony. Perhaps topping that event was one initiated by the Williams Island resort community in Florida, which hired 150 symphony orchestra musicians under the baton of Antonio de Almeida to promote the "topping off" of its first completed residential tower. Grouped along balconies of the tower's 31 stories, the musicians performed at the ceremony.

FREE ADVERTISING OPPORTUNITIES

Free advertising opportunities for the arts abound in some interesting and perhaps unlikely places. America's craftsmen and the June 1986 conference of the American Craft Council were promoted throughout March and April 1986 in free advertising printed on the sides of millions of Safeway shopping bags, distributed to shoppers in over 700 of the chain's supermarkets. The Kentucky Center for the Arts captured the attention of potential supporters, thanks to a slide show on its activities installed without charge on the second floor of a popular Louisville restaurant, Charley's. In New York City, the Museum of American Folk Art showcased objects from its per-

92   manent collection in the American Festival Cafe. Another museum, Impressions 5 in Lansing, Mich., benefitted from an ad campaign undertaken by Kroger supermarkets which included museum admission "two-fers" in newspaper ads. The supermarket chain also printed and distributed family membership coupons for the museum and 5,000 copies of the "Amazing Michigan Maze Booklet," prepared by the museum's graphics department.

In one of the more unusual yet effective business advertisements, the Pima Savings and Loan Association in Tucson, Ariz., had works from the collections of four leading area museums shot by a top photographer. The bank then issued a new line of custom checks in four designs, each featuring a photo of a grouping of artifacts from one of the museums on its face. The reverse side of the checks provided background information on each of the museums. In addition to this promotional support, the museums received donations from the bank.

THE PRINT MEDIA

Magazines and newspapers have provided arts groups with free space. They have also entered into joint promotional campaigns to provide funding for the arts and new subscribers for themselves. *Argus*, a Seattle weekly, donated six ads per issue for two years to local cultural groups seeking to promote their events and raise money. *Corporate Monthly*, in the Philadelphia area, found corporate sponsors to purchase space for nonprofit cultural groups.

In 1962, long before the arts were recognized by business as a useful marketing resource, I helped introduce a new subscription-builder for *Show* magazine through my public relations firm, Related Arts Counsellors. The concept was simple yet workable, tying subscription sales to donations to participating arts groups. Cultural organizations offered their supporters subscriptions to the arts-oriented magazine at discount rates and, with each subscription sold through the offering, the arts group received half the proceeds. To give greater impetus to the offering, department stores in several cities served a third-party role as patrons of the arts. Neiman-Marcus in Dallas did a mailing to its charge customers on behalf of the Dallas Theater Center; Hengerer's in Buffalo bound the *Show* magazine offer into its Christmas catalogue on behalf of the Buffalo Philharmonic; and the Albright-Knox Art Gallery and Halle Brothers in Cleveland mailed to 15,000 top charge customers in support of the Cleveland

Orchestra. In Hartford, Conn., Mayor William E. Glynn proclaimed   **93**
the period between November 20 and 26 as Performing Arts Week,
with *Show* sponsoring a luncheon in Hartford to kick off the week—
both arts leaders and magazine advertisers were invited—and to announce its subscription plan to benefit the Connecticut Opera, Mark
Twain Masquers and the Hartford Symphony. To strengthen the relationship, *Show* introduced an October through May Performing Arts
Calendar for Hartford, which it distributed free of charge. The plan
has since been adapted in recent years by such publications as *The
Wall Street Journal* and *Horizon*, but without the promotional involvement of local third-party supporters. These local boosters not
only can provide a lift to the promotional effort, but can win their
quid pro quo through the recognition they receive as arts supporters.

BUSINESS MARKETING TIE-INS

Arts groups also can benefit when major coordinated advertising campaigns undertaken on their behalf are tied to a business's
overall marketing concept. Philadelphia's INA Corporation not only
undertook sponsorship of 26 weeks of Philadelphia Orchestra radio
concerts during the 1981-82 season, but tied in its sponsorship to
a company-wide "Performance in Concert" employee incentive campaign designed to boost the productivity of over 6,000 of its workers
in offices throughout the country. The insurance company, which
also made major donations to the orchestra, built its campaign around
a musical theme, disseminating posters and printed materials featuring musical instruments. It also offered music scholarships in the
names of its agents who had the greatest success during the
campaign.

At about the same time, a Canadian cigarette company initiated
a long-range marketing program designed to benefit Canada's nonprofit professional theatres. Vantage cigarettes, in association with
the 85-member Professional Association of Canadian Theatres (PACT)
and the 67-member Les Association de Directeurs des Théâtre in
Quebec, launched the Vantage Arts Academy, whose initial activity
was in support of theatre. The five-year campaign, launched after
market surveys showed that the Canadian theatregoer's profile
matched that of the Vantage smoker, included 30-second commercials aired during CPAir's in-flight film urging travelers to "get out
and go to the theatre," and an electronic message center in Toronto
featuring free promotional messages by local theatres. A hoped-for

94   promotion which would have resulted in the printing of mini-profiles of theatres throughout the country on millions of packs of Vantage cigarettes didn't materialize. Company lawyers felt that the individual profiles might violate the tobacco industry's code by implying that the theatres were endorsing Vantage. The cigarette company also began presenting an annual $20,000 award to a PACT member company and launched a giant, consumer-oriented Theatre Pass contest, with entry blanks available to Vantage buyers at thousands of outlets in Canada. The contest, which heightened awareness of the participating theatres, offered such prizes as gold passes good at any of the theatres, and theatre weekends for two anywhere in Canada. Unfortunately, the five-year project didn't run its course. According to Curtis Barlow, PACT's executive director, the project was creative and ambitious. "But," he said, "after several years it became apparent to both parties that business realities made it clear that the contract's objectives could not be achieved within the established time period." However, the $20,000 award continues to be given annually to a PACT theatre.

Indicative of the fact that where there's smoke there must be money, another Canadian cigarette supporter of the arts, du Maurier, initiated a unique advertising support campaign during the 1985-86 season in behalf of a single company: the Royal Winnipeg Ballet. The cigarette company, which was underwriting a 25-city national tour of the dance troupe to the tune of $125,000, wanted to ensure an audience for the tour. The result was the du Maurier's marketing department, at a cost estimated to be twice that of the tour, put together a total marketing program designed to lure audiences to each of the 66 performances. Removing the promotional burden from the dance company, the du Maurier pros developed and placed ads in local media, initiated local promotions and worked with the press in each of the cities to boost coverage of the performances.

Because advertising is such an integral facet of business activity, opportunities for arts involvement may be greater than many cultural groups surmise. Lines inserted into a business ad to promote a production or exhibition are not uncommon; nor are arts "piggybacks" within business mailings. An area that has opened up considerably in recent years is the ad or series of ads undertaken by businesses specifically to extol the virtues of arts groups that they support. Typical was the large advertisement placed on the "Op-Ed" page of *the New York Times* by the Chemical Bank several times in 1985, with the headline, "At Chemical, financial performance isn't the only kind we're interested in." The ad, which featured a picture of a scene from an Ensemble Studio Theatre performance, went on to ask, "How can New York's playwrights, directors, actors and designers experiment without having to worry about finances? One of the ways is through The Ensemble Studio Theatre—and that is why Chemical Bank supports it."

One of the more memorable business ad campaigns in recent years reaped major acclaim not only for the arts groups whose activities were lauded, but for the business that paid $50,000 for the space. The business was the American Savings Bank in New York City, and the beneficiaries of the series of newspaper ads were six leading arts organizations. Each ad featured a photo of the arts group's leader along with a brief quote and a statement about the organization's artistic purpose and program. In small print at the bottom of the ad was the bank's name and logo. The campaign, which featured such groups as the Dance Theatre of Harlem and the Brooklyn Academy of Music, attracted so much attention that the bank was asked for and gave its permission to run the ads as public service insertions, minus its own credit, in several major magazines.

THE BROADCAST MEDIA

A very adaptable advertising concept, "What's Next" was the brainchild of a Denver ad agency, Arnold & Company, (now known as Arnold Media Services, Inc.). It grew out of a concern by agency heads that local cultural organizations had a hard time winning free public service announcement time from radio stations during hours that potential audiences might be listening. The agency asked its clients if they might not be willing to purchase prime time on a regular basis for messages promoting a cultural institution and its program. The commitment was for $1,850 a month, covering production costs and purchased time, for 60-second spots which, while highlighting a cultural institution and soliciting audiences or funds, *also* included brief opening and closing statements from the corporate sponsor. In its first year alone, the project won commitments from sponsors of over $100,000 in purchased air time and, at last report, it was still going strong.

One area frequently overlooked by those seeking to donate advertising to the arts has been prime-time network television. While it would be nice to see a major corporate sponsor donate his time during the Super Bowl broadcast for a message on behalf of a worthy arts group, it is highly unlikely that this will happen. Still, the arts have scored some successes. When Mobil sponsored *The Life and Adventures of Nicholas Nickleby* in prime time over four consecutive evenings several years ago, it replaced its product commercials with public service messages lauding the work of five nonprofit organizations, two of them arts groups.

ARTS ADVERTISING CONCEPTS

Aware of the power of advertising, some enterprising arts organizations have been able to turn it to their own use at no cost to themselves. The Kansas City Symphony, for example, looking for a way to promote its players and its program, adapted the well-known advertising format used by a liquor company, the "Dewar's Profile." The orchestra found local businesses, like the Scandia Down Shop, to sponsor newspaper ads. Each ad, patterned after the Dewar's concept, profiled a different orchestra musician, and along with the player's picture, listed his or her hobbies, most memorable music, latest accomplishment, a personal quote and a profile statement concluding with a tag line telling readers where that musician would next be performing. Each business sponsor received only a single line of credit acknowledging the contribution. Blown up posters of the ads were also placed in the concert hall lobby.

Although they have not been widely used by arts groups as yet, film and videos seem certain to become more common advertising and promotional tools in the coming years. While few cultural organizations could hope to successfully invade the MTV domain and woo rock-oriented audiences, visually exciting, well-executed videos can reach and attract specific markets. In an attempt to boost their education programs, several symphony orchestras—Chicago and Cleveland among them—have successfully used videos as classroom tools to prepare youngsters for concert attendance, and underwriters have often paid for their production. The Akron Symphony has had good reaction thus far to its three-part video series aimed at students and teachers, *Meet an Orchestra Musician.*

A number of arts organizations have used the advertising medium to tell their story to a much larger audience than they usually reach, and to recruit members and raise funds. Full-page newspaper ads in leading dailies, often purchased with money donated by business benefactors, have been effective selling tools. When underwriters have not been available, some groups have purchased full-page ads on a "space available" basis at greatly reduced rates. When

the Greater Hartford Arts Council purchased a 12-page supplement   **97**
in the *Hartford Courier* at favorable rates—production costs were paid
by Connecticut Bank & Trust Company and Aetna—it used that supplement to explain its funding needs and articulate its rationale and
mission. It also used the supplement to publicly thank its contributors.
Interestingly, donations were up by 15 percent following publication.

The power of advertising, when combined with an imaginative
approach, was clearly evidenced in 1984 when an arts group was
forced to take dramatic steps to compensate for a near fatal mishap
which was not its fault. Planning for its first subscription series at
Town Hall, Philharmonia Virtuosi leaders were shocked to learn, 60
days from the opening, that a bulk mailing of 125,000 pieces had
evidently never reached its intended targets. "We had purchased
some good lists," recalled music director, Richard Kapp, "and when
we only received a total of 13 responses, all from five zip codes, we
knew that something had happened to the mailing." (To date, the
mystery has never been solved.)

At an emergency meeting of the executive committee, various
options were weighed concerning ways to reach potential subscribers
for the five-concert series in a hurry. Adding to the urgency of the
situation was the fact that the musical group was faced with a rare
opportunity to reach new audiences since it had received a $90,000
grant from General Foods to pay for the season's talent, rehearsal
and production costs, thus freeing funds for promotional use that
might otherwise have been unavailable. But with much of that money
already spent on the "phantom" mailing, and time a factor, another
costly direct-mail campaign to reach the goal of 500 to 600 subscribers
had to be ruled out. When Kapp suggested that perhaps it might be
cheaper to offer everyone who showed up $10 than to pay the ex-
penses of a traditional marketing campaign, his board chairman
picked up on it. The group purchased a quarter-page ad at regular
rates and a full-page ad on a stand-by basis in *The New York Times*,
and also bought time on two of New York's key classical music stations, WQXR and WNCN, to present a unique offer. (Because of its
stand-by basis, the rate for the full-page *Times* ad was greatly reduced,
but there was no guarantee as to when within a period of several
weeks it would run, or even if it would run at all.) The ads not only
offered subscriptions for $40 instead of the usual $64, but had a
unique bonus—anyone presenting a ticket stub at the end of a concert would be given $5 in cash for cab fare home.

Both print ads ran in September 1984, along with some 50 radio
commercials, and the results were astounding. Within a week after

98   the ads were first seen and heard, orders were pouring in. "Our offer was limited to the first 1,000 who applied," said Kapp, "but we couldn't turn it off in time." In all, 1,113 subscriptions were sold within a week, far exceeding all expectations. The following season, when General Foods again funded the production costs, a similar subscription offer was made along with the $5 a concert rebate. This time however, Philharmonia Virtuosi got off to a much earlier start. The campaign was initiated in late spring with a stand-by print ad and a more modest mailing of 35,000 pieces—which actually arrived in potential subscribers' homes—and a follow-up advertising and promotion program conducted in the fall. As opposed to the previous year, when the best seats were offered on a first-come basis, the house was scaled for three different locations. This time around, 840 subscriptions were sold, about 300 of them new.

Far from being unhappy with the drop-off in subscribers from the previus season, Kapp was very pleased with the response. "Normally, it would take five years to build up the kind of large audience we've developed in two seasons," he said. An added plus was the fact that Philharmonia Virtuosi experienced a large increase in single-ticket sales during the 1985-86 season, and a number of subscribers turned their rebates into contributions.

Designing a "crash" advertising program to win immediate results presents one kind of problem. But when a cultural organization is developing a major advertising project such as publication of a newspaper advertising supplement to reap large financial rewards, there are different kinds of concerns. Then the group should be sure that it has a lot of volunteers to work on the project, a careful plan of action and sufficient time to carry the plan through. For more than 20 years, the women's committee of the Toronto Symphony has made a key project out of the publication of a special symphony supplement to a leading Toronto newspaper, which they usually purchase at cost from the paper. Working for months, volunteers handle virtually all aspects of the supplement, from selling ads to individuals and local merchants—many of whom are not regular symphony supporters—to writing ad copy and doing layouts and photography. In the early years, many of the models in the ads were members of the committee, with some photographed in their own homes along with the advertised products. In more recent years, however, local celebrities, businessmen, artists and sports figures have been recruited as models, and occasionally an international notable—one year it was Itzhak Perlman—has agreed to pose. Planning begins nearly a year in advance of the April publication date, and the heavy adver-

tising sales effort takes place between September and January. The
committee's success is evident in the results: In 1964, the supplement raised $27,000; 20 years later, it netted $89,000 for the
symphony.

"It's a tremendous undertaking and it's enormously labor intensive," claims Natalie Little, who chaired the successful 1984 effort.
"You need an awful lot of hard-working volunteers to succeed." But
when you do succeed, as the Toronto Symphony has, it is very clear
that it pays, in fact it pays very well, to advertise.

CHAPTER 6

Don't Just Applaud: Send Money

102

I'm not sure who "R" is, or just which Joe it is who's been writing to me, but within the space of several weeks I heard from both of them. Scribbled on promotional fliers I received in the mail were "personal" messages from R and Joe. Quite simply but emphatically, R had written across a flier advertising a newsletter, "Great Offer! R." On an ad offering a business information service, the inked message was almost as terse, "Sounds like a great idea for you------Joe."

There's no way that I can discover who R and Joe are, but the chances are that I know neither of them. But since everybody knows *someone* with the intial R, and nearly everyone has met a Joe at some point in his life, the messages could lead me to believe that a friend or business acquaintance was trying to be helpful. A Felix would never write me such a note; nor would a Clarence or Hepzibah. But good old Joe certainly would.

In their quest for responses, direct mailers will try any technique they can to win an immediate and positive reaction and get a check back by return mail. Arts promoters are no different. Once a prospect has gone far enough to open a mailing piece, a positive action in itself, the next trick is to get that prospect to read and, most important, to react.

Direct mail is one of the easiest ways to reach funding prospects—and one of the hardest ways. It is one of the cheapest ways and one of the most expensive ways. It may require the least effort or the most effort. As the saying goes, it all depends. All of the ingredients that go into direct mail—the targeting of audiences, the selection of appropriate mailings lists, the physical appearance of the mailing piece, the wording of the message, the time of year it is sent, how it is sent, the urgency of the case, the signer of the letter—contribute to the effectiveness or ineffectiveness of the effort. If any one of the ingredients is below par, the entire effort will suffer.

For groups without much of an existing donor base, direct mail can be very expensive and take time and more than one effort to succeed. Also, competition for a recipient's attention is a key factor. On any given day, an arts mailing piece may arrive in the company of myriad other pieces of unsolicited mail, all of which can make the most understanding recipients wonder why they have the honor of being on so many different mailing lists.

The positive aspects of direct mail, however, can far outweigh their drawbacks. Direct mail offers entry into someone's home with a message that says precisely what the sender wants it to say. Barring unforseen circumstances, it arrives about when the sender wants it to arrive. And if all the ingredients are in place, not only can it result

in meaningful responses, but the recipient base can become a fertile   **103**
field to plow over and over again in anticipation of good results.

Direct mailers have been searching for years to discover what techniques work best and, obviously, if there were one single simple answer, everyone would automatically be successful. In fact, what has been shown over and over again is that what works best at one time or for one organization may not work as effectively at another time or for another organization. Testing, assessing, targeting a particular approach to a particular audience and even, at times, breaking all the rules may be the answer to the success of a particular mailing. *Consumer Reports* magazine, for example, in its 1985 and 1986 subscriber mailings, went to a green and yellow color scheme as part of a deliberate attempt to avoid using primary red, because too many direct mailers had been using the red on their envelopes.

ORIGINALITY

Direct mail in the arts offers organizations the opportunity to be original and personal, beginning with the outside envelope discussed in a previous chapter. When peer speaks to peer in a language understood by both, the mailing can be quite effective. A light touch may not hurt either. Some years ago, when the Grand Opera House in Wilmington, Del. had targeted a particularly affluent audience—physicians—for a funding pitch, it went to a peer group to make the pitch—other doctors. A letter with the heading "Medical Committee for the Grand Opera House" listed the names of nine doctors and their wives, offering, presumably, at least one medical name familiar to each recipient. The salutation was equally on-target: each letter was addressed, "Dear Colleague."

But it was the body of the letter that was most effective for in it, each recipient was addressed in language that made the flattering assumption that he or she knew something about music. It played up to—rather than down to—the recipients. Instead of telling them that "opera, like medicine, doesn't have to taste bad" or "for your continued good health, we prescribe a season of music," as one such arts appeal did, it reached them by perhaps causing a chuckle or two and arousing their sense of involvement. It also used at least one word that only a doctor would understand.

The letter began, "The association between music and medicine is an old one. Brahms tried out new scores on Bilroth. Freud analyzed Mahler in one afternoon (presto analysis). Illness pervades the

104 last act of more operas than can be quickly counted. One can imagine the disastrous last act of *Bohème* had Mimi, instead of phthisically [a medical term referring to a debilitating disease of the lungs] wasting away, sustained a sudden cardiac arrest. In short, medicine has been there when music needed it.''

The appeal went on, ''Now there is a new call for our help. The Grand Opera House needs our support, in the form of money . . . If you choose to join your colleagues and fellow citizens, we hope you will endow at least two auditorium chairs by pledging $600 over three years.''

At times, the pitch can be tellingly provocative, especially if there is something besides a letter in the envelope, and if the circumstances are unusual. When the Chamber Orchestra of New England, a small ensemble with a budget well under $100,000 a year, requested and received a $3.5 million cash gift from Parker Brothers in 1979, it provided the musical group with the rationale to launch a direct mail appeal to its individual donors. In addition to a letter from music director James Sinclair, each envelope contained a special bonus: a $500 or $1,000 bill. The bills, of course, like the cash award from Parker Brothers, were—play money—from the company's game, "Payday." Recipients were reminded that "handling the finances of a professional chamber orchestra is no game. We take it seriously." Press releases headed "$3.5 Million Gift Launches Fund Drive," were widely picked up and helped call attention to the fund mailing. While the mailing was only moderately successful in terms of the amount raised, the promotion gave the orchestra a good deal of first-time visibility— especially since many of the names on the mailing list were new— and set the stage for follow-up funding efforts.

THE PERSONAL TOUCH

The offbeat approach makes use of whatever resources are available and applicable to an arts organization, and especially whatever appears to be on target. The personal touch can be especially meaningful in the right situation. During the 1985-86 season, J. Robert Hillier and Phyliss Marchand, both board members of the McCarter Theatre Company in Princeton, N.J., and co-chairmen of the Major Individual Development Committee, decided to try a new approach on "major individuals," donors of $250 or more to the theatre, with the support and consent of the theatre staff.

"Bob and I were personally overwhelmed with the number of requests we receive for donations from various organizations," claimed Marchand, "so we decided to be different, a bit theatrical, and not send the same old worthy cause letter." The result was a one-page theatrical "script" from "Bob and Phyliss for McCarter Theatre." Although the basic script was the same, with lines "read" by each of them, specific lines in each letter were changed to assure that the particular letter was specifically on target for the individual recipient, especially lines that referred to the donor's previous gift and the amount suggested for the current year's gift. As one script read:

Phyliss: Last year you were pretty MAJOR to us with your generous gift of $1,234. This year you could be even more MAJOR; it would be great if you could give us $2,345 . . . or we hope more.

Bob: This is not the capital campaign for the renovations to the theatre; this is our annual fund. Your gift lets us stage very special theatre at a lower ticket price that lets a lot of people see it . . . which makes it worth staging and worth supporting. Donations support 33 percent of our budget.

The reaction was excellent. Some donors even called Marchand at home to say they were increasing their donations because of the "refreshing" approach taken. In fact, the response was so strong that the co-chairmen followed up with two additional mailings. An "angel" script told lapsed givers how they could be "saved" by re-entering the ranks of McCarter donors. A mailing to those who had never before contributed to the theatre was a straight letter rather than a theatrical script, but it was liberally sprinkled with theatrical terms such as "join a stellar cast." According to development director Pamela Sherin, "the response was much quicker than for the usual individual mailings. People reacted very positively to the innovative approach." As the season neared its end, with contributions still coming in, it looked like the theatre would easily reach its goal for individual donations.

A script was also used that same season by New York City's Symphony Space, but in that case the "participants" in the drama were a Concerned New Yorker (CNY) and a Still, Small Voice (SSV). In the dialogue, CNY voiced the desire to "be doing something significant with my money. Something that will make a difference." The assurance by SSV that a contribution would be "a vote of confidence for one of the good things in life" led to an embrace and a contribution "as the music swells and the lights fade."

A personal letter can take many forms. Sometimes the personal touch comes not from the sender's relationship to the recipient but from the sender's relationship to the beneficiary of the mailing. A letter with an enclosed pledge card from actress Blythe Danner, on behalf of a dance company, that opened with the line "I went to school with

Meredith Monk. I take great pride in that fact," had an excellent chance of catching the reader at the outset.

NON-TRADITIONAL APPROACHES

Arts groups have been daring enough over the years to try new and imaginative ideas, even when they seemed to fly in the face of traditional beliefs. One of the more imitated concepts, since adapted over the years by many other arts groups, was the Brooklyn Academy of Music's 1975-76 "Reasonable Request" campaign. Although most professional fund-raisers advise against spending much time or energy on small donors, BAM launched a campaign aimed specifically at new donors, who would be asked to contribute $5 and only $5. The pitch was made to a list of non-contributors who had either purchased tickets to Academy events or had asked to be placed on its mailing list. The thinking was that if interested recipients could be made to cross the line into the donor category, even at such a small amount, they would be funding targets for much larger contributions in the future.

The campaign was specifically tied to $5 because BAM, during that period, had offered tickets to many of its events for that amount. It was therefore, "reasonable" and fitting to ask recipients to turn the $5, BAM's asking price for many of its tickets, into a $5 gift. In a thoroughly professional approach, BAM pre-tested two different mailings to the same audience, one asking for $5 only, and the other leaving recipients the option of increasing the amount. When the test mailing showed that audiences clearly responded more favorably to the unique concept of a $5-only gift, the die was cast for the campaign.

A very soft-sell letter reminded donors of BAM's historic relationship to the $5 figure, and highlighted the fact that asking for $5, no more, no less, was indeed a very "reasonable request." An accompanying pledge card gave donors the opportunity to participate by checking off one of a series of both serious and tongue-in-cheek reasons for making the contribution, or even adding a personal reason in a space left blank for that purpose. Included as check-off reasons were such BAM attractions as Twyla Tharp, the Boston Symphony and the Pennsylvania Ballet, and such non-attractions as the old Brooklyn Dodgers and the leaks in BAM's roof.

By the time the campaign ended, over 2,000 new donors had contributed more than $10,000 to the arts center, a somewhat incredible 14 percent response to the 15,000-piece mailing. The BAM thank-you note appropriately began, "Dear one-of-our-largest con-

tributors. We couldn't have done it without you." In the follow-up   **107**
campaigns aimed at the same audience, BAM, of course, was no
longer quite as "reasonable."

THE TOOLS OF BUSINESS

Some arts funding mailings have been patterned after commercial efforts. The American Museum of Natural History, one year, followed the example of many magazines and asked recipients to "insert a token in the slot" to become a member. A public television station sent out letters with a drawing of a chain on the envelope, and indicated that since this was a "chain letter" it hoped that those who received it did not break the chain. Choreographer Merce Cunningham went a step further and along with composer John Cage actually mailed a chain letter on behalf of the Cunningham Dance Company to one person in each of the 50 states, suggesting to recipients that they donate $1 to the company and then mail copies of the letter to 10 other prospective donors. While less than $1,000 was raised from the effort, it did get the dance company a lot of good publicity, and helped it to reach some future funding prospects.

A business-like approach to fund-raising has prompted several groups to utilize the tools of business. Fund mailings over the years have featured facsimile stock certificates suggesting that audiences invest in an arts council or theatre. The George Street Playhouse told its audiences in such a mailing to "get bullish about GSP," while the Joffrey Ballet, for its 20th anniversary season, sent out, "prospectuses" to potential donors. In one funding flier with decided business overtones, the Minnesota Orchestra focused on such topics as "the return on your investment" and the "in-go and out-go simplified." The brochure cover perhaps intrigued some readers with its message, "One very solid investment Sylvia Porter would probably never recommend. The Minnesota Orchestra."

LETTER INSERTS

In their quests for funds via the mail, arts groups have been known to sweeten the kitty with something beyond letters and fliers. Some of the inserts and stuffers have been totally unexpected, frequently amusing and often quite productive. For a fund pitch designed to tie in with its 20th birthday, the American Place Theatre in New York decided to ask audiences to help it celebrate 20 years by par-

108   ticipating in its China anniversary. Along with a brochure featuring a Chinese drawing and the word China on the cover, the theatre included a pair of chopsticks. Its logic? The theatre suggested that audiences "call a Chinese restaurant and order your favorite dishes sent in. Turn on your television set and tune-in to one of the networks—any one will do. While you're waiting for the food to arrive and saying to yourself, 'Gee, is this the only kind of entertainment there'll be if the American Place Theatre goes broke?' get out your old checkbook and become a supporter. About the time you finish writing our check and sealing it in the enclosed envelope, your food will arrive. (They always forget the chopsticks, hence our gift.) Eat. An hour later you'll crave a meaningful theatrical experience; and we'll be on our way to providing just that, thanks to you."

With its mailing of tea bags, the Philadelphia Settlement Music School could have joined forces with the American Place to add another embellishment to the Chinese dinner. But its tea bags served a more practical purpose. They were a reminder to those receiving them that they were invited to attend "A Stay-at-Home Tea Party," live over Philadelphia station WFLN-FM that the school was hosting. Held each March since 1985, the Tea Party is a two-hour concert that also includes conversations about the school with its faculty, students and friends. Participating in 1986, before a live audience, were Metropolitan Opera soprano Benita Valente, pianist Jorge Bolet and former Phildelphia baseball star Tug McGraw, who turned singer for the night. Along with the invitations and the tea bags, courtesy of the Milford International Tea Company, recipients also received pledge cards. The invitation to stay at home and tune in was heeded, and during its first go-round in 1985, over 1,500 listeners, 1,100 new to the school, sent in donations totaling more than $20,000 in small gifts. A year later, tea party contributions increased to $28,000.

The American Boychoir School in Princeton, N.J. used chocolate kisses as a sweetener and symbol for its $75-a-head after-dinner fund benefit in 1984, fittingly titled, "Just Desserts." The kisses, which arrived in foot-long silver tubes, were accompanied by invitations to the event, described as a "mouthwatering fantasy evening" featuring entertainment and dancing and highlighted by champagne and desserts. In another interesting use of an insert, in 1983, the New York Shakespeare Festival's Public Theatre sent a target audience of 30,000 a flier that featured a shiny dime on its cover with a legend around it reading, "Take the Dime to Call the Public." (New York phone rates have since risen to 25 cents.) The $3,000 the public invested in dimes proved its worth, as better than 10 percent of the recipients responded positively to the subscription offering.

An insert can be a fun way to attract the attention of direct mail recipients and elicit a favorable response, but obviously it's not the only way. Copy plays a key role—a shocking theme line can make a difference—and so does the mail piece's visual appeal, especially if it's unexpected. To dramatize its quest for funds to renovate its concert hall, the North Carolina School of the Arts sent out fliers with a cover line reading, "Some colleges seek gifts for endowed chairs." When the fliers were opened, the chairs came to life as miniature pop-ups rising from the page, over the words, "Your $850 will purchase one endowed seat," The Syracuse Symphony came up with a fun approach to funding with an imaginative concept which, unfortunately, presented one unforseen obstacle. A dramatic flier which featured the word "dough" on the cover in bright pink on a black background opened to read, "Re, Mi, Fa, So, La, Ti, Dough!" Opened once more to its full 16″×22″ size, the flier read, "We Need Play Dough." Beneath the legend was a picture of the orchestra's conductor sculpted in pink Play-Doh, the colorful modeling compound used by children, on the face of a Play-Doh $20 bill. Copy near the top discussed the orchestra's funding needs and asked for audience contributions.

According to reports, the orchestra received such an immediate response to the mailing that the flier is now a collector's item. Indeed, it is not only scarce now but was scarce within weeks after it was mailed. The reason, unfortunately, had nothing to do with its effectiveness as a fund-raising tool, but it does suggest strongly that before arts groups adapt commercial products to their own needs, they do some checking in advance. For although the flier was dramatic, telling and response-oriented, it also was in violation of a trademark belonging to Kenner Products, the makers of Play-Doh.

There are many ways to apprise an audience of a funding need, and while stressing the urgency of the cause is judicious, threatening the audience isn't. Notices that inform recipients, "We'd hate to end the next performance at intermission" or "We'd hate to ask you to leave," as several mailings have, tend to set up adversarial situations. The reader feels threatened by the very organization that he or she is being asked to support, and also feels enveloped in a cloud of gloom and negativism.

THE LIGHT TOUCH

Nobody doubts that an arts need is real, but how much better it is to present that need in a lighter way, with the threatening tone

110   or message obliterated. To dramatize the fact that box office receipts and grants paid for only two thirds of its budget, and that the remaining third had to come from individual contributors, the Long Island Symphony sent a visual reminder to its supporters—one third of a letter, the bottom third. Other groups, such as Milwaukee's United Performing Arts Fund, have sent two parts of a torn ticket that fit together, with one part reading, "Your contribution will complete this ticket." Somewhat along the same "complete this" line, the Queens Symphony made a pitch for increased giving by existing "Friends." To attract donors to sponsor chairs for the 1984-85 season, the Symphony mailed a flier listing Bach, Beethoven and Brahms on its cover, but with several letters in each of the names missing. The copy read, "We need you to fill in the missing pieces." The opened fliers showed three seated musicians amidst a sea of five empty chairs. The approach, which included special benefits for chair sponsors at donations ranging from $500 to $5,000 for the conductor, worked very well: $10,500 was raised for the chairs, and there was a 34 percent increase in overall Friends funding.

The New Orleans Opera found a light yet extremely effective way to press its funding needs upon its patrons at Christmastime in 1985. The cover of its spirited flier showed caricatures of figures from four of its upcoming operas accompanied by the line, " 'tis the season of giving . . ." When opened, the flier revealed the same four opera characters—Lohengrin, Leila from *The Pearlfishers*, Musetta from *La Bohème* and Lucia di Lammermoor—all on bended knees, begging for funds with words from their own arias. "My voice implores thee," begged Leila. "Ah, send the letter now," intoned Lucia. A fold above the drawing indicated the categories of gifts and the designations for givers, ranging from Scrooge at $0 to elf at $25, reindeer at $50, Christmas angel at $75 and Santa Claus at $100 and up.

"It was the most successful fund mailing of its kind that we've ever done," claimed Esther L. Nelson-Rapp, the opera's public relations director. "We got 50 percent more money than we ever received from any similar mailing."

A HARDER SELL

A somewhat different approach to a mail campaign launched just prior to Christmas, and quite a controversial one (although it was equally successful), was taken by the George Street Playhouse in New Brunswick, N.J. during the 1984-85 season. Because the theatre had just moved into newly renovated quarters and had incurred $150,000 in capital expenses as a result, its administrators knew that they need-ed to make more than their usual low-key appeal to individual donors. With the goal for individuals increased to a record high of $35,000, the decision was made to take a hard-sell approach.

The result, while hard-sell and striking, never actually threatened the individual reader with a loss of theatre services. But it did attract attention. In fact, the message turned into a war, literally. The placid tone of the cover of the Playhouse's fund brochure showing the en-trance to the new George Street Playhouse, described as "beautiful, spacious, better-equipped, more exciting than ever before," was harshly interrupted by the blunt question, "Then why are we at WAR?" Without mincing words the copy on the inside panels came right to the point. In a column headed "This means war!" the message read, "The George Street Playhouse must close a $150,000 projected income gap quickly before it becomes a deficit at the end of our fiscal year." Further down, in bold type, the message read, "THE GEORGE STREET PLAYHOUSE NEEDS MORE SUPPORT. Will you join us in the fight to wipe out this $150,000 income gap in our premier season in this beautiful new facility?" Silhouetted in blue on the back cover of the brochure was the figure of an armed soldier.

The initial mailing, along with a cover letter from the theatre's producing director Eric Krebs, was sent to about 8,500 current and past subscribers, single-ticket buyers and current and lapsed donors on November 30. A second mailing to new prospects went out in January. The response was immediate and excellent, with over $17,000 in contributions drawn from the November letter alone, but the campaign was not without controversy and dissent. Several theatre supporters, including board members who were not aware of the mailing in advance, criticized the theatre for using a war theme, especially during the Christmas season. In a subsequent newsletter article titled "War is declared on Playhouse income gap," the theatre, sensitive to the concerns of some of its supporters, explained why it took the approach it did. "If we've succeeded in getting you to open the brochure and read our message, then we hope you'll forgive our Machiavellian approach. We want you to know how important it is to us to raise the money. We're fighting this gap with every weapon we have, and we're sure to step on a few toes in the process, but you know the old saying . . . 'All's fair in art and war.'"

The same war theme was repeated later that season in other mail-ings and in a telemarketing campaign. The results of the somewhat unorthodox approach proved, according to development director Kim Nelson, that the end justified the means, especially since the campaign had been presented firmly but tastefully. "We took a gamble in coming up with the war symbol," she said, "especially since the theatre's image is very important. But the controversy wasn't that great, since, aside from the board, we received only a handful of negative letters. And we got recipients to open the flier and, as a result, many donated."

When the "war" ended at the season's conclusion, the theatre had netted $42,000 from the campaign, easily topping its $35,000 goal. Moreover, the campaign raised 26 percent more than the previous year's fund drive and matching gifts increased proportionately. Now, who was it who said "War is hell"?

INVOLVING THE RECIPIENT

A number of arts groups have had success with mail campaigns that try to involve recipients with the organization, stressing the "you" along with the "us." In one such campaign, built around the theme, "Give Yourself a Round of Applause," the Vancouver Symphony invited recipients to "perform" with the orchestra. Brochures in the form of "application forms" accompanied by an offer of a pair of free tickets for new contributors or givers of over $25, read, "Now is your golden opportunity to perform for the orchestra—No musical training necessary." Backed up by a strong telemarketing pitch to 25,000 households by paid canvassers, the campaign more than doubled the number of individual contributors and raised well over $100,000 more than the goal for individuals.

Another "you" campaign, in the much smaller community of McAllen, Tex., stressed donor involvement with the Valley Symphony Orchestra. With its budget doubling to $64,000 for the 1982-83 season, the symphony's flier featured a cover message, "Keep Your Symphony in the Black," set in white type on a black background. The message inside focused on individual participation, with one panel headed, "You Helped Us Begin" and the other panel reading, "You Can Help Us Grow." Within four days of receipt, the mailings pulled in nearly $1,300, a record draw for the tiny orchestra.

Sometimes personal mesages are quite terse. In a footnote at the end of an informational mailing, the Universal Jazz Coalition stated simply, "You say that you love us. Have you sent in a check to help us? Please mail to 380 Lafayette St., NYC 10003. We love you." The Williamstown Theatre Festival in Massachusetts has used personalized picture postcards to reach donors. One such card showed Dianne Wiest and Austin Pendleton in a scene from a 1985 WTF production

of *Uncle Vanya* on the face. On the reverse side, next to the address   **113**
box, the message read, "Your continued support will be greatly ap-
preciated. (signed) Judy Peabody." Judy Peabody is a board member
of the theatre.

HOW THE MONEY WILL BE USED

Although most arts groups tell recipients why their money is
needed, some fail to mention precisely how it will be used. Of course,
it's nice to just have the money come in to a general operating fund,
for use as the organization sees fit, but some donors are curious. They
like to think that perhaps there is a particular need in an area that
interests them, for which their money will go. The Westerly, R.I.
Center for the Arts, in a flier based on the theme, "You Make the
Magic," told its audiences that "you" are "singing along with Burl
Ives" and "bringing Rudolph Serkin to play Beethoven." It then went
on to tell what each contributing membership paid for, from two
months of piano tuning for a $100 donation, a teacher's salary for
one class for $250, a day's operating cost of the Center for $500, up
to the Center's insurance costs for a year for a $5,000 donation. The
Cultural Arts Council of Plano, Tex. published a 26-page, illustrated
"Gifts to Share Catalogue," along with an order form, to offer donors
the opportunity to specify exactly what they would like their donations to pay for. Each of 17 different cultural organizations presented
"wish lists," describing the activities or needs they would like to have
funded. Included among the 172 items listed were a $3,000 gift to
turn the Plano Ballet Theatre stage "into the land of sugarplum
fairies" and a very modest $15 for the conductor's score for the Plano
Chamber Orchestra.

TEST MAILINGS

Arts mailers should be open-minded and willing to experiment
with direct mail efforts since, although many ground rules have been
established over the years, there may be times when the best ground
rules are no ground rules. That's where testing and professionalism
are important. Before committing itself to a major financial investment, an arts group should be prepared to test its mailing concept
first. The results could be surprising or even shocking. In a bid for
donors in 1980, the San Francisco Ballet sent solicitation letters to
3,000 past givers. In a random sampling designed to test the impor-

114   tance of offering a premium—the Margot Fonteyn book *The Magic of Dance*—80 percent were offered the premium for contributions of over $100, while 20 percent were not offered any premium. In a result surprising to many, the return from those not offered premiums far surpassed that of those offered them. Although they comprised only 20 percent of the donor list, the non-premium recipients contributed 33 percent of the donations received, matched the dollar returns for donations of under $100 and exceeded the percentage of returns for donations both under and over $100.

Confronted with this surprising result, the bible of the ad field, *Advertising Age*, surmised, "We can only conclude that the offer of the book to those contributing over $100 turned off those who couldn't contribute that amount, and may have affronted or confused others who might have been big contributors."

The outside envelope has been mentioned previously as a teaser for many recipients of direct mail solicitations. A key word or phrase on the face of the envelope or a very prominent name in the upper left corner can be lures to get readers to open the envelope. Among the enticements used by arts groups have been such phrases as "An Invitation for You" (a membership lure for the New York City Ballet Guild), or "Gift Offer Inside" (a flier from Providence's Trinity Repertory Company suggesting that recipients purchase gift certificates for Christmas).

NON-INVITATIONS

One group used its envelope to proclaim "Tickets Enclosed." Inside the envelope were two tickets telling readers, "You are cordially invited not to attend an evening at the Theatre Premiere Benefit Performance," but soliciting their donations. The non-event has a cherished place in arts lore, and if the mailing piece and back-up promotion are handled with the appropriate light touch, it can be quite effective. When Young Audiences' New York chapter held its very successful "Make Believe Benefit" in June 1985, it included reservation cards with designations for both "performers" and "audience," including such categories as soloist at $1,000, prompter at $500 and chorus at $250, and audience seat designations ranging from loge at $125 down to standing room with a blank space for price. Allied Arts of Seattle's "Not to Attend" committee invited supporters to participate in the "I'd give anything not to attend another fund raiser" and sent them donation cards which listed nine local events they wouldn't have to attend. All they had to do was circle any of the events they'd least like to attend, with prices ranging from $5 up to $100, and enclose a check for the cost of tickets to those events.

In an interesting twist on the non-event concept, Stouffer's Cincinnati Towers Hotel decided to celebrate the 1978 opening of its new tower by *not* having a party and instead donating $10,000 to the Greater Cincinnati Fine Arts Fund. In his "invitation," the hotel manager requested "the pleasure of your absence." The Fine Arts Fund capitalized on the situation with some imaginative publicity. One staged news photo showed two sleeping "non-chairwomen" who were "pursuing their responsibilities."

MAILING LISTS AND COMPUTERIZATION

As good as the mail piece and its envelope might be, the mailing list must be equally effective. Hitting on-target audiences is a key to winning a better response, both for funding requests and for subscription offerings. For a number of years, savvy arts groups have been targeting certain zip codes or mail routes where their prospective audiences were most likely to live, as indicated by education and income demographics. Geography can be used in other ways also, as the experience of an organization in another nonprofit field indicates. Because it was located near a local airport, St. Vincent College in Latrobe, Pa., recruited new students through a mailing to 25,000 airplane owners in the 13-state area around it, who, surveys showed, had a high level of income and education. When the Brooklyn Academy of Music decided some years ago that its adventuresomeness would be a key element to stress in its selling campaign—it presented attractions that weren't presented elsewhere, and its location was off the beaten path in Brooklyn—it chose the lists of *New York* magazine, a publication geared to the new in New York, over the list of the arts-committed audience of the Metropolitan Opera.

Computerization has changed the nature of direct mail activity and may change it even more in future years. With the advent of word processing and data bases, personalized letters can be regurgitated by the thousands, and lists can be broken into any number of configurations. But even with technology at its command, the mailing must still compete with everyone else's technology, and sometimes the extra touch may help set one group's letter apart from another's. The word "free," for example, has been a boon to commercial mailers, and if arts groups can learn how to package their offerings to include "free," it can be helpful. A P.S. is a useful adjunct to a letter also, since it stands apart from the rest of the text and is easily noticed. As small a touch as a secretary's initials can help to make a computerized letter look individually typed. And one important fact about direct mail that arts administrators have learned should never be ignored: a direct mail piece is an advertisement for the organization as well as a selling vehicle. Even if it is thrown in the garbage after opening, if someone has looked at it and remembered something about the organization, the direct mail piece may have done its job.

TELEMARKETING

An adjunct to direct mail that can't be thrown out like an envelope is the phone call. In recent years, telemarketing has become a big tool of arts organizations, both to sell tickets and to reach donors. But telemarketing has also become a major technique of businesses and organizations in every area, and the competition for the human ear has become fierce. One friend told me about a call he received from Charlton Heston on behalf of the Statue of Liberty or some other charity. Even though my friend knew the message was taped, he recalled wondering how he could say no to Moses.

Although telemarketing is here to stay in the arts, it has its doubters and its critics. While it is a personalized medium, it also is a disruptive one. "We get a lot of complaints from people who were called at the wrong time," claims Edye Rome, the advertising and public relations manager of Toronto's O'Keefe Center. "They'll tell us that we got them out of the bathtub." It can also be expensive, requiring either the hiring of an outside organization, or in-house training and hiring of canvassers. It requires careful advance scripting designed to introduce the program, indicate its benefits, provide a series of options as responses to various objections and, one hopes, to close the call with a commitment. Sometimes, outside agencies hired for the job deliver less than they promised. Also, as arts consultant Joseph W. Ziegler claims, the vast majority of new ticket purchasers wooed into buying don't renew, perhaps, he indicates, because they're not part of the regular audience.

When telemarketing works, however, it can be one of the most effective weapons in the arsenals of cultural institutions. Personal phone calls following up on a fund mailing, for example, establish a direct contact with the prospect and can result in instant positive decisions. And in those instances where, unlike the usual telemarketing campaign, the caller has clout or local fame—as in phone "blitzes" using volunteer celebrities—the results can be outstanding.

One group that has had great success with telemarketing in fund- **117**
ing and subscription campaigns is San Diego's Old Globe Theatre,
which has made it a key part of its marketing strategy since 1982.
The theatre believes it has been successful for two key reasons. First,
it targets only in-house lists for its calls—subscribers, donors, ticket
buyers, people who've inquired about programs, and lapsed donors
and subscribers from the previous 36 months. Second, the theatre
trains and pays its own canvassers who work virtually year-round
on a salary-plus-commission basis. "We offer them security and they
feel like they're a part of our staff," claims marketing director Joe
Kobryner.

Although the Old Globe was hesitant at first to use telemarketing
because of the negative reaction of so many people to receiving calls
at home, it soon discovered that because its calls were aimed at an
in-house list, they were perceived not as annoyances but as a personal service of the theatre. Calls are made seven to ten days following a mailing and, Kobryner indicates, "People have told us that they
were waiting for us to phone, and they've thanked us for following
up." In the four years since the program started, both to sell tickets
for two seasons a year and to raise funds for special needs, the in-
house base has built from 25,000 to 51,000 households.

When the Old Globe suffered a major tragedy, a fire which
destroyed its Lowell Davies Festival Theatre, in 1984—the theatre's
second fire in only a few years—it went back to the same in-house
list it had hit with subscription offerings in the past to ask for funds.
That telemarketing campaign, launched around Christmas—a time
when the competition for attention is particularly intense—was a major success. Nine callers working over a four-week period won 1,041
responses resulting in donations totaling $48,336. That kind of cam-
paign has quite a pleasant ring.

CHAPTER 7

At Your Place
or Mine?

120   In their search for the elusive dollar, arts groups have tried an incredible variety of ways to hit the jackpot. The orchestra that transforms a concert hall into Old Vienna one year might turn the same site into a Roaring Twenties speakeasy or an Old West saloon the next. The theatre that sponsors a successful benefit performance one spring might discover that a garage sale is its big money-maker the following season. And in their fervor to help their local theatre, opera company or museum, arts supporters are doing everything from jogging to cruising at sea, from removing their clothes (with elegance, of course) to visiting designer-decorated homes. They buy junk they don't need and purchase clothing they'd never dare wear. In service of cultural charity, unlikely things have happened. Middle-aged couples have gone pub-hopping for an opera company, and the town's most fashionable couple has dressed like hobos for a museum benefit.

Special events are the *sine qua non* of arts fund-raising. They are the glue that helps hold members and volunteers close to an organization, and the magnet that attracts audiences—and sometimes celebrities—who might never otherwise get involved. Special events give every arts organization the opportunity, at least for an evening or even several days, to be something other than what they really are. They inspire newspaper coverage in such sections as society or sports, where arts activities aren't normally reported. They can be fantasy or they can be fun, but the bottom line is deadly serious. In order to be successful, they must make money and, through involving participants, set the stage for making even more money.

In a January 1986 *San Diego Tribune* society page round-up on arts fund-raising, several local cultural leaders discussed some of the ancillary benefits of social fund-raising events. Janet Rice, deputy director of the San Diego Museum of Art, commented, "Special events serve to get members involved in the museum and make them feel very much part of the family," while Ian Campbell, general manager of the San Diego Opera claimed that such events "not only allow regular supporters to assist the company but also act as a great conduit to involving other San Diegans in the life of the opera." But, while fostering togetherness, special events also foster increased funding. From three special events alone in 1985—dinner-dances to coincide with an exhibition opening, a black-tie fine arts ball and a three-day celebration of arts and flowers—the San Diego museum raised $150,000. The San Diego Opera, which netted $80,000 from its opera ball and over $100,000 from other special events, also discovered that these social activities were a great help in raising the institution's membership base, which increased by 47 percent in 1985.

While special events are vital to the overall funding effort, they

can be a drain on the resources of the organization, requiring a **121**
tremendous amount of time and effort and sometimes, a considerable
advance outlay of money. Theatre Communications Group, which
in 1985 surveyed its affiliated theatres on special events, found that
a simple rule is often followed in evaluating special events. According to many survey respondents, the ideal event should gross three
times its cost: a third to pay for itself, a third to pay for another event
and a third to put in the bank.

A well-constructed volunteer and membership program, one in
which affiliate guilds or volunteer groups undertake, develop and present special events, can cut time, energy and costs considerably. Sponsorship by an organization or business can reduce expenditures and
help draw in many more participants. Because so many special events
sponsored by so many different nonprofit organizations are competing
for attention, anything that makes an arts group's event stand out
is likely to increase its attractiveness in the marketplace. The more
an event relates to an organization's artistic program, such as a
Shakespearean theatre company's Elizabethan dinner or a symphony
orchestra's bus tour of a musical instrument factory, the greater its
likelihood of success.

CELEBRITY ATTENDANCE

Another benefit booster is an announcement that a major celebrity will attend. Although not every group can come up with President
and Mrs. Reagan, as the Joffrey Ballet did for a top donor private dinner party in Los Angeles some years ago, personalities of every type,
from Lena Horne (for the Negro Ensemble Company) to Christopher
Reeve (for The Second Stage) have donated their time and their
publicity value to arts groups. Rumor has it that when Robert Red-
ford went around to shake the hands of those attending a fund-raising
dinner for the now-defunct PAF Playhouse on Long Island, at least
one woman refused to wash her hands for several days.

PUTTING VISION IN A SITE

Special event options are staggering, and it seems that over the
years, arts groups have successfully tapped nearly every possibility.
Just as site selection can be a critical factor in an organization's decision to build a new facility, so can it be as critical a factor in determining the nature and theme of a special event. When the nearly com-

122 pleted Public Affairs Center was made available to the Springfield, Ill. arts council in the early '80s, the council logically decided to host a "Building of the Arts" gala for its annual Patron's Party, complete with invitations designed as blueprints and hostesses wearing hard hats. Leaders of the Williams Center in Rutherford, N.J. decided to use the fact that its old Rivoli Theatre was undergoing extensive renovation as a positive rationale for a fund-raising party. With three tiers of temporary wooden platforms built around the peeling paint and exposed brick walls, the theatre provided an authentic setting for a very successful "Phantom of the Opera Ball," held on Halloween night in 1985 and featuring, in addition to entertainment, screenings of the old movies, *Dracula* and *The Phantom of the Opera*.

The availability of railroad stations has presented several arts groups with interesting and different approaches to fund-raising events. To tie in with the construction of a somewhat controversial Light Rail Rapid Transit System in Buffalo, N.Y., whose construction was ripping up the downtown area, members of the Buffalo Philharmonic's Women's Committee decided to take advantage of the pro and con attitudes in the community. Their method was to let their supporters be the first to really experience what was happening, through the "Symphony Express." As the result of a year-long planning effort, the committee was able to put together a festive evening which included first-ever rides in the new subway cars to the party site—the transit system's maintenance building at its yard and shop facility—with enroute entertainment by musical ensembles. The party itself featured an orchestra concert, dinner and dancing. Curiosity about the rail system and interest in being the first to ride the new cars resulted in the largest and most profitable ball the symphony had ever held, with net income of $66,000, tremendous press attention and a waiting list for tickets.

Some years earlier, an old rather than a new rail facility provided the inspiration for a successful Wichita Symphony benefit, despite its being held on one of the worst evenings in the city's history, complete with several tornado alerts and a driving rainstorm. After months of discussion with railroad officials, the orchestra won permission to use the long-closed, once elegant main waiting room of Wichita's Union Station for its "Symphony Station Stop." The railroad theme was sustained throughout the evening with baggage carts, station scales and shoeshine stands turned into bars, a large railroad mural serving as a photo backdrop, tours of a restored caboose and, in addition to music, food and entertainment, the continuous showing of two silent train films.

In a decidedly less elegant but equally successful event on its own terms, the Thronateeska Heritage Foundation in Albany, Ga., staged a "Hobo Fish Fry." To focus on its efforts to turn the town's old railroad depot into a museum and planetarium, impress members with the building's potential and spur their continued support, the Foundation decided to hold a party at the depot, which it had partially repaired. Featuring railroad signs familiar to hobos, taped railroad sound effects, guests decked out in hobo garb, and fish fried by local businessmen who served as volunteer cooks, the Fry attracted 300 members and their guests.

An indication of how an unusual and offbeat site can also provide the user with an exciting, attention-getting theme can be gleaned from the experience of one arts group that was presented with the opportunity to use its city's 120-year-old, abandoned water works enginehouse as a party site. To volunteers of the Louisville Orchestra, the water facility suggested a very familiar and lively party theme which was reflected in the invitation to the benefit. "Go," read the front panel of the fold-out invitation, over a big red arrow. It then unfolded to reveal, in four more panels, details on the black-tie event as well as pictures of the playing tokens from a "Monopoly" game. The last panel showed a picture of the familiar Water Works card from the game, along with the words "Water Works." Enclosed with the invitation were two small cards duplicating playing cards from the board game. The "Chance" card, when returned with a $50 check, allowed recipients to "advance to the Water Works," while "Community Chest" read, "I wish to donate but cannot attend."

The game theme was carried out at the party. In return for city permission to use the water works for a $1 rental fee, the facility was completely cleaned up by volunteers for public use. On the floor of the facility, a giant game board was drawn with local place names substituted for Monopoly street names. On a wave of nostalgia for a game remembered from childhood—and to the accompaniment of tremendous local publicity—the ball proved an irresistible lure to the people of Louisville. It drew double the attendance and produced twice the income of the previous year's funding event.

THE EVENT THEME

The right theme can be as important to an event sponsor as the right setting, although both in combination are even better, of course. When the Oklahoma Theatre Center and Oklahoma City Arts Center came up with the idea for a California beach party in August 1983, the landlocked city did not seem to offer the best setting for such an event. No problem. With support from Coors beer and local radio station KATT, enterprising planners took over a downtown area, filled it with 20 truckloads of sand and erected a stage, waterfall and lifeguard stands. Over 6,000 beachgoers turned out for the fund event, which raised $12,000.

Downtown had a different use in Columbus, Ohio, where symphony orchestra volunteers raised $22,000 through "A Night on the Downtown" featuring three simultaneous parties on the same evening, each in a different bank lobby and each featuring its own music, food and decorations. Attendees, who could visit any of the parties for a single admission fee, enlivened a downtown area at a time when it was usually uninhabited while at the same time enriching orchestra coffers.

Many arts groups have intentionally departed from the norm in their funding events and, at times, this move has provided the spark that excited patrons. To counteract the numerous formal balls held in its community, one arts group transformed a ballroom into a frontier town for its fund-raiser, complete with backdrops of a Western jail, general store and saloon; while a normally sedate orchestra, the Springfield, Mo. Symphony, harkened back to the time that it was founded, 50 years earlier, to host its anniversary ball in a rural restaurant that had once been a speakeasy. The Speakeasy Ball included bathtub gin and a casket among its decorations. A Chicago theatre featuring *Bagtime*, a play written by a supermarket bagboy, held its opening party in a supermarket. The least expensive seats were in the frigid ice cream section.

Fun themes tend to attract people who want to have fun—and they are frequently willing to spend a few dollars to have it. Adopting a leaf from the pages of show business, New York City's Organization of Independent Artists built a successful fund-raiser around a "roast" of one of its own leaders. The subject of the roast was OIA board chairman Rubin Gorewitz, an accountant for arts groups and a leading arts lobbyist. The event attracted such noted roastmasters as artist James Rosenquist, opera star Richard Fredricks and New York University president John Brademas, all of whom were pleased to have fun for a good cause. The event, which raised more than $10,000 for the arts group, attracted a good deal of attention from the art world and drew an audience of more than 600 people.

A party idea used by arts groups to involve the so-called Yuppie generation, is the "Get Up and Go Party." One such event, sponsored by the Milwaukee Barre Asociation, a group of younger volunteers of the Milwaukee Ballet, invited attendees to arrive at a downtown office site decorated as an airport, prepared to depart on a trip. At midnight, four names were called and the winners, who, along with others in attendance, contributed $12,000 to the ballet company through their attendance, left on an all-expense-paid weekend trip to San Francisco.

One institution that has been noted for its tongue-in-cheek approach to fund-raising parties is The New York Art Theater Institute. Since 1981, the Institute has attracted attention and support with such imaginative, light-hearted fund-raisers as an "Arties" benefit patterned after the Hollywood "Oscars," which honors the company's actors; a rhumbas-only party; and a Viennese waltz party featuring offbeat decorations and women's gowns made of plastic trash bags and foil wrap. Its 1985 ball, dedicated to Pierre Auguste Renoir, featured two commissioned fake Renoir drawings as decorations, cardboard silhouettes of palm trees and 30 women, all involved with the company, wearing gowns made of plastic, mylar and vinyl, put together by the theatre group's enterprising designer.

According to Donald Sanders, artistic director of the avant-garde theatre group, all its funding events are devised to be consistent with the image the theatre wishes to project: "Rather than limiting ourselves to a dull fund-raising event, I thought that it would be great if we did something that had wit and charm and integrated what we did in the theatre into the event. People who came would then be able to participate in the artwork itself. The parties express our character and reflect our personality." The parties are also very successful, with attendance and funding increasing every year. Many newcomers are attracted to both the theatre and the parties because of the tremendous publicity the events receive. The 1985 fest attracted 175 people who paid $125 each to attend. With nearly everything contributed and expenses minimal, the event netted over $20,000.

Although cultural organizations are traditionally associated with good taste, a strictly-in-fun assault on good taste, if done with the proper verve and spirit, can attract paying patrons and attention. One arts group, with tongue firmly placed in cheek, has deliberately mocked good taste with its annual, very tacky party, "The Swine Ball." Sponsored by the Sierra Arts Foundation in Reno, Nev. to reward old members and attract new ones, the Swine Ball has featured a sty motif, "pig-out time" beginning with cocktails, and such door prizes as a champagne tour of a pig farm, a swine sculpted out of pure pork sausage and a gift shop's cuddly pig. Guests, asked to wear blue jeans, coveralls or barnyard wear, have been invited to gather at the trough to have "a real swill time." The group's newsletter, *Encore*, has pro-

126   moted the event with pictures of the hefty chairpig, an actual swine, meeting with the humans on his planning committee. In 1986, perhaps in deference to the sensibilities of some members of its audience, the Foundation decided to change the party theme to the "Cotton Club," set in the Speakeasy period. In retrospect, the Swine Ball, according to the membership committee, "was found to be a piggish and tasteless affair at best."

Some arts parties have been successful precisely because of provocative themes that turn out not to be what they seem. What would appear from its title to be in very bad taste, "A Clothes-Off-Your-Back Ball," actually turned out to be a successful and tasteful, as well as appropriate, fund-raising party for the St. Louis Art Museum. Held to help fund the costs of bringing a traveling costume exhibition, "Vanity Fair," from New York's Metropolitan Museum to St. Louis, the benefit invited patrons to "come as you were" and "leave as you are." In addition to paying for party tickets at $15 each, guests were asked to donate "your attending attire as you leave." As the invitations read, "Be prepared to leave your finery with us. The clothes you wear (your vintage attire or newest bib and tucker) will be sold at a later date."

More than 500 guests entered into the spirit of the evening, with men wearing everything from formal clothes to military uniforms, including one coat of armor. Women wore designer gowns as well as old family treasures. At the conclusion of the ball, the guests entered portable dressing booths where they shed their outerwear and, after receiving plastic bags to don, as well as tax deduction forms, gave their clothing to committee members for auctioning off several weeks later.

THE HOLIDAY SPIRIT

Holidays present built-in themes for arts funding parties. Carnegie Hall used Valentine's Day 1986 as the *raison d'etre* for a benefit to help its restoration fund. Held at the Pace Gallery, where the work of artist Jim Dine was being exhibited, the event drew some 125 couples at $1,000 per couple, who received, in addition to heart-shaped hors d'oeuvres and cocktails at the gallery and a buffet dinner at one of six sites afterwards, a limited-edition five-color lithograph by Dine.

On a somewhat more plebian note, Tulsa's American Theatre Company has had several Haunted House benefit tie-ins at Halloween, including a "Journey to Galaxy 33" on a "space ship" of the theatre's design which was based at the Tulsa State Fairgrounds for five days. Visitors, who paid $2 each, toured a "previously unexplored planet" to the accompaniment of video tape, laser beams and light and sound effects. The San Diego Symphony has used the traditional German celebration of Oktoberfest for a major annual four-day event featuring beer-drinking, eating, dancing and singing contests as well as clowns, jugglers and mimes. The event, held under a giant tent in Balboa Park, grossed nearly $200,000 in 1985. In the absence of other holidays, an arts organization's own significant anniversary date could provide reason enough for a funding event.

THE EXTENDED EVENT

With the right kind of volunteer participation, some fund-raising parties can become extended events, stretching beyond a single evening into several days or even weeks. With their well-organized guilds, symphony orchestras have been particularly adept at developing these kinds of events. In Tulsa, for example, the Volunteer Council of the Philharmonic, initiated an entire funding series, "Entertaining for the Philharmonic," early in 1986. Thirteen locally celebrated hosts and hostesses were recruited to host parties, each with a different theme, menu, location and attendance cost. Stretching from February 22 to April 4 (with several held on the same day), the events ranged in price from $10 for a "Mothers, Manners, Tots and Tea" children's party, limited to 20 mothers and 20 children, to $20 for a cooking demonstration for 50 people, to $50 for a St. Paddy's Day dinner and authentic Irish party for 10 people.

One of the most successful of all of the extended parties has been "Odyssey," a three-day affair hosted by the Oklahoma Symphony Orchestra's Women's Committee. Held every two years, the event has raised as much as $600,000 over a long weekend. Bult around a special theme—"Three Days on the Riviera"—the 1985 Odyssey was put together by a team of 300 volunteers and included separate events on each of its three days. All were related to the overall theme, and several were done with special glitter and panache. It began with a Thursday noon fashion show at "St. Tropez," the Marriott Hotel, continuing with a Friday champagne buffet in "Cannes," the elegant mansion of a symphony supporter, and a Saturday night in "Monte Carlo," the ballroom of the Skirvin Plaza Hotel, where gambling and an auction supplemented dining and dancing. Another year, the chef

128   from the world-famed 21 Club in New York prepared the gala dinner. And once, Maude Chasen of California's Chasen's Restaurant made her celebrated chili.

THE ELEGANT EVENT

Obviously, not every arts party has to have an element of fun or lightness to succeed. For many groups, elegance, even sumptuousness, is the cornerstone of the winning benefit. The elegant party begins with an elegant invitation listing the names of the many notables serving on the benefit committee; it has, among its key ingredients, an evening promising classic food and drink, music, a tasteful setting with special attention paid to color scheme and decor, and perhaps a fashion showing or performance preceding or following it. For its annual ball, one symphony orchestra mailed invitations which, when opened, greeted recipients with a burst of music. The orchestra described its ball setting as having "theme colors of jade and coral complementing the decor of the ballroom . . . The tables featured hurricane lamps filled with coral roses around which geese nested." The elegant benefit is pegged towards the donor who can afford it, and often features, as an extra reward, the presence of some especially notable guest, such as Her Royal Highness Princess Margaret, who graced the $300 to $500-a-person Sadler's Wells Royal Ballet gala benefit at the Brooklyn Academy of Music.

Although elegant funding events are most often hosted by larger, more established arts organizations that can afford the investment and can frequently rely on the involvement of a major corporation to help underwrite them, smaller groups have also had their flings with elegance. The Quincy Society of Fine Arts described its Black and White Ball, held during Illinois Arts Week in 1985, as an evening that began with music and cocktails, "followed by an elegant 'designer dinner' created especially for the ball."

BUSINESS SPONSORSHIP

Some larger organizations have been fortunate in attracting corporate support for their funding events because they can promise the kinds of audiences that some businesses are very interested in reaching and the kind of posh setting with which the businesses can identify. To tie in with the New York Philharmonic's "An Evening in Vienna" benefit ball in 1985, Tiffany & Co. sponsored a pre-ball cocktail reception and viewing of pieces from the Tiffany Classic Diamond Collection in its Private Jewel Salon and Tiffany Room. A year earlier, Dom Perignon underwrote benefit parties in each of seven cities to celebrate the openings there of the American Ballet Theater's then-new production of *Cinderella*. In addition to a gift of $200,000 to pay for the Cinderella Balls, the company also contributed about $100,000-worth of cognac and champagne. With this kind of support, ABT was able to net over $650,000.

Here is how *The New York Times* described the setting for the champagne supper with dancing for 800 guests—at $500 and $1,000 a guest—following the ABT opening at the Metropolitan Opera House: "All the decor was white—tablecloths, candles, napkins, flowers—except for the few pale pink blossoms and the little pink ribbons that were tied around the napkins in the manner of toe shoes. White flowers were also massed in a gigantic Cinderella slipper on the grand staircase." The supper menu "included smoked salmon with Saran Nature, a wine made from the first pressing of the Champagne grapes; veal with chanterelles and wild rice, accompanied by Simi cabernet sauvignon from Moet's California vineyards [Moet-Hennessy owns Dom Perignon], and crème brulée, with Dom Perignon 1976. There were also such trifles as little chocolate slippers filled with champagne truffles from Neuchatel. And as a finishing touch, Hennessy Cognac."

In addition to business sponsors, there are philanthropic organizations in some cities that host major funding events and donate the proceeds to one or more local nonprofit groups. In San Diego, for example, Las Patronas, an organization of 50 La Jolla women who host an annual Jewel Ball, made the San Diego Opera some $40,000 richer by naming the group as a major beneficiary of its 1985 ball.

THE SELECT FEW

Larger arts organizations may limit attendance at some benefits to a select few because the program is so special that it would be difficult to accommodate large numbers, and because only the few will be willing to pay enough for the privilege of attending a truly exclusive event. The National Symphony's special gala weekend in Washington, D.C., aimed at national trustees from throughout the country and their associates and friends, has been one such event. Built around the symphony's annual ball, a large fund-raising event in itself, the weekend is limited to 40 couples who pay $3,000 each for a round of very special events running from Friday afternoon through Sunday noon.

130   During one such weekend, the select group of 30 couples began the festivities with a Friday pre-luncheon cocktail reception attended by the Secretary of Health and Human Services and the State Department's Chief of Protocol, followed by a luncheon and briefing hosted by President Reagan's assistant for National Security Affairs, and continuing with a private cocktail reception and white tie Symphony ball reception. Saturday's program included luncheon with the Secretary of Agriculture and a black tie dinner-dance at the French Embassy, followed by a Sunday brunch hosted by the Attorney General and his wife.

THE ARTISTIC BENEFIT

One of the staples of arts fund-raising is the benefit program built around an artistic event, frequently an opening night gala. Of course not every group can fill three tiers of its concert hall (not many groups *have* three tiers), as the Metropolitan Opera did following the opening night of *Porgy and Bess*, and raise close to $350,000 in the process. But an arts group can attract attention with its benefit event if its program has some ingredients that set it apart from other programs, and if the event is preceded or followed by a reception or party for which additional donations can be asked. The Shakespeare Center in New York City, for example, built a three-layer event around a staged reading of Dickens' *A Christmas Carol* narrated by Helen Hayes, several weeks prior to Christmas in 1985. Tickets for the performance alone were $20, for the performance and a champagne reception immediately afterwards, $50, and for all of the above and a special holiday banquet at the then-new Marriott Marquis, $125.

Frequently, the nature of the artistic presentation will provide its arts sponsor with an opportunity to package related special events around it and build an entire integrated evening, thus justifying a boost in prices. To highlight the Ubu Repertory Theater's production of the rarely seen Pablo Picasso play *Catch Desire By the Tail*, presented as part of its conference on avant-garde art and literature, Hofstra University built a Gala Avant-Garde Evening around it. It began with a "surrealist buffet and cocktail party" and a preview of art exhibitions, including works from a special collection of avant-garde art and literature. Following the performance, guests (who paid $125 each for the evening, $1,000 for patrons) attended a gala after-theatre supper. To add further glamour, the event was held under the patronage of the ambassador and consul general of France and the French ambassador to the United Nations, and included as

honorary chairmen two of Picasso's children and both New York   **131**
senators, Daniel Moynihan and Alfonse D'Amato.

For a first-ever benefit for the experimental theatre company Mabou Mines, host Joseph Papp of the New York Shakespeare Festival staged a three-tiered, interrelated funding event, offering patrons the opportunity to select whichever option best suited their pocketbooks. "Uptown" tickets at $500 each included a benefit show at the Public Theater, dinner at an elegant nearby restaurant with Mabou Mines members and all the celebrity performers, and luxury transportation to a new, about-to-open disco. "Midtown" tickets at $100 included everything but the dinner, and "Downtown" tickets, priced at only $10, "because the company chooses not to ignore any of the groups that have supported us over the years," were available for the disco alone.

Sometimes the artists participating in a benefit program are of such stature or so rarely seen in public performance that their presence alone is sufficient to draw an audience. This was especially true when the International Writers' Congress, to help raise the nearly $1 million needed for its 1986 gathering in New York City, staged a series of eight literary evenings at a Broadway theatre, featuring as speakers such literary luminaries as Saul Bellow, Eudora Welty, Kurt Vonnegut, Arthur Miller and Norman Mailer. The eight-event program, with two writers participating in each of the Sunday evening readings, sold out almost immediately at $1,000 per series subscription, and subsidized almost the entire cost of the conference.

PUTTING THE BENEFIT TOGETHER

Specialists have formulated many principles for putting a successful benefit program together, and they are worth following. Every event needs carefully pre-determined goals, a program focal point, a suitable site and date and an overall plan that includes a timetable, working budget, controls on spending, a chart of accountability and a coordinated direct mail and publicity effort. Most important, however, the event needs people—and the right people—to work on it. The adage "peer speaks to peer' may have its greatest validity when it is applied to special events that must attract people willing to spend a good deal of money to attend. Perhaps this is why so many event planners are concerned at the outset with getting a top-drawer chairman and high-level committee actively involved. In fact, with the right kind of leadership, some of the rules can even be violated and the event can still be a financial and artistic success.

132 One of the most glittering arts benefits of the 1985-86 season was the concert performance of *Follies* presented just after Labor Day at Lincoln Center, for the benefit of the New York Philharmonic and the Foundation of the Dramatists Guild's Young Playwrights Festival. Featuring a once-in-a-lifetime cast, including such stars as Licia Albanese, Carol Burnett, Betty Comden, Barbara Cook, George Hearn and Mandy Patinkin, the program—at prices ranging from $100 to $500 a person—raised over $210,000. Thanks to major gifts-in-kind, expenses were kept down to less than 25 percent. This success was achieved in spite of the fact that the event "broke every rule in the book," according to fund-raising consultant Carole Southall, head of the Southall Group, who coordinated the benefit.

  "The experienced wisdom is that you don't try to do anything over the summer in New York City because everyone is away," noted Southall, "yet the benefit campaign was launched in June for a September 6 performance." Also, the benefit committee, a critical element in the success of any program, was put together in a somewhat unorthodox manner because of the late start and the difficulty of getting people together just before the summer. "Because we didn't have time to have a kickoff party with a committee invited by the chairman to attend, as is usually done, we did what is normally absolutely forbidden," added Southall. "We got the up-front commitments by mail."

  In spite of these presumed drawbacks, the program worked exceptionally well, mainly because of the human factor. On June 28, letters from the well-known and well-liked benefit chairman Mary Rodgers were sent to some 1,500 key individuals. They were invited to become vice chairmen for donations of $500 and upwards, or committee members for donations of $100 and upwards, and were asked to respond before July 8, when the invitations were to be printed. The mailing list was drawn from top Philharmonic and Dramatists Guild donors and from the personal lists of Rodgers, honorary chairman Michael Bennett, *Follies* composer Stephen Sondheim and others close to the event. Phone calls helped turn up names as well, and Southall claims that she was on the phone with composer Marvin Hamlisch for over an hour as he went through his Rolodex looking for appropriate people to invite.

  Each letter included one of five handwritten postscripts from Rodgers, (depending on her familiarity with the recipient) ranging from, "Please be an angel and help me with this. Love, Mary" to, "Listen, this is going to be terrific and you've got to help! Please . . .? Love, Mary" to, "I swear to you this is going to be the most exciting evening all year. Come and bring everyone you know! Best, Mary."

The mailing to the 1,500 key people was very successful and brought in half of the benefit money. Somewhat incredibly, considering the short time available, the benefit invitation, with the names of 36 vice chairmen and 58 committee members printed on it, was mailed to a list of some 13,000 names on July 15, only a few weeks after the initial letter had been mailed.

Although summer mailings are normally considered taboo, this one worked. "People are far more reachable during the summer than you might think," commented Southall, "and this mailing stood out from the crowd because the people on most benefit lists receive so little mail of this type during the summer."

On September 5, *Follies* kicked off the New York social season before an audience of more than 1,000. Months later, millions of people saw a taped version of it on the Public Broadcasting System. As a fund-raiser, *Follies* was no folly.

CHAPTER 8

Game or Gamble?
Why Not Both?

An arts contest is a game, and, like Monopoly, the money that's used may be for play only. But, unlike Monopoly, the rewards to the winner are very real indeed. Over the past few decades, arts groups have learned what casinos have long known: that while the players may have the fun and the excitement, in the long run, it is the house that always wins. The most savvy organizations have further learned that while playing by the rules can bring excellent results, it is the unexpected twist or the slight deviation from the rules that can bring the very best results.

When the London, Ontario Symphony was planning a raffle with 10 vacation trips as prizes several years ago, it made a calculated decision to limit the number of ticket purchasers to only 200. In that way, it reasoned, players would have an extraordinary one-in-twenty chance of winning. Fliers proclaiming the favorable odds read, "We are a very small organization in a small city. We are quite happy to issue only 200 tickets. This means your chances of winning are a phenomenal one in 20, think of it, one in 20!" Although tickets moved slowly at first, once the ice was broken the rush was on. Within five weeks, all 200 tickets at $125 each were sold. The result was a large $13,000 net profit for a not-so-large group.

Although gambling may be frowned upon by puritans, anyone who has ever started a new program in the arts is very aware of the need to take risks. But when it comes to using gambling or gaming as a means of raising funds, arts groups are in the dealer's seat. If cultural leaders are somewhat uneasy about mixing gambling with the arts, and using raffles, auctions or games of chance to part patrons from their money, they might take comfort from the words of Michael Michalko, director of California's first state lottery, who said, "In my mind, technically there is no denying that the vehicle we are using is gambling. But it's not gambling for the sake of gambling. It's really a means of raising money for education." A Massachusetts spokesman might say the same thing about that state's lottery to benefit the arts, which has been held for several years. Raising money is what gambling and gaming for the arts is all about.

Raffles and auctions have been popular arts money-makers for years, and for some larger organizations they are virtual bonanzas. The Metropolitan Opera, for example, won $800,000 in 1979 as the result of a raffle in which 54,000 people, many of them multiple ticket buyers, sent in donations of $2 each in order to be eligible for one of more than 1,000 different prizes. Six years later, in 1985, the Met offered 3,333 prizes in two raffles (between 100 and 150 of the prizes were substantial), and raised a little over $2 million. But not every organization is as large as the Met, and few can afford to distribute a million raffle brochures. For many of these organizations, the difference between a real financial return and a relatively insignificant reward may involve such factors as an unusual and promotable theme; a good publicity effort; low expenses; a good plan of action; unique or expensive donated prizes; and strong volunteer involvement.

The importance of keeping expenses as low as possible was pinpointed in Theatre Communications Group's 1985 membership survey of special events. The informal poll showed that of 19 auctions held—out of 161 theatre funding events—the average cost was $20,182 and the net return was a little over 100 percent. However, the eight most successful auctions, netting profits of over 200 percent, cost an average of only $9,460 each.

While raffles and auctions are two of the most popular and successful arts funding events, they may appeal to different kinds of audiences and draw different kinds of responses. Basically, a raffle as a game of chance is the more democratic of the two, because each ticket-holder has the same chance of winning. Conversely, in an auction (unless it is a silent auction), chance has little to do with it. The bidder who spends the most money will be the winner. Consequently, to get the high bidders in the right frame of mind, auctions are usually tied to an event such as an elegant dinner.

RAFFLES

Raffles or sweepstakes are wonderful ways of involving a great many people, and the participants do not necessarily have to attend an event. But raffles demand a means of getting the word out, and getting the response device, such as a reply envelope, in the hands of the potential player. Most often this requires a direct mail effort which highlights the gift or gifts to be awarded and ties participation to a donation to the sponsoring organization. Since regulations on games of chance differ among states, it is essential that any organization considering a raffle first check with its state attorney general's office to find out whether raffles are allowed and, if so, whether there are any special requirements or disclaimers, such as, "Of course, there is no obligation to make a contribution in order to enter."

The suggested contribution amount is far from an automatic choice. In most instances, the amount relates to the value or uniqueness of the gift, the limitations, if any, on the number of entries, the size of the mailing and the prestige of the sponsoring organization. It also relates to the objective of the organization. If it is to draw the

138   greatest number of entries—and the mailing is a giant one—then the suggested donation may be low. Prestigious groups such as the San Francisco Symphony have had raffles with $2 contributions, while much smaller groups such as the aforementioned London Symphony have had limited drawings with $125 contributions.

A raffle needs hype, a catchy title or some unusual personality feature to distinguish it from the events touted by myriad unsolicitated pieces of mail which arrive daily in the average mailbox. The American Ballet Theater called one of its raffles the "Million Dollar Match" to tie it in with a National Endowment for the Arts grant, and a later raffle, "The Manhattan Fantasy Sweepstakes."

The envelope may be a good starting point in getting noticed. To promote its raffle, the New York Public Library featured a blue strip above the window address on its envelope with the words, "Open immediately to see all you can win in the Friends of the Library Raffle." Below and to the right of the address, the library listed such prizes as a luxury London vacation for two; a Jacuzzi whirlpool bath for home or apartment; a glamorous designer dress by Bill Blass; a cocktail party for 50; "and scores of other prizes." The self-mailer of the Jewish Museum featured the word "PRIZES!" three times in giant red letters on its face. Inside, along with ten raffle coupons at $2.50 each, a list of the prizes was included.

Some smaller organizations with limited prizes available have offered raffle tickets as subscription or donation inducements. The 1986 New York Gay Film Festival offered one sweepstakes coupon, good for two free admissions, with each six-admission pack of tickets purchased, while The Yard Theatre on Martha's Vineyard offered, along with such benefits as opening-night tickets and party invitations, one raffle ticket for $100 donors and three tickets for $450 donors.

THE SINGLE, SPECTACULAR RAFFLE PRIZE

To attract ticket purchasers, some arts groups have focused in on special themes, such as the Arizona Theatre Company's travel raffle to several exotic locales, while other groups have limited their raffles to a single, spectacular and promotable prize, such as a luxury automobile. One advantage of an automobile drawing is that a car, moved to different locations, can become a vehicle (no pun intended) for publicity. Both the Winnipeg and Edmonton symphonies have been partial to Mercedes Benz 380SL sports cars, a $50,000 plus "dream" auto and—because of the involvement of volunteers—have been able to sell thousands of raffle tickets for these cars at $25 to

$30 each. Even with expenses of $60,000 one year, including the cost of purchasing the car (a portion of the cost was donated) the associates of the Edmonton Symphony netted over $80,000 from the car raffle. That the prize Mercedes had formerly been owned by Edmonton's hockey superstar, Wayne Gretsky, didn't hurt the 1984 raffle. Gretsky himself participated in the drawing for the winning number.

When the Kentucky Opera wanted to wipe out a $100,000 deficit in 1985, it hoped to ride the road to solvency in a Maserati Biturbo. Previous company raffles, begun three years earlier, had awarded vacation trips as prizes and had been generally successful, but planners felt that by offering a $27,000 luxury car, the ante could be upped significantly. It was, and raffle ticket prices were raised from $25 each in 1984 to $100 a ticket the next year. As board president Diane Mayer indicated in an interview, the ticket price hike was no cause for worry. "Last year and the year before," she said, "most of our tickets were sold in $100 blocks. We have an audience willing to pay that amount. . . . Because this is a much more valuable prize, we feel that we will be successful in selling the tickets at $100 apiece."

Because of the high price of the tickets, much of the sales effort, utilizing 150 volunteers organized in teams, was on a one-to-one basis. The campaign was kicked off dramatically: tickets were placed on first-time sale at the opening night of a Kentucky Opera production of *The Pearlfishers*, and the Maserati was on view in the theatre lobby. Although the 693 tickets sold fell short of the projected 1,000, the $69,300 in sales was a leap upwards from previous raffles, and raised nearly $55,000 for the company, once the cost of the car—at a deducted $15,000—was included. Pleased with the results, the opera company maintained its $100-a-ticket price for its 1986 raffle, although it made one significant change. The car offered the following year was a Jaguar.

FOOD-ORIENTED RAFFLES

While the appeal of snazzy foreign cars is great, there are some audience members who would rather eat than drive, and arts groups are more than willing to pamper their stomachs. Hence, the food-oriented raffle which, interestingly enough, need not be limited to gourmet diets in order to succeed. At Princeton, N.J.'s McCarter Theatre, the restaurant raffle has become an annual event aimed at luring large numbers of contestants, who pay only $1 a ticket for the chance to win dinner for two at up to 15 top area restaurants. To promote the event, and to promote the restaurants that contribute the

140 dinners, the theatre displays menus from each of the participating restaurants in its lobby.

When the gastronomic rewards are even greater, the entry fee may be higher. For its gourmet fantasy sweepstakes, the American Ballet Theater invites audiences to vie for a dinner a week for an entire year, at different top Manhattan restaurants. "Imagine," says the ABT flier, "for $20 you could have not one but 52 meals fit for a king."

Although most food-oriented raffles rely solely on meals donated by gourmet-quality restaurants, the East End Arts and Humanities Council in Riverhead, N.Y. came up with an interesting variation on that theme several years ago which made them $3,700 richer. Instead of just seeking out a few top restaurants, the arts council went for quantity. It solicited virtually every eating establishment in its area for a donation—from haute cuisine French restaurants to fast food outlets. Raffle tickets were sold at $1 each, offering chances on every kind of eating experience, from a quiet sit-down dinner for two in posh surroundings to a Sunday brunch, a fast pizza or breakfast at a coffee house, with well over 100 eateries and their offers listed in the raffle booklet. To win the commitments from restaurants, scores of volunteers, organized into committees in several local communities, solicited the establishments they regularly patronized.

THE ONE-OF-A-KIND PRIZE

At times, arts groups may come up with such a distinctive one-of-a-kind item that a raffle will draw tremendous audience interest and attention. For the Buffalo Philharmonic in 1984, that item was a custom-designed, hand-stitched quilt that replicated the orchestra's 1983-84 poster, featuring nine different program cover designs from the season. The spectacular finished product, designed by a local quilting studio and crafted by master needlewomen, was hung at the orchestra's performance base, Kleinhans Hall, to attract the attention of potential raffle ticket buyers during concert intermissions. Coupons, sold at $2 each, earned over $7,000 for the orchestra. For the Syracuse Stage in 1983, that unique item was a four-color lithograph of Maurice Chevalier by Charles Kiffer, which was displayed in the lobby throughout the season.

EXTENDED SWEEPSTAKES AND LOTTERIES

In addition to one-time raffle drawings—with momentum, interest and, one hopes, sales building until the prizes are drawn—some cultural organizations have decided that a good thing is worth extending. CSC: City Stage Co. in New York City had a modest in-house lottery one season, with weekly drawings at $1 a chance for prizes donated by board members and friends. More ambitious is the season-long sweepstakes promotion that awards major prizes on a regular basis in well-publicized drawings. One of these was held some years ago by the Sacramento Symphony (which has since switched to a raffle for a Mercedes). Supporters, in return for a $10 donation, received coupons for a monthly prize drawing, as well as a large wall calendar showing the prizes—each worth $500 or more—and the dates when they would be awarded. The contest received a promotional boost each time a winner was announced. It also earned some extra income through the sale of the calendars as Christmas gifts.

While the major purpose of a raffle is to earn money, it can also be very useful in helping an organization build up its mailing list, as the New York-based Theatre Development Fund discovered. As part of a fifth anniversary promotion, TDF held a sweepstakes soliciting donations of $10 and up in return for eligibility in a contest offering more than 175 prizes. Using other arts lists in addition to its own, TDF drew responses from newcomers, although at a lower rate than from its own list, and raised over $25,000. But in a separate aspect designed specifically to build its mailing list, TDF distributed sweepstakes forms—without requests for donations—to people waiting on line at its discount TKTS booth in Manhattan. Within four months, over 100,000 entries had been received.

AUCTIONS

Raffles and sweepstakes rely on mail response, but an auction is definitely a live—and hopefully lively—event, unless, of course, it is being held in a radio or television studio and phone bids are solicited. (Even then, there is usually a live audience on hand.) While the prizes to be awarded play a critical role in the success of the auction, the theme, setting, program, and above all, the auctioneer, are all contributing factors. The presence of major celebrities, especially if they can be announced in advance, can also be very helpful.

One of the oldest and most successful arts auctions is Camelot, the "Cultural Auction of Many Extraordinary Lots of Treasure," held since 1968 as a benefit for the Arts and Education Council of Greater St. Louis. One of the city's top social events, Camelot drew a turnaway audience of over 600 in 1985, at $125 a head for cocktails, an elegant dinner and live auction at the corporate dining room of the

142   Monsanto Company. The site was specially decorated in the colors of the evening, pink, silver and gold. Sponsored by Famous-Barr department store, which has supported the event since its inception, the evening featured a silent auction during cocktails and live bidding following dinner. Spirited bidding, on such items as a trip to France underwritten by Ernst & Whinney which sold for $2,000, and 12 bottles of rare wine contributed by the widow of local business and civic leader Morton D. May (selling for $4,000), was supervised by well-known auctioneer Bruce Selkirk. One of the highest winning bids, at $6,200, was for an "Agatha Christie" trip on the Orient Express underwritten by Peat Marwick Mitchell & Co. "It was the most successful auction we've ever held," recalled Arts and Education staff member Ann Shutek. "It netted nearly $200,000."

Not every arts auction can net $200,000, but many groups have realized very respectable returns, and promoted themselves as well, through imaginative, elegant, unusual and even funny auction programs. The settings have been as varied as hotels, department stores, convention centers, school gymnasia, night clubs and office buildings, and even a state fairgrounds, in Des Moines, Iowa, where a "Carnival Auction of the Uniques," benefitted the Des Moines Metro Opera. Guest auctioneers have included Art Buchwald for the American Repertory Theatre and comedian Henny Youngman for Manhattan Punch Line, while Lily Tomlin, appearing as "Mrs. Judith Beasley, Cultural Ambassadress of Calumet City, Illinois," assisted Christopher Burge, president of Christie's, in a sale to benefit Carnegie Hall. Tomlin also bid $5,500 for a trip to Nashville's Country Music Awards. Celebrities, such as Helen Reddy for the Denver Center for the Performing Arts and Marsha Mason and Neil Simon for San Francisco's American Conservatory Theatre, have graced the auctions of cultural groups—and several have volunteered their services and names as honorary chairmen.

Because every arts auction has its own personality, it is difficult to come up with a standard format. Although many auctions include a glittering program, frequently featuring dinner, and charge a hefty price for admission, some, such as the Celebrity Auction to benefit the Strand Theatre in York, Pa. in 1985, have offered free admission in order to attract as wide an audience of bidders as possible. The York program, billed as a "fun-for-the-whole-family" event, was held from 6:00 p.m. to midnight on a Saturday night at the theatre.

Good organization and volunteer involvement have been important elements for most successful auctions. The annual Tamasha auction of the Cultural Activities Center in Temple, Tex. is a case in point. Over 150 volunteers work for months on some 15 committees—

decorations, dinner, silent auction and acquisitions among them— to make the auction a reality. As a result, as much as $65,000 has been raised through the four-hour event, even though Temple's population is only about 50,000. At more than a $1 per capita profit, that's a very effective auction.

Successful auctions have also featured interesting themes—often relating to the sponsoring group's program—and unusual prizes. For its annual auction, the Manhattan Punch Line, which bills itself as "New York's Comedy Theatre," has not only utilized comedians such as Henny Youngman as auctioneers, but has auctioned off items consistent with its comedic image, such as a custom-made obituary "ready to go whenever you are," and a Caribbean cruise . . . for one. New York City's New Dramatists auctioned off the doodles of noted theatre personalities and promoted the event through an advance window display at a leading store. Befitting its role in the world of music, Carnegie Hall auctioned off 12 "Passport to Music" prizes, featuring a monthly, one-of-a-kind international music experience throughout 1986, complete with private entrée and behind-the-scenes privileges. Included were a New Year's Eve trip to the Vienna Opera House and a four-day trip to the Herbert von Karajan Easter Festival in Salzburg, which drew winning bids of $14,000 and $12,000 each.

In many instances, auction prizes are experiential and arts- or community-related, rather than tangible items. The American Repertory Theatre has auctioned off an "All in the Family" script signed by Norman Lear and a day at Suffolk Downs including a horse race named for the successful bidder, while the WPA Theatre has hawked a walk-on movie part and "a fabulous dress worn by a major Broadway star in an ill-fated musical." The Lethbridge Symphony has offered bidders an opportunity to throw a pie at a local personality, while the Children's Museum of Denver has afforded some lucky attendee and his or her youngster a visit by Mayor Pena to the child's classroom. The Asolo Theater in Florida was able to tie in an auction item to its production of *A Thurber Carnival* by having cartoonist Dik Browne, of "Hagar the Horrible" fame, do an original drawing based on a Thurber cartoon; while the Washington Project for the Arts marked its 10th anniversary in 1985 with an auction featuring a "Surprise Box," a hand-made cloth-covered box containing a variety of small works by artists participating in its art auction.

Good promotion is essential to drawing audiences to an auction event. One of the more successful promotional devices used by arts groups is the participation of local celebrities in the program. When Binghamton, N.Y.'s Roberson Center for the Arts held an art auction some years ago, it turned to famed local cartoonist, John Hart

("Wizard of Id" and "B.C.") for help. To promote the advance sale of "building blocks"—certificates redeemable in lieu of cash at the art auction—Hart drew his cartoon characters piling up building blocks on the face of the certificates. The theme, repeated in posters and promotional materials, gave an immediate identity to the auction.

Food has been just as potent an arts tool in auctions as it has in raffles. Theatre London in Canada has raised as much as $30,000 from its annual Gourmet Dinner Auction by featuring in its silent and live auction, wrapped around a "gastronomical orgy," such biddable items as gourmet restaurant dinners and a six-foot salami. The Pennsylvania Ballet's epicurean auction featured such unusual culinary rewards as a private plane ride for six to dine anywhere in the Eastern United States, a picnic in a Goodyear blimp and breakfast at Tiffany's with a Philadelphia celebrity.

A unique concept or theme can play a key role in selling an upcoming auction, and if the concept is successfully carried out, audience word-of-mouth will help sell an organization's future funding programs. One of the more intriguing auction concepts in recent years was a murder mystery auction, conceived and developed by the Portland Stage Company in Maine. The audience, seated in a local high school gymnasium, was surrounded by three different stage sets, each a setting for one act of a short three-act tongue-in-cheek murder mystery written and presented by a local comedy team. At the end of each act—one set in a living room, another in a sun room and the third in an attic—the audience was invited to bid on the props featured in that particular act and set. The bidding, for such items as an oriental rug, paintings and sporting equipment including tennis rackets and skis, was spirited, and since the playlet and live auction were compressed into less than two hours, things moved quickly. The evening, which opened with a silent auction, netted $14,000 for the theatre group and set the stage for the next annual auction. Also held in a gymnasium, the 1986 fund event employed a similar concept to display the items up for bidding. The theme? A three-ring circus.

BROADCAST MARATHONS

In recent years, there has been a growth in the use of radio and television marathons to benefit cultural groups. Auctions and other on-the-air funding techniques have become an integral part of these events, whose greatest proponents have been symphony orchestras, opera companies and public television stations, although arts councils, theatres, music schools and other cultural institutions have been getting on the bandwagon. According to WFMT-FM, a Chicago radio station which has sponsored live Chicago Symphony marathons for a decade and averaged nearly $500,000 a year in funds raised, over $20 million has been raised for music groups from radio marathons since 1968, when the first such funding event took place in Syracuse. Although many marathons last only a day or less, some stations have devoted as much a week to a particular arts group, spotlighting the organization and its needs on many of its programs, interviewing its performers and administrators and playing its records frequently, as New York's WQXR has done during Metropolitan Opera Week.

A key to the success of broadcast auctions has been the solicitation of gifts to ensure audience interest in bidding. The Chicago Symphony has been able to win such one-of-a-kind items in years past as cartoonist Milton Caniff's drawing of maestro Sir Georg Solti and Mikhail Baryshnikov's inscribed ballet slipper. One year, TV personality Gene Shalit donated an item with which he is closely identified, his bow tie, along with a personal message which read, "Come to New York and we'll tie one on together. I am bass and vile."

Center Stage, a Baltimore theatre which has been holding radio auctions since 1978 and has made as much as $65,000 in an 18-hour session, has been able to offer over 500 items in its 8:00 a.m.-to-midnight auctions over WBAL radio. These have included prizes with material value—a seven-day cruise on the Queen Elizabeth and round-trips for two to London—as well as more personal items, such as becoming batboy-for-a-day with the Baltimore Orioles. Well in advance of the auction, the theatre solicits scores of local businesses for items, promising, in return, on-air promotion during the days leading up to the event and plugs for 16 hours on auction day.

Advance promotion, to supplement spots that a participating station may be running, has been critical also. Some groups, such as the New York Philharmonic, publish gift catalogues with pages describing the gifts available to "buy, bid or pledge." For the higher priced items to be auctioned off, the Philharmonic publishes minimum bids and the approximate auction time. That familiar standby—food—had a special place in a recent catalogue with a listing of 200 different restaurants offering meals to benefit the Philharmonic, at prices ranging from $15 to $450. In Windsor, Canada, the symphony promoted one of its "dream auctions" with help from the city. A Mayor's luncheon launched Symphony Week, and the city renamed the downtown section of Riverside Drive "Symphony Drive."

While auctions and broadcast marathons sound like easy fundraisers, they are far from automatic. Not only do they require a lot of work and good organization, but even with careful planning things

146   can go wrong. When seven Brooklyn arts groups joined to present a televised auction in 1976, the hoped-for bonanza turned out to be a financial flop, with only 40 of the 250 contributed items sold. Although unforseen TV production expenses cut into the earnings, the greatest problem came from a rash of fake telephone bids, triggered by the unrealistic bidding for one of the first items offered, a rug worth $400. Bidding on the rug was allowed to continue until it reached an absurd $59,000. And then the crank bids started coming in.

Improper timing can also have a strong negative effect on a program's financial success, as the Albany Symphony discovered some years ago. The most listened-to radio station in the city, WROW, had offered an on-air giveaway in behalf of the orchestra. It began with a drawing for 100 pairs of symphony tickets for "WROW Night at the Pops" and concluded with half-hour appeals for funds on the Monday and Tuesday before the Saturday concert. However, the promotion was presented just a week before the local public service classical music station presented its own on-air fund marathon. Also, the weekday symphony fund appeal failed to reach many weekend listeners, and the nearly week-long lag between the ticket giveaways and the requests for funds caused the promotion to lose its momentum. The result was slim monetary returns.

GAMES AND CONTESTS

While raffles and auctions are rewarding, some arts groups get their kicks out of playing games. Casino nights (with fake money, of course) and admission donations have been quite successful for some organizations, although groups have learned to check local regulations before initiating such activities. Theatre Virginia has held a "Casablanca Night" with play money featuring Humphrey Bogart's picture and volunteers portraying characters from the well-known movie, while Hartford Stage Company has featured a Monte Carlo Casino, a black-tie affair at $100 a person which includes a raffle and auction. It netted the company $76,647 in 1984.

Les Grands Ballets Canadiens drew 1,000 people to its "casino" in November 1985, and netted over $40,000 from the effort. The Cincinnati Ballet, which hosts an annual Monte Carlo Night, ties live and silent auctions to the preceding action at the blackjack, craps and roulette tables, by allowing winning gamblers to use their chits at the auction. One special auction item, incidentally, is billed as a "No Hassles" item. "Bid high enough on this one," audiences are told, "and no one from the Ballet will ask for a donation for one year."

Game or Gamble? Why Not Both?

Arts groups have been ingenious in devising games to promote their programs and part audiences from their money for a good cause. From the mundane weekly bingo game—which was anything but mundane in its execution, earning profits of over $100,000 a year for several years for the L.A. Public Theatre—to treasure hunts, to some very mysterious games, to celebrity contests, arts organizations have made money and headlines. As far back as 1963, the Pittsburgh Symphony was the "prize" in a radio station's "win an orchestra contest." In that competition, contestants who vied for a free orchestra concert accompanied each entry with a donation to the orchestra's maintenance fund campaign.

More recently, arts contests have served a range of needs, including program promotion, ticket sales and funding. In many instances, contests have been tied to an organization's program and personality. Washington's Folger Shakespeare Library, for example, has sponsored an annual Shakespeare birthday card contest since 1980, with prizes donated by local merchants. To hype its subscription sales blitz over station KTRK, the Houston Symphony sponsored a "battle of the conductors" with local celebrities, Olympian Carl Lewis and football hero Earl Campbell among them, leading the orchestra in a work of their choosing; in San Francisco, the symphony launched its summer "pop" season in 1984 with Bay Area personalities participating in a competition to see which of them could "pop" a champagne cork the greatest distance.

Local business also can play a role in arts contests. In Fort Wayne, Ind., the Lincoln National Corporation sponsored a competition among its employees which not only encouraged their arts involvement but bolstered the company's role as an arts patron. Lincoln offered 50 free seats to a performance of the Fort Wayne Philharmonic to employees submitting the best statements completing the sentence, "I think Lincoln National should continue to support the fine arts in Fort Wayne because. . . ." The Canton, Ohio Ballet enlisted the services of the local offices of Prudential-Bache and Merrill Lynch to compute the results of an unusual contest it sponsored, and which the brokerage firms underwrote. Contestants, who paid entry fees of $25, were asked to select five stocks they thought would grow in value during the coming quarter, and invest a fictitious $10,000 in them. The event, which netted about $3,000 each of the years it was held, awarded cash prizes to the top five winners.

Many of the arts contests held in recent years have been for fun as well as for funding. The Changing Scene, a Denver experimental theatre, attracted a lot of attention in the community (although not too much money) with its city-wide treasure hunt called "The Game." Contestants, organized into teams of four who paid $30 a team for

148 the privilege of competing, scoured the city to find the answers to a series of complex clues, and win prizes. Held for several years, The Game was discontinued a few years ago because it became too much work, and the company didn't have enough help to pull it off.

Newspapers have been willing participants in arts games, to the delight of many cultural development and promotion directors. Several museums, such as the Founders Society Detroit Institute of Arts, have reaped large financial rewards from the Family Art Game. Published annually since 1978 as a Sunday supplement to the *Detroit Free Press*, the game is similar to the advertising supplements described in an earlier chapter, with one notable difference—the game aspect. While the museum buys the supplement virtually at cost from the newspaper and sells space in it to local corporations, reaping substantial financial rewards in the process, through the game, the supplement has a promotional and educational aspect as well. Readers are asked to find the answers to questions about artists and their work which are hidden among the many color reproductions of museum works featured in the supplement. Prizes are awarded for correct entries. In addition to the more than one-and-a-half million readers that the supplement reaches, it is also distributed to thousands of schoolchildren. And it has netted an important $45,000 to $65,000 a year for the museum.

Another newspaper game, this one appearing for the first time in the Portland *Oregonian* in May 1985, served as a potent audience development tool for several mid-sized local arts organizations. The game, "Body of Art," was a murder mystery spoof and puzzle contest which appeared for six consecutive Sundays in space donated by the paper. Each of the weekly puzzles was a page-long story detailing the investigation into the murder of an art efficiency expert. The interesting aspect of the game was the fact that Portland arts groups, all members of the Portland Cultural Alliance, were part of it. In each script, the fictional detective assigned to the case quizzed Alliance member groups about their programs and activities to come up with clues to the murder of the efficiency expert who had advised such stringent budgetary procedures as cutting out lines of dialogue in plays to speed up the action. In addition to teaching readers about the arts groups in the course of the game, the newspaper featured a weekly listing with pertinent data on each Alliance member group, and advised readers that additional clues were available, in person, at each institution, a suggestion followed up by some 1,500 readers. Prizes contributed by local businesses were awarded to readers with the best solutions to all six puzzles.

Murder has been a profitable game for several other theatres as

well. To promote the Repertory Theatre of St. Louis's production of   **149**
Dial M for Murder in 1985, the Backers Board, a theatre support
group, sponsored a contest with prizes built around the murder of
an unknown fictitious victim. Clues were placed in newspaper ads
for the theatre's production, playbills, on stage (built into the set) and
in the subscriber newsletter. Washington, D.C.'s Source Theatre Company has committed murder on stage to earn money and promote
its program. In addition to producing "Murder Mystery Weekends"
at several Washington hotels, the company has presented mysteries
at sea on several Sun Lines cruises, and in 1985 presented its first
murder mystery benefit at $50 a head at a mansion in nearby Virginia.
Proctor's, a Schenectady, N.Y. theatre, not only developed its own
murder mystery weekend to raise funds in 1986, but put together
several packages to sell to other nonprofit organizations. Buyers could
purchase the production with cast or, for theatres with their own actors, they could buy use of the script along with a detailed plan ex-
plaining how to market and sell the production for fund-raising
purposes.

Perhaps, indeed, crime does pay—for the arts.

CHAPTER 9

More Ways to Skin a (Fat) Cat

152   In their funding efforts arts groups should not hesitate to solicit whatever help they can from whatever unlikely sources they can find. But only, of course, if those sources are legitimate. An outside presence, especially if it's a celebrated one, can lead to inside presents. The drawing power of celebrities has been demonstrated over and over again, and when a noted personality is pressed into engaging in an unexpected activity, then the audience appeal is undeniable. Picture, for example, as the audience did, Erica Jong entering the ring on an elephant's back at a circus performance benefit for Poets & Writers, or Norman Mailer reciting poetry while balanced on a board atop a rolling wheel at the same event. For the top donors to Atlanta's High Museum of Art, the special draw was a first birthday party for the museum's new facility featuring as a special guest, film star Sophia Loren, blowing out the candles on a giant birthday cake in the shape of the museum building. Loren appeared on behalf of J.C. Penney, the party's sponsor. For friends of the Hudson River Museum in Yonkers, N.Y., the drawing card was aerialist Philippe Petit, who had gained instant celebrity by walking on high wires between the World Trade Center's twin towers. Petit walked on high wires stretched over the museum floor to highlight a benefit heralding the opening of a museum exhibit on "Flying."

THE CELEBRITY DRAW

The friends, relatives (remember Billy Carter?) and even the pets of certified celebrities can be just as useful. Washington, D.C.'s Capital Children's Museum scored heavily with the Capital Canine Follies, a funding benefit built around the dogs of cabinet members, ambassadors, senators and journalists. In addition to raising about $10,000, thanks to underwriting from Kal Kan, a pet food firm, and from the curious who paid $10 to attend, the event received major press attention. Included among the coverage was a bylined article in the *Washington Dossier's* "Bark of the Town" column by Jasper Meese, the celebrated schnauzer of Attorney General Edwin Meese, III.

By the same token, an organization or institution, or even a government agency or official, acting in unexpected fashion to benefit an arts group can be a major lure for donors. Also in Washington, the appearances of Lady Wright, the British ambassador's exuberant wife, in acting roles at fund benefits for local arts groups are eagerly anticipated. In the same politically conscious city, the unique opportunity to feast on Chinese delicacies at the Embassy of the People's Republic of China drew over 300 supporters of Arena Stage's Living

Stage Theatre Company. As "a special gesture of friendship," Ambassador Zhang Wenjin and Mrs. Zhang Ying feted the theatre group.

Drawing celebrities to funding events isn't always an easy job, but one way to do it is to honor them. Not only does that usually assure the celebrity's attendance, but it frequently helps to draw his or her equally notable friends and associates to the event. The relatively small National Italian American Foundation was able to draw no less a personality than President Reagan to its anniversary gala because the organization was presenting its Life Achievement Award to the President's long-time friend, Frank Sinatra. On a somewhat more modest level, the New York Philomusica honored George Plimpton for his contributions to the world of music, and drew such a galaxy of notables as Jackie Onassis, Kitty Carlisle Hart, Betty Comden and Anthony Drexel Duke.

An organization with a talent for luring celebrity support, the New York Public Library, may even have topped its past efforts with a February 1986 dinner to benefit its performing arts branch at Lincoln Center. The library named 24 luminaries from the performing arts—Andres Segovia, Beverly Sills, Jerome Robbins, Leonard Bernstein and Garson Kanin among them—as "Lions of the Performing Arts." Admission to the event honoring the attending celebrities was limited to purchasers of tables, at $10,000 each. Twenty tables, for a total draw of $200,000, were sold.

Seeing celebrities is one thing, but having the opportunity to do something with them, such as bowl or play tennis, is an even more potent lure. Sporting events, both participatory and spectator, constitute an increasingly successful arena of arts funding, and there are few sports that haven't been tapped. For one of its major fund-raising events of 1986, New York City's Second Stage held an All-Star Bowling Classic at the Madison Square Garden Bowling Center. Donors were invited to contribute $200 for the opportunity to play two games (and perhaps land in the gutter, in a bowling sense) with the likes of Robert De Niro, Mandy Patinkin, Christopher Reeve, Gregory Hines and Kate Nelligan. Four corporations paid $2,500 each for the privilege of letting their employees bowl with the stars, helping contribute to the $50,000 that the theatre company raised from the event.

In fashionable Boca Raton, Fla., a more genteel activity drew $60,000 into the coffers of National Public Radio. The Celebrity Croquet gala, held at the posh new St. Andrews Country Club in April 1984—which also raised $20,000 for the Croquet Foundation of America—drew such participants as Zsa Zsa Gabor, Joan Fontaine and George Plimpton, as well as as several stars from the Miami Dolphins football team. The entire event, which served to introduce the country club to many notables, was underwritten by the club's chairman, who flew in and housed all the guest celebrities, as well as covering various other expenses.

THE SPORTING TOUCH

One of Milwaukee's household names, and a name familiar to most television viewers, sportscaster and TV celebrity Bob Uecker, is the drawing card for Uecker's Ride for the Arts, a bicycle event that benefits Milwaukee's United Performing Arts Fund to the tune of over $50,000 a year. Held annually since 1981, when it was known as Arts Peddlers, the event was conceived by the arts fund's marketing and promotions committee chairman, advertising executive Jack Birchhill, who drew one of his clients, Blue Cross and Blue Shield United of Wisconsin, into the event as its sponsor. For its second year he was able to get Uecker, the announcer of the Milwaukee Brewers baseball games and a star of Lite Beer commercials, to act as event host. The event name was then changed to reflect his participation. Held every June, the ride attracts several thousand cyclists who pay entry fees of $8 each to ride one of four routes, 1.3 miles, 15 miles, 25 miles or 50 miles. Participants are encouraged to have sponsors pledge dollar amounts for the distances they ride. The 1.3-mile route was added for the first time in 1986 to attract arts supporters who weren't in good enough shape to ride 15 miles. Families can ride for $16, and corporations can compete for $100 and up with a 10-rider minimum. Prizes are awarded for the most entrants and pledges.

"Bob Uecker really makes a difference," claims Evelyn Vitek, the Arts Fund's special events coordinator. "He's very well-known and he attracts people." Uecker does public service announcements gratis to promote the event, and acts as starter for all four of the rides, which begin at half-hour intervals in front of the Blue Cross building.

Arts supporters who don't bike may run for the arts. Scores of cultural organizations have organized runs, similar in concept and structure to the biking event, under such names as San Antonio's ArtsRun, to benefit public radio station KPAC, the San Diego Symphony's Quarter Note Classic and the Federated Arts Council of Richmond's Run for the Arts. Corporations, sensing the identification benefits of sponsorship, have underwritten such runs as the Natural Lite Run for Washington, D.C.'s Arena Stage, the Perrier Symphony 10K for the Dallas Symphony and the Dannon Dinosaur Dash for the Cleveland Museum of Natural History. The runs include such local amenities as routes designed to pass by cultural facilities, performers entertaining along the way, musical walks, and concerts and other entertainment at the event's conclusion. In Knoxville, as part of its Artfest, the arts council has sponsored an annual Great Champagne Race, featuring teams of waiters and waitresses from local restaurants. In Houston, the well-organized Interfirst Symphony Run sponsored by the Inter First Bank has attracted 5,000 runners and raised as much as $90,000 for the orchestra from a single day's events. The fun begins several days earlier with a pre-run sponsors' party for which the attire is black tie and running clothes.

Even non-bikers and non-runners need not feel excluded from the action, because somewhere there is an arts organization that has still another variation on the theme. In Philadelphia, the New Freedom Theater benefits from the pledges raised through its annual Walkathon, while in San Diego, on the California coast, the Old Globe Theatre has been boosted in a time of need from a Surf-a-thon organized by one of its supporters. Proving that arts groups know how to relate to their surroundings, the Creede Repertory Theatre in Colorado, an area of great winter sports activity, has held an annual Ski-a-thon since 1983.

Tennis has also involved a great many people eager to pay for the privilege of competing in tournaments specifically organized to benefit arts groups. In Santa Rosa, Calif. at one such tournament for the local symphony's benefit, more than 100 players paid $25 each to compete, and a fashion show, breakfast and lunch were added as part of the day's events. Since 1982, New Jersey arts groups have split about $160,000 annually—the recipients change each year—as beneficiaries of the Governor's Invitational Tennis Tournament, an event held at his official residence in Princeton. Corporations, competing in teams, pay to enter the charity event.

For those supporters more inclined to watch than participate, arts groups have concocted some exotic as well as traditional sporting possibilities. In Oklahoma City, the Oklahoma Alliance for Arts Education benefits from an annual Darts for Arts Tournament held in cooperation with the Oklahoma Darting Association, while in McFaddin, Tex., the Victoria Regional Museum has been the beneficiary since 1981 of "A Sporting Afternoon," an annual event including an auction, luncheon buffet, a military precision drill and parade, all leading up to a championship polo match.

An ice show has been one of the Denver Symphony's big fund-raisers in recent years, as the orchestra capitalized on both the event's proximity in time to the 1984 Winter Olympics and the homecom-

156 ing of Olympic figure skating champion Scott Hamilton, who had just made Denver his permanent home. Co-sponsored with the Presbyterian/Saint Luke's Medical Center, "Classics on Ice," which included a black-tie dinner and dance the night before the ice show/concert, drew an audience of 11,500 people and netted $100,000 for each organization. The event was especially unique since it involved the arts group's partnership with a hospital involved in cancer research. The alliance came about because Hamilton wanted to do something for his new city and also help fight cancer, the disease that had killed his mother.

Horse racing, the sport of kings, has brought royal returns to some arts organizations. Greyhound racing has also. Although arts administrators have not been known to frequent pari-mutuel windows, several racetracks, interested in attracting arts audiences, have given arts groups a day at the races. For several years, Woodbine Racetrack in Toronto gave Toronto Arts Productions the opportunity to host "The Run for the Arts." For its day at the races, the arts group was allowed to sell admission tickets to the racetrack and keep most of the money. It was also permitted to sell specific races to corporate sponsors at $5,000 a race; the race then bore the sponsor's name. Additional revenue came from such at-the-track activities as luncheons, the sale of food, drink and souvenirs by volunteers, and a raffle of donated prizes. The event netted about $50,000 each year it was held. In a somewhat similar arrangement, the Sacramento Symphony held "Symphony Goes to the Races" at Golden Bear Raceway annually from 1980 through 1984, netting between $25,000 and $45,000 each time. "It worked quite well," said Alzada Forbes, the orchestra's marketing director, "but it took a lot of volunteer effort. After a while it just ran its course and it was time to do something different."

One cultural group that has been deeply and successfully involved with horse racing, in an entrepreneurial sense, for several years is the Kentucky Opera. With the sponsorship of leading corporations, particularly Brown-Forman Corporation, the distributor of Bolla Wines, the opera company annually presents the Hard Scuffle steeplechase races at Hard Scuffle Farm, just north of Louisville. Like many arts groups who have developed a successful funding concept, the opera company has built an entire series of events around the Saturday day of racing, which culminates in the $40,000 Bolla Steeplechase. The event, which attracts horses and riders from around the world, is preceded by a Friday night ball and pre-race parties featuring wine donated by Bolla. With boxes selling from $650 to

$1,000 in 1986, up from the $300 to $650 several years earlier, the effort, involving hundreds of volunteers for months, has reaped close to $100,000 annually.

Perhaps the most unusual arts relationship to horse racing turned out to be something of an unexpected bonanza for the Baltimore Opera. In 1979, members of the Meyerhoff family, then owners of one of the all-time great thoroughbreds, Spectacular Bid, as well as major supporters of the opera, combined their two interests. They assigned all rights to the Spectacular Bid trademark and all the royalty income from sales of promotional materials relating to the racehorse, as well as commercial use of the horse's name, to the opera company. For several years (until the horse was syndicated), annual royalties of about $10,000 flowed into opera coffers from such income-producing ventures as the sale of bronze sculptures of the horse.

PLEDGES FOR THE ARTS

While sporting events lend themselves to winning pledges from donors spurred on by the accomplishments of their friends and relatives, arts organizations have been imaginative in winning pledges for virtually every kind of activity. Such "thons" as a piano-thon—a marathon 48-hour fund-raiser that began with formal concerts and featured local music teachers and students playing into the wee hours—raised thousands of dollars in pledges for the Carroll County, Md. Arts Council through $10-a-minute pledges. A Bard-a-thon, a five day nonstop reading of Shakespeare's works, raised $19,000 for the Fine Arts Theatre of the College of Marin in Kentfield, Calif. Pledge income was supplemented by admission charges for hearing celebrated alumni readers such as Robin Williams and David Dukes read the Bard. For sheer monotony, however, probably nothing topped the 1983 Presteigne, Wales performance by two organists of Erik Satie's 17-hour, tuneless and endlessly repetitious work, "Vexations," described as "the most boring musical work ever written." The work was played in an attempt to win pledges to support a fall arts festival that "promised more exciting music." It's not certain, of course, if listeners paid to hear the work or pledged money in an effort to get the musicians to stop.

Even the physical condition of an arts executive or, more properly, the lack of it, can result in pledges of support. "Big Joe" Wilfer, the five-foot-eight, 215-pound director of the Madison, Wisc. Arts Center, lost 37 pounds and helped win pledges of several thousand dollars for his organization in 1978 while Douglas Duncan, the 350-pound manager of the Des Moines Metro Opera, shed 57 pounds and won $8,500 in fat-free pledges for the opera company in 1983.

DESIGN FOR FUNDING

Although it is not a reflection on arts planning, cultural groups have won a great deal of money by design—home design. Given the curiosity of most people to visit elegant homes and compare the work of noted decorators, it is no accident that designer showcase fund-raisers and other design-oriented activities have proved so lucrative for so many organizations, netting in some instances hundreds of thousands of dollars from a single endeavor. The typical showcase is built around such essential ingredients as an historic or architecturally interesting house that will attract thousands of visitors, the involvement of top local designers to decorate the various rooms, the active involvement of scores of volunteers over a period of many months, a far-reaching promotional program to attract the interest of organizations as well as individuals and a plan that includes provisions for a series of related, income-producing events.

Showcases, which usually last about a month, have been planned around such elegant facilities as an English Tudor mansion in a country setting, a majestic early-19th-century estate overlooking the Hudson River and a townhouse once owned by top movie executive. In San Antonio in 1984, the Symphony League convinced the builders of a new, not-yet-completed ultra-luxury condominium of the public relations value of loaning two $1.2-million penthouses as showcases. As in this instance, most homes are loaned to the sponsoring organization for its use, and designers and design firms contribute their services in return for the opportunity to win tremendous exposure and future clients.

In addition to paid admissions ranging from $6 up—attendance of over 10,000 is not unusual—showcases also reap the financial and promotional rewards of such volunteer-run activities as the sale of lunch and refreshments, raffles of donated items, sales-oriented boutiques, jewelry showings, gourmet dinner parties, food tastings and changing art exhibitions. Virtually every successful showcase is kicked off with one or more opening benefits, such as one group's "Sneak Peak" party. For its 1986 showcase of three condominiums in a new downtown office/condo tower, the Des Moines Symphony had a "bare bones" party in the undecorated apartments six weeks prior to the event's official opening, as well as a $125-per-person cocktail, dinner and tour preview party in the completely decorated **159** condominiums the night before the kickoff.

While showcases can be lucrative, many groups have discovered that they are also expensive to produce, involving outlays of considerable sums for printing and promotion and for maintaining heat and electricity during the showcase period. To compensate, in addition to planning income-producing events, many groups have made special efforts to involve the community and win in-kind service donations and underwriting from local businesses.

Just how successful an event can be, and how much effort can be involved in producing it, are evident in the case of the 1984 Decorators' Show House presented by the Womens' Committee of Washington, D.C.'s National Symphony Orchestra. Held at a mansion owned at different times by both the Iranian ambassador and a member of the Corning Glass family, and loaned by the State Department which now has custody of it, the month-long event attracted over 30,000 visitors. The house, which opened with a black-tie preview, featured a designer-decorated tea room and 12 boutiques. During the month, 10 special events, ranging from parties to a wedding reception, were held. The Show House netted $270,000 for the symphony.

Arts administrators have also been known to create variations on successful funding themes, as in the case of the "Suite Life" concept offered by another Washington-based arts organization that same year. Sponsored by the League of Washington Theatres and TICKETplace, Suite Life afforded ticket purchasers a tour of some of Washington's most luxurious living accommodations, the rarely seen suites of seven of Washington's most opulent hotels. For the $12 admission price, transportation among the hotels and edible refreshments at several of them were available, thanks to the sponsorship of American Express. The credit card company further tied in its interests to the tour by offering tour-takers a "Taste of the Suite Life" booklet which included special privileges at the participating hotels and the League's member theatres—when using the American Express card.

Design has other fund-raising uses as well. The American Conservatory Theatre in San Francisco is one of many groups that has raised thousands of dollars annually through Christmas-oriented design programs, featuring such projects as ornate table settings created by designers for noted hostesses and celebrities, and fantasy-decorated Christmas trees. San Diego's Museum of Art has made as much as $45,000 from a three day celebration of arts and flowers.

Appraisal programs also appeal to design-minded patrons. Well-

160   known auction and appraisal houses, Sotheby Parke Bernet and Christie's among them, interested in discovering new items to offer their own customers, have volunteered their services to arts groups for appraisal clinics. In a typical program of this type, Morton M. Goldberg Auction Galleries in New Orleans held appraisal clinics for fine arts, porcelain and silver items at its premises every day of the week between November 1 and 18, 1985 to benefit the New Orleans Symphony. Symphony supporters paid $5 to have one item appraised and $3 for each additional item. All the money went directly to the symphony. Additionally, for an auction held several weeks later, the symphony received 100 percent of the sale price of items donated totally for its benefit, and a percentage of the selling price of items placed in the auction on consignment.

CHAPTER 10

Selling Trips and Anything Else That Can Be Sold

———————————————————

164   Tourism is an area of growing importance to the arts. Not only do travel programs offer good opportunities for fund-raising projects aimed at members and supporters, but travel programs offered in conjunction with hotels, airlines, convention bureaus, conference planners and state and city tourism agencies can attract out-of-town visitors. Moreover, because of the interest that travel-related businesses have in attracting visitors, very often they will bear not only the costs of promotion but will frequently sweeten the kitty for the arts groups with whom they wish to work.

In Houston, the Guest Quarters-Post Oak and Guest Quarters-Galleria West Hotels had a month-and-a-half promotion tying their guests to the Museum of Fine Arts. If any guest mentioned a donation to the museum during this period, the hotels donated 50 percent of the revenues, for stays of up to three nights, to the arts institution. In Salisbury, Md., the Salisbury Wicomico Arts Council produces a calendar of events, under a unique arrangement which lists not only arts activities but other commercial and tourist activities. The expanded calendar was suggested by the Southern Eastern Shore Travel Council, which arranged to have the state's Department of Economic and Community Development, Office of Tourism pay a third of the costs. Other funding for the calendar, which now goes to 7,500 restaurants, hotels and motels in addition to the council's list of 4,500, comes from a local bank. Also, as mentioned earlier, airlines have provided major support to the arts through contributions made to cultural organizations when passengers have flown certain routes. They have also offered free tickets to the staff and performers of arts groups in return for designation as a group's official carrier.

The opportunities for cultural involvement with tourism are great because, as a growing number of arts groups are recognizing, the travel industry needs the arts as an attraction for tourists. In some states, the significance of the arts to tourism is reflected in hotel-motel taxes, with local governments reserving the option of giving a portion of the tax—millions of dollars annually, in Texas and California—to the arts. Also, many municipal and state leaders see the arts as a way to help attract convention business, which brings millions of dollars to a community. Indianapolis Mayor William H. Hudnut, III, in fact, led a group of local leaders to New York City in 1983 for a Friday night Carnegie Hall concert by the Indianapolis Symphony and Saturday and Sunday performances by other Indianapolis-based performing arts groups. The special invited guests at the Friday concert and lavish reception at the Russian Tea Room that followed were the heads of New York-based trade associations.

The arts draw is further illustrated by the experience of the Seattle Opera, which estimated in late 1985 that, of the 6,000 people it expected to attend its two complete Wagner *Ring* cycles the following summer, 3,900 would be tourists. Based on its past experience in presenting the *Ring* in both German and English—one summer both the *Ring* and the King Tut exhibition were in town together, prompting the wonderfully promotable tourist slogan, "The Ring and the King"—opera executives estimated that these tourists could be expected to spend $5.3 million. Even larger amounts have been spent by tourists drawn to communities by blockbuster museum exhibitions. According to a visitor study conducted for the Metropolitan Museum of Art, the museum's 1984 "Van Gogh in Arles" exhibition "drew more than 443,000 visitors, more than half of them from outside the city. These out-of-towners spent more than $223 million while they were in New York—for hotels, restaurants, entertainment, transportation and shopping."

The working relationship between culture and tourism accelerated beginning in the mid '80s. An August 1985 article in *The Travel Agent*, a key trade publication, pinpointing the emerging rapprochement was aptly titled, "Cultural Tourism Boom: Arts Institutions Introduce Packages Geared to Travel Industry." Large New York City groups such as Lincoln Center, the Metropolitan Opera and the New York City Opera have put together special packages including hotels, tickets, restaurants and such special amenities as Lincoln Center's "Meet the Artist Plus." In Reno, the Sierra Arts Foundation contracted with El Dorado Teleguide to create three pages of advertising promoting its arts attractions. Terminals placed in prominent locations throughout the state listed the events. National conferences and working seminars were developed to help arts groups reach into the travel market. The six-part seminar series presented by New York's Alliance for the Arts from October 1985 through April 1986, "Arts and Tourism: Building New Partnerships," explored such relatively unexplored areas of arts opportunity as how to tap the group travel market, how to package cultural attractions and how to work with travel writers and utilize familiarization tours.

The fact that state offices of tourism were spending more money than ever before to attract tourists—from $98.1 million in 1979 to $189 million in 1984—and that some, such as New York with its "I Love NY Celebrates the Arts 1985," were building entire promotional campaigns around the arts, indicated the importance and scope of the travel market. Figures from the United States Travel Data Center substantiated this, showing that spending by American tourists increased from $140.7 billion in 1979 to $217 billion in 1984. Yet, in

166   spite of this potential, the relationship between arts and tourism was not as well developed as it might have been.

According to a November 1984 survey of state travel promotion literature by Sandra Lorentzen, then director of the Mid Atlantic States Arts Consortium, "It would seem that the arts should be playing a more significant role in the tourism development efforts of state travel offices than this survey indicates they are." Lorentzen pointed out that arts opportunities were growing because state travel offices were beginning to focus "considerably more attention than in the past on attracting the higher-spending vacation traveler and the conventioneer, recognizing that to save their quality of life they must fill hotel rooms, not just campgrounds. Realizing that it is better to attract 10,000 visitors who spend $1,000 each than one million visitors who spend $10 apiece, they are now trying to attract more who fly instead of drive, stay in hotels, eat in restaurants, and who partake in more sophisticated pleasures." Lorentzen concluded, however, that many states omitted vital information about the arts and excluded many cultural resources from their materials, sometimes interpreting the request for information about "cultural activities" to mean historical museums and historic houses only. "Based on what is in the travel literature," she claimed, "it appears state travel offices need to see more clearly what is in their best interests if the arts are going to be put to use in helping to achieve their tourism goals."

While the opportunities for greater arts involvement in travel exist, many cultural groups, some working with travel packagers and tour agencies, have sweetened their coffers considerably with sophisticated and lucrative travel programs. In Atlanta, the Ballet joined forces with the Ritz-Carlton Hotel to introduce the "Nutcracker Sweet Offer" for the 1985 holiday season. For $95, each hotel guest received a room for two, two tickets to the Atlanta Ballet's production of "The Nutcracker" and a gift from Davison's/Macy's. In St. Louis, the Symphony introduced a $195 weekend tour package built around a Saturday evening concert which included a room at the Breckenridge Inn, shopping trips to the Plaza Frontenac shopping center, meals, a concert ticket and a post-concert reception. The promotion, which sold 60 such packages in its first year, cost the orchestra next to nothing, as the shopping center and the hotel picked up the symphony's mailing costs. In Des Moines, the Metro Opera developed two-night packages, offered on three different weekends, that included opera tickets, hotel, meals and local daytime sightseeing for $145 a person.

Museums have learned how to wrap themselves into a complete

visitor-oriented day. Since 1983, the Brooklyn Museum has successfully sold its Connoisseur's Choice program, which offers visitors a choice of full-day packages including private coach transportation between Manhattan and Brooklyn, tours of both the museum and the adjacent Botanic Garden and lunch at the Montauk Club. The Franklin Institute, a Philadelphia museum, joined with the Gallery shopping mall and the Frog Restaurant to offer a Fabulous Philly Day which, for $15 a person, included visits to all three sites.

The New York City Opera, which has developed an extensive travel program featuring tours, meet-the-artist programs and restaurant options, has been able to reach travel agents by having its message included along with many non-cultural attractions that the agents regularly learn about. In a mailing from a marketing company to travel agents, offering free literature on "hotels/resorts, cruise lines, convention and visitors' bureaus and airlines," some 50 return cards were included. The New York City Opera's was the only one from an arts organization.

In many communities, a key to the success of arts travel promotion programs has been the willingness of cultural organizations to join forces in presenting new concepts. The museums of Boston unite every October to offer "Museum Goers Month," an array of exhibitions, demonstrations, performances, lectures and films, while in New York State, 12 galleries in Oneida County have cooperated on an Art Discovery Weekend. In Miami, five arts groups cooperated on the Miami Arts Sampler, a "two-fer" offer distributed to area hotels by the Dade County Tourist Development Council. In New York City, the New York City Opera and the Museum of Modern Art joined forces to offer group packages for 15 or more. The package included a visit to the museum, lunch or dinner and a ticket to the opera.

TOURS AND CRUISES

Tours and luxury cruises, many oriented to the disciplinary cultural interest of the sponsoring organization, have been big money-makers for arts groups. Tickets bought at bulk rates by arts groups are frequently sold at higher individual rates, and usually, a donation is added to the ticket price. Typical of many was the McCarter Theatre's London/Stratford Bath theatre tour, led by artistic director Nagle Jackson in 1985, which included tickets to productions, visits to theatre sites and discussions with actors, directors and critics. Some groups go further off the beaten path in an effort to entice their

168   audiences. The Michigan Opera Theatre sponsored an $1,895 "Opera Behind the Iron Curtain" tour in spring 1986, which included visits to cultural sites and performances in Prague and Budapest. The Lyric Opera of Kansas City's 1986 "All Star Music Tour of Australia" included attendance at four operas, one ballet and the Adelaide Festival of the Arts, priced at $1,830 for the land portion and $1,660 for the airfare.

Even more exotic was the American Ballet Theater's 1985 European trip built around a gala New Year's Eve party with prima ballerina Cynthia Gregory, aboard the famed Orient Express from London to Venice. Part of a tour that began in London and included luncheons and other parties, the trip afforded the dance company the opportunity to sell out the entire train at $2,700 a person; $1,000 of that was a tax-deductible donation to ABT. Although the train was opened to others when seats remained, the 30 ABT supporters who took the trip helped pay for a lot of toe shoes. A year earlier, the National Symphony rewarded donors of $10,000 or more with a much shorter (but perhaps more exclusive) trip, a ride down the Potomac on the 141-foot yacht Imperator, which featured Monets, Lautrecs and Seurats among its other adornments. The yacht was loaned to the symphony for the evening by trucking magnate Arthur Imperatore.

Cruises can be especially lucrative because of the high tariffs they bring and the opportunities they present for the relaxed wooing of donors. Arts groups usually block out a certain number of cabins at group discount rates, and benefit from donations built into the price. The Baltimore Opera, fortunate to have a top travel executive on its board (Mrs. Lourdes Morales, president of World Travel Associates), topped earlier cruises with a 1986 Queen Elizabeth II cruise to the Caribbean, with cabin prices ranging from $1,219 to $4,011.

The financial rewards of a cruise can be seen in the 1977 experience of the Los Angeles Philharmonic. For its Mediterranean performance tour, the orchestra used the liner M.S. Danae as its means of transportation between performing sites. Many of the paying passengers, however, were orchestra supporters whose fares included a 25 percent contribution to the orchestra. The extra fees paid for all the tour expenses, including orchestra players' cruise costs and airfares from Los Angeles to Nice, where the cruise began, and added thousands of dollars more to the orchestra treasury.

Some arts groups have actually performed at sea as part of various cruise fund-raisers. According to Charlene Baldridge, national media director of San Diego's Old Globe Theatre, her organization

viewed its March 1986 "Theatre at Sea" cruise on the Pacific Princess
from San Diego down the Mexican coastline not only as a fund-raiser
but as as way to involve its supporters in the theatre. The cruise included scenes from *Dear Liar* performed by two of Old Globe's
associate artists, and theatre discussions led by executive producer
Craig Noel. Although each fare sold through American Express travel
Service in La Jolla, Calif., which conceived the "Theatre at Sea" concept, resulted in a substantial $150 donation to the theatre, Baldridge
also felt that "it gave our patrons a little theatrical bonus while they
cruised to Puerto Vallarta, Mazatlan and Cabo San Lucas."

The National Foundation for Advancement in the Arts was the
beneficiary of several of the most lucrative tours ever launched involving a cultural organization. Thanks to the support of Ted Arison,
a board member and major benefactor of the organization, the Foundation was able to sponsor the inaugural cruises of two Carnival
Cruise Lines ships, the M.S. Holiday in 1985 and the M.S. Jubilee
in 1986. Arison, the owner of Carnival Lines, offered some 70 percent
of the ships' cabins, more than 500 in all, to the Foundation without
charge, holding the remaining cabins for press and promotional use.
The Foundation, in turn, offered the cabins as a benefit to all new
members contributing $1,000 or more to the organization. The 1985
cruise, billed as "ARTSfest at Sea," included an extra bonus in addition to the more than $500,000 it raised. New members were able
to learn more about the organization during the two-day cruise and
meet with many of the young artists involved in the Foundation's
national Arts Recognition and Talent Search program.

PERFORMING FOR TOURISTS

Tourism can also be built into the regular performing schedules
of arts groups. Washington, D.C.'s Source Theatre Company has
financed some of its tours by presenting mystery dramas on cruise
ships, while ensembles from the Savannah Symphony performed
every month for several seasons at a posh resort hotel, the Cloisters,
in nearby Sea Island, Ga. The International Chamber Orchestra of
New York, a group comprising both professional musicians and
amateurs, has established something of a tradition with one or more
overseas tours every year since 1983. The musicians pay their own
travel expenses for the privilege of presenting concerts in places where
live orchestras have never before performed, including Anoghia, Crete.
The orchestra nucleus, musicians who have been on all the tours and

170   play with the ensemble in New York engagements, are supplemented by musicians from throughout the country.

THE SALES GAME

Some of the best salesmen in the country are the staff members and volunteers of arts organizations. One reason may be that they have the best product to sell, but even when they're not selling theatre subscriptions or museum benefits and the product is more mundane, they are persistent, persuasive and goal-oriented. Over the years, arts organizations and their volunteers have sold everything from books to old cars, from fine arts to fine food, from Oriental rugs even to their own companies and performers.

At the height of the so-called gas shortage some years ago, the enterprising Seattle Opera decided to help motorists and themselves at the same time. Aware that many motorists were buying smaller cars to save gas, the opera company asked its supporters for donations of the big gas-guzzling automobiles they no longer wanted. Several dozen donated cars were later sold to people more interested in buying inexpensive autos than saving money on gas, realizing more than $5,000 for the company. Old items other than cars have sales value as well, which is why some groups, such as the Seattle Repertory Theatre, have held annual "rummage" sales of items contributed by their members, friends and business supporters. Named the "Elegant Elephant," the Seattle Rep sale brings in about $50,000 a year.

Often, even an arts organization's own items have sales potential. The Old Globe Theatre times its annual sale of no-longer-needed costumes from its collection to coincide with Halloween. Held on a Saturday several weeks before the holiday, the sale continues until everything is sold. The Metropolitan Opera dipped into its extensive history to hold its first Metropolitan Opera Archives Bazaar in March 1986. Helping the event and stirring up considerable nostalgia was the presence of six former Met divas who autographed purchased books and photos. Among the items available for sale to those who paid $5 admission for the afternoon event were programs, catalogues, posters and originals and copies of costumes.

A change in program orientation can also leave a cultural institution with some saleable but no longer needed items. When Orlando, Florida's John Young Museum and Planetarium changed from a general museum to one concerned specifically with science and technology some years ago, it found itself with masses of items it could no longer use. With America's Bicentennial celebration looming immediately ahead, the museum decided to capitalize on the excitement and kick off the holiday weekend with its own "First Super Colossal John Young Museum and Planetarium Garage Sale and Auction." Held on July 3, the event offered scores of items that had been catalogued and appraised by a local antique dealer. The garage sale of less valuable items was held in tents outside the museum, while an auction of more valuable items was presented in an adjacent auditorium. The idea of a museum having a garage sale drew tremendous press interest and, with thousands of people turning out for the event, over $15,000 was cleared. As an extra dividend, many of the buyers visited the museum once their shopping was completed.

For an arts organization, art itself is a potent commodity to offer for sale, especially when the art is related to the institution's specific or broader interest. For a number of years, Chicago's Lyric Opera has realized about $150,000 a year from the sale of limited edition Jim Beam ceramic bottles designed to resemble such opera characters as Carmen and Figaro. Donated by the liquor company, the collectors' items have sold for well over $200 each. The Fashion Institute of Technology in New York City has turned to its area of interest for a successful annual sale of sample cuts of fabrics, donated by some of America's best-known designers. While it may be difficult to characterize them as art, the items made by members of the Thunder Bay, Canada Youth Symphony and offered for sale to orchestra supporters were in their own way a cultural expression; the orchestra's first Won Ton and Egg Roll sale featured Chinese delicacies. In North Carolina, volunteers for the Fayetteville Museum of Art scour the community for months to come up with 100 donated pieces of artwork for the museum's annual Collectors Choice event. Every item is sold, but with a twist. To attract 100 purchasers to buy the $100-a-couple tickets for the event, the museum offers an incentive. Every ticket-buyer receives one of the donated items—portraits by local artists, Chinese rugs, pieces of sculpture, among them—both as a bonus and as a "come on."

Something of greater value results when one art helps another Art. When Montreal's Les Grands Ballets Canadiens was facing a major funding need, it turned to 100 visual artists in Quebec for help. It asked them to contribute personal handwritten statements on their feelings about art. Each resulting statement, some including sketches, was reprinted in a signed, limited edition of 1,000 on seven-by-ten inch parchment and sold for $2. The Wilmington, Del. Opera Society commissioned artist Cynthia Doney to sketch scenes from four of

172 the operas performed by the company and then reproduced the sketches on notepaper. They were sold along with matching envelopes in sets of eight for $2.25 per set.

Some arts sales are gigantic and become productions in themselves. The Michigan Opera's Grand Estate Sale features items collected from area estates for over a year, while the Cleveland Play House's annual Treasure Sale offers some rare antiques and collectibles for sale over a three-day period. The Los Angeles Music Center's biennial selling fair, Mercado, which brings as many as 75,000 people to the Music Center on a June weekend and nets upwards of $750,000, is a giant discount marketplace. In addition to the merchandise on sale it includes entertainment, food and auctions. In 1986, Mercado added a huge book fair to the program, and volunteers collected more than 200,000 new and used books to be offered for sale. To add to the luster of the event—and realize some additional income as well—the Music Center organized and presented four panel discussions featuring prominent California authors on the two mornings of the book fair.

One of the granddaddies of arts selling events, the Italian Street Fair sponsored by the Nashville Symphony's Guild has grown from a flea market netting $5,000 in 1954 to one of the city's annual traditions, drawing about 50,000 people over the four-day Labor Day weekend each year. Put together by nearly 2,500 volunteers working for months to collect items for sale—about 800 businesses make contributions—the fair features 75 booths manned by volunteers, selling everything from handicrafts to music to clothing to virtually every kind of Italian food imaginable. Rides, entertainment, photos and children's games are also offered. In addition to the money it earns from sales and entrance fees of $3 for adults and $1 for children, the fair includes several auctions and two leased areas for carnival rides and for over 100 arts-and-crafts booths. The Guild earns a percentage of the gross sales from the leased operations.

"It's a massive job," claims Carol Catington, co-chairman of the 1985 fair. "It kept me busy practically full-time from the January before it started until Christmas, several months after it ended, meeting with committees and driving back and forth all over Nashville to pick up donated items." The job had its rewards, however, in addition to the $289,000 it netted in 1985. "I was so proud during the fair's four days," added Ms. Catington. "It seems like all of Nashville was there."

Arts building campaigns have been successful in selling items related to the facility. Seat sales have been a tradition in performing facilities. For example, the Tampa Bay Arts Center, preparing for its inaugural season in 1986, offered a choice of plaques to be placed on the backs of seats in return for donations of $500, $1,500 and $2,500. But some groups have gone beyond seats to sell other facility areas.

To help finance repair of its roof and dome, the University of Pennsylvania's University Museum sold over $7,000-worth of clay roof tiles for $2.50 each, on which donors could inscribe their names. Instead of selling tiles to add to a real facility, the leaders of the Fort Stockton, Tex. Historical Society had a model of their soon-to-be-renovated museum built by a carpenter, without a roof, and sold small shingles which were inscribed with donors' names and tacked onto the model. The Stanley Theatre in Utica, N.Y. had a "buy a light bulb" campaign for $5 donations to help fund its restoration. The Old Lyceum Theatre in Clovis, N.M., which had previously sold all its seats to donors, sold ceramic tiles at $10 each when it had to replace its sidewalk. Theatre London in Ontario, Canada sold building bricks for minimum donations of $150 each for the renovation of its Grand Theater. It placed the bricks, engraved with donors' names, in an interior wall of the mezzanine lobby which it renamed the Donor Gallery.

Among other unusual items offered for sale were the individual piano keys that the Carroll County Arts Council in Maryland invited its supportes to buy for $200 each, to help defray the cost of a $14,000 Steinway grand piano. Buyers, who selected the key of their choice, had their names recorded on a large cloth piano keyboard which was hung in the hallway of the county arts center. And when the Oklahoma City Performing Arts Cultural Center and Industrial Development Trust was financing a theatre center, it sold $500 tax-exempt revenue bonds printed on art paper with limited edition prints by local artists on the reverse side. The hopes were that at maturity, buyers would keep the bonds for their art value instead of redeeming them at their face value.

Almost everyone sells cookbooks, and if you have Nancy Reagan and four former First Ladies contributing recipes, as the Washington Opera did, it can't hurt sales. But there are even more personalized items that groups can sell. In fact, some groups have put themselves and their performers up for "adoption," as the Orchestra of Illinois did in its 1984 Adopt-a-Musician program (see Chapter 2). The Alliance of Resident Theatres/New York picked up on the concept during the 1985-86 season, and put each of its 82 member-theatres up for adoption. Adopters paid $2,000 each for the privilege, and there were a number of takers. They received free opening night seats, invitations to parties, program listings and official adoption certificates.

PERSONAL SERVICES

Personal services are a good way to make money, provided that the services are worth buying, or that the sellers of the services are so well-known that anything they offer will be saleable. Some groups have had volunteers wash cars to raise funds. In Montana, where the spaces are wide open, money was raised for a week-long poetry residency with a local adaptation. Instead of a car wash the event was a horse wash. Everyone likes to be served by a celebrity, and when former football star O.J. Simpson tended bar at a Buffalo Philharmonic benefit, it helped to lighten the mood and the pocketbooks of attendees.

Health and welfare organizations have been extremely successful in using celebrity waiters to collect tips for their programs. In fact, according to a report in the *Nonprofit Marketing Insider*, local chapters of the Leukemia Society of America were expected to raise several million dollars from Celebrity Waiter luncheons featuring local businessmen and politicians as waiters. In an American Lung Association luncheon in Cleveland, $9,000 in tips was collected in 90 minutes by 70 celebrity waiters, who also found time to sign autographs, pour water and pose for pictures. While no arts groups have reported this kind of success as yet, the arts are learning. At a kick-off party for the San Diego Symphony's first annual symphony weekend, a group of top city business executives, some of them orchestra board members, won plaudits and tips as waiters.

MOVIE PREMIERES

An activity that can be somewhat lucrative, a movie premiere, is not the easiest event to schedule, because it requires a cooperative arrangement with the filmmaker. It also requires the arts group, once it has been designated for a first showing, to get into a business with which it's not ordinarily involved. An appropriate theatre must be booked, the event must be promoted and seats must be sold. It helps, of course, when the film to be premiered is either an eagerly awaited one, such as any of the Woody Allen movies, or contains subject matter relating to the sponsoring arts group's interest. *The Dresser*, for example, with its backstage theme, served as an appropriate benefit for both the American Conservatory Theatre in San Francisco and the Living Stage Theatre Company in Washington, D.C. in 1984. Years earlier, *The Agony and the Ecstasy*, based on the life of Michelangelo, was premiered in several cities by leading museums.

Jack Rollins, who along with Charles Joffe is an executive pro- **175**
ducer of Woody Allen's films, indicated that his company receives
requests for benefit premieres each time a new Allen film is about
to open. Decisions are made based on knowledge of the organization,
the marketing plans for the particular film—which could limit the
number of screenings—and sometimes the appropriateness of the
organization to the film. "We provide the print free of charge," said
Rollins. "It's up to the organization to find and book a theatre, promote the opening and sell the tickets. They decide what to charge,
but we retain the right to approve their decisions."

Sometimes an arts group's relationship to a film makes it a logical
choice for a benefit. The Whitney Museum, for example, which served
as the setting for several scenes in the Allen film *Manhattan*, was
awarded the benefit.

The ingenuity of cultural groups in finding people and groups
to help them in their funding efforts is seemingly endless. And when
human resources fail, then it's time to look elsewhere, as the Science
Museum and Planetarium of Palm Beach County, Fla. has done.
Regularly appearing on behalf of the museum at fund-raising benefits,
shopping centers and conferences is the four-and-a-half foot tall Sir
Plus. Aptly named, Sir Plus is a robot built from spare parts for less
than $700 by museum staff members.

The funding quest must be endless, because the funding isn't.
As cast members of New York's Equity Library Theatre so aptly sang
in one of their intermission pitches, "We can't live on passion, so
please put some cash in the hat."

CHAPTER 11

Where's the Beef?
Or, Eat Your Art Out

---

178   To paraphrase Shakespeare, if music be the love of food, then lay on the vittles when you raise funds. The relationship between fine art and fine food is a long and honored one, and cultural organizations have been more than willing to play the role of culinary Cupid in the cause of fund-raising. Clearly, as so many of today's arts groups have learned, one of the best ways to an audience member's pocketbook is through his stomach.

MULTIPLE DINNERS

As enterprising cultural organizations have demonstrated in recent years, one dinner may be lucrative, but multiple dinners may provide a financial bonanza. The rationale for such culinary funding events is understandable. While the benefitting organization must round up a number of hosts who agree to hold dinners on the same night, and coordinate the sale of tickets to these feasts, the dinners themselves, and the cost and effort of preparing and serving them, are borne by the hosts. Moreover, the job of getting dinner donors may not be as hard as it seems. Many notables who might not be available for other kinds of volunteer activities are pleased to show off their homes and their hosting skills for a good cause, even if, as in many cases, they don't do the cooking themselves.

The Nevada School of the Arts, a relatively small institution, benefitted from four gourmet dinners in private Las Vegas homes, an effort that netted the school $22,000, while the Hoff-Barthelson Music School in Scarsdale, N.Y. spurred the sale of $100 benefit performance tickets with pre-concert dinners for the 100 buyers at several different board members' homes. Guild Hall in East Hampton, N.Y. has done even better. For its "Joys of Summer: A Weekend of Feasts by the South Fork," the cultural center convinced 24 different hosts to undertake events throughout a weekend. Partygoers, nearly 400 of them, paid $100 each (a nice round $40,000) to choose from an array of food-oriented activities running virtually non-stop from Friday evening—a Danish smorgasbord, Chinese feast and Indian banquet were all on the menu—to Saturday afternoon parties oriented to children, to Saturday evening feasts, to Sunday brunches and hunt breakfasts. For its second annual "Joys" in 1985, the number of hosts grew to 26 and the paying guest list topped the 400 mark.

In Los Angeles, 50 Joffrey Ballet boosters, spread throughout Southern California, ran festive culinary events on the same June 1985 evening to benefit the dance company. "The Night of the Joffrey Dinners" included tables spread for as few as four people and as many as 150. Sites ranged from private homes to such elegant restaurants as Chasen's and L'Ermitage to a garden bistro, from dinner and a baseball game in the private box of Los Angeles Dodgers chairman Peter O'Malley, to a dinner party and projection room film-showing at the home of arts patron Armand Deutsch, to a gourmet beach party with special guests from the world of politics. Tickets, at $150 each, were sold on a first-come basis. Attendees were asked to select six choices in order of preference, and the benefit committee promised to let them know which dinner they would attend several weeks prior to the event.

A spur to attendance was the roster of special guest celebrities who committed themselves to coming to or hosting the various parties. Gene Kelly guested at an Oriental Palais dinner, Angie Dickinson and Glenn Ford appeared at a dinner/dancing party held at a private club, and Gordon Davidson, artistic director of the Mark Taper Forum, and his wife Judi, were special guests for dinner and an evening of theatre talk for 10 guests at the 7th Street Bistro. Three nights following the dinners, one special party remained, a Sunday supper for 36 guests with former President and Mrs. Gerald R. Ford.

Perhaps the one blockbuster eating event that makes all others pale in comparison, however, is the New York Public Library's "Night of One Hundred Dinners." In addition to tables being set all over New York City, hosts as far away as Venice also do their bit for the library. As in other such affairs, the flier listing the dinners available to purchasers not only includes the dinner hosts and the culinary theme, but also suggests the type of dress appropriate for each setting. With the cost of attending set at $200 a person in 1985, and the hosts contributing food, wine, space and amenities, the annual event raised about $200,000 for the library.

The multiple dinner fund-raiser has many variations. In some communities, the dinners are held over a period of several months, as with the "Opera to Go" programs sponsored by several opera companies. Opera/Omaha's festivities during the 1985-86 season included brunches, lunches and dinners, two speakers, an open dress rehearsal, three opera previews and a *La Traviata* party. The "Opera to Go" offered by the Saint Louis Opera during a recent season included 11 culinary events ranging from $25 to $100 a person, touching virtually every imaginable palate. Included were a dessert and coffee opera trivia party, a pig roast with opera singers "fiddling" with blue grass, a Gilbert & Sullivan Mississippi cruise with Southern cooking, and a Neopolitan picnic with Italian fare and arias. Schubert & Friends, limited to 35 people at $35 each, was a 19th-century soirée with *lieder* and art songs, German wine and cheese.

In Akron, dinner benefits for the Ohio Ballet have commenced with a common cocktail party at one home for as many as 350 donors. Following the party, donors dispersed for dinner to any one of 10 to 15 homes, each offering a different ethnic meal. Afterwards, all the diners and their hosts gathered at yet another home for dessert. In Lubbock, Tex., where the "Epicurean Experience" has been a Symphony Guild fund-raiser, each of the proffered dinners has had a specific artistic theme tied to the architectural style of the home where it was held. One year, the "South Pacific" dinner included a Polynesian buffet, floating centerpiece and grass serving hut, while "Camelot" came alive with a giant round table of food and decorations.

Packaging can help to merchandise a food event. The Abilene Cultural Affairs Council in Texas promotes its series of food events, held in both restaurants and homes over several months, as "The Great Chefs of Abilene," and includes among the listings a "Stay at Home Dinner." Supporters not caring to attend a party are invited to "spend a lovely quiet evening at home surrounded by all the things you love" and "help support the Cultural Affairs Council by sending your check if you decide to stay at home."

Single food-oriented events have relied on unusual food, settings and themes to win audiences and money. The Scottsbluff, Neb. Arts Council is perhaps the only arts group in the country to host an "Incredible Bean Festival," which features such events as a Bean Bake-Off, Bean Melodrama, Children's Bean-Glue-On Contest and a Bean-a-Rama. The program is underwritten by the local Farmers Bean Co-op to benefit the arts. A memorable Pennsylvania Ballet benefit, "Culinary Capers at the Granary," was held at a former railroad grain elevator. With noted choreographer and hobbyist chef George Balanchine as honorary chairman, the evening featured cooking demonstrations by local celebrities and judges presiding—where else?—at the bar.

THE ARTFUL DINNER

Cultural organizations have been imaginative in tying food events to their artistic programs and reaping both monetary and publicity benefits. A special draw to patrons of the Lyric Opera of Chicago is the annual business meeting and dinner, held on stage at the Civic Opera House before a backdrop from one of the company's operas. The 1986 meeting, held within the stage setting for Handel's *Orlando* and billed by the company as "the world's most glamorous annual corporation meeting," drew more than 400 "stockholders" (contributors) to dine, hear financial reports and listen to tenor Jon Vickers perform.

For years, the Baltimore Symphony has hosted an annual Picnic Competition to launch and promote the opening of its open-air park concert series. Audiences have been invited to tailor their picnics to themes inspired by the evening's opera selections, with prizes awarded to the most imaginative picnics. They have responded with fervor and flair in recent years with such entries as a "Mephistopheles Temptation" with "devilishly delicious breads." A picnic inspired by *Madame Butterfly* included Japanese food and floral arrangements, and picknickers wore kimonos and a Lt. Pinkerton uniform.

Dinners offered immediately prior to arts presentations are usually somewhat traditional, although some groups have packaged the dinner-performance into more attractive offerings. The Old Globe Theatre's "Summer Gourmet," at $30, has included dinner with wine at one of three nearby restaurants, transportation to the performance and transportation back to the restaurant following the performance. The Pittsburgh Opera has included a post-performance return to the dinner restaurant also, and has added one item to the list of desserts offered—a visit with the artists who have just performed. As part of the package for its eight-concert Gourmet Music Series, the Cincinnati Symphony offered subscribers a free dinner at each of eight different restaurants. Subscribers were allowed to attend the restaurants in any order they chose, immediately prior to concerts.

One of the more unusual packages, in tiny Wilkesboro, N.C., tied the Wilkes Community Theatre to the college's hotel and restaurant management program for a theatrical feast. Included for a single price were a pre-performance buffet of soups and chowders, attendance at two one-act plays, a return to the dining hall for the rest of dinner, a third one-act play, and then a dining room encore of dessert in the company of the cast.

Specific productions may suggest food-oriented tie-ins. The Cincinnati Playhouse, which regularly offers pre-performance buffets, came up with a "Man Who Came to Dinner" dinner before its production of that name, while New York's Gryphon Theatricals served Darjeeling tea and scones before each peformance of a Rudyard Kipling play. In California, the Redlands Symphony used its version of a United States passport as the subscription brochure for its six-concert series. Each concert, which focused on works from a different country, was preceded by a dinner featuring the food of that country. In quite a natural but unlikely tie-in, New York's La Mama E.T.C. included its audience *in* the culinary offerings included within one of its productions. For its 1985 nine-performance presentation of Ulrich Braker's *Life for Sale*, a play about peasant life in 18th-century Europe, the cast of three prepared an actual six-course dinner as part of the drama. At the appropriate moment, the audience of 30, which had been seated around a large dinner table onstage throughout the performance, was joined by the actors. Together, audience and actors ate the dinner that the actors had just prepared. And all this for only $25 a person.

The Toronto Truck Theatre has offered free brunches "that reflect the flavor of the current production," including fish and chips prior to *Beyond the Fringe* and haggis and short bread before a play set in Scotland, while in a more earthy offering, the Fort Wayne Symphony handed out discount coupons courtesy of Pizza Hut following its Family Night concert featuring the "Pines of Rome." Perhaps the Michigan Opera had the most intriguing tie-in in recent years. It featured a "Sweeney Todd and Mrs. Lovett's Meat Pie Party" with an imported New York chef to do the cooking following the company's performance of the Sondheim musical. One can only assume that the chef was not inspired to emulate Mrs. Lovett's recipes.

JUST DESSERTS

While performance-oriented dinners have been around for quite a while, it is only within recent years that arts groups have discovered the fund-raising potential waiting at dinner's end in the dessert, particularly chocolate. Proving that anything can be packaged into a special event, arts groups have followed the lead of other nonprofit organizations in fattening up their donors with events bearing such who-counts-the-calorie titles as a "Taste of Chocolate Festival," "Suite on Chocolate" and "Designs for Chocolate Lovers."

Thanks to the largesse of chocolate manufacturers, who are eager for large audiences to sample (and later buy) their products, arts groups such as the Colorado Opera Festival have held two- and three-day festivals featuring free chocolate tastings, chocolate exhibits, chocolate-making demonstrations, lectures on chocolate, cooking classes and even meetings of "Chocoholics Anonymous." The Lyric Opera of Kansas City, which has held annual chocolate fests since 1984 and kicked them off with such events as a $60-per-person champagne and chocolate reception and a "Choc Hop" dance, has raised as much as $25,000 from a single program.

Certainly, the most fitting host for this kind of event is the aptly titled Chocolate Bayou Theater Company in Houston, named for the river near which the company originated. Since 1983, the theatre has **183** sponsored an annual benefit with a chocolate theme. The 1985 "Designs for Chocolate Lovers," at $75 a person, included such rare experiences as a Monte Carlo area "coated in chocolate," a space voyage with giant robots serving chocolate, and a Temple of Divinity wherein the goddess Aphrodite shared her secret passion, Chocolate Divinity, with theatre supporters.

In still another expression of financial chocolateering, the Rochester Symphony won support from the noted candy maker Fanny Farmer, a firm which had been founded in Rochester. To tie in with the orchestra's annual presentation of *The Nutcracker*, the confectioner created a new 9.5-ounce bar of solid chocolate, packaged and designed it to resemble the Nutcracker, named it the Nutcracker and printed the Nutcracker story on its wrapper. Most important, it donated 50 cents from each $10 bar sold to the orchestra.

Even I succumbed to the lure of chocolate. Because the annual three-day conference I direct, the Professional Arts Management Institute, has been called a "high intensity" meeting, it seemed logical to convince Tobler, the noted Swiss chocolate firm, to help replenish the energy levels of our attendees. As a result, Tobler has become the first officially designated chocolate bar of an arts meeting, and our conference-goers, placed on a two-bar-a-day chocolate diet, have added to both their energy levels and their waistlines.

Another dessert, ice cream, has provided the inspiration for many arts funding events. In 1979, the St. Louis Arts and Education Council helped initiate the first St. Louis Ice Cream Festival as a way to commemorate the invention of the ice cream cone at the 1904 World's Fair. Pleased with the results and the $40,000 raised for the arts through the event, the council retitled the event the St. Louis Ice Cream and Arts Festival, and developed a weekend program that drew some 75,000 people and earned even more money for the arts. Built around the theme, "Get Your Licks at the Arts and Ice Cream Festival," the event included performances by many of the council's member organizations, samples of ice cream and such ice cream-oriented contests as a "milk-off," "taste-off" and "Dream Sundae" competition. In a similar vein, the San Diego Opera held one of its most successful 1984 funding events, a "Family Ice Cream Fundae," featuring, among other activities, a Celebrity Ice Cream-Eating contest.

Proving that the variety of desserts is virtually inexhaustible, New York City's Symphony Space found a way to utilize one of today's better known dinner-enders, fortune cookies, in its funding program. After testing a range of homemade messages on other arts ad-

184 ministrators, such as "Help, help, I'm a prisoner in the development office of a community-oriented performing arts center," the center developed some potent new messages to aim at its own audiences. One such message read, "You're about to develop a meaningful, deeply satisfying, important relationship with Symphony Space." Others included, "Many are called, few actually fund" and "Computer say: He who supports Symphony Space, Lives Long Life."

COOKBOOKS AND COOKING DEMONSTRATIONS

The fascination that cooking holds for many arts supporters can lead to money in the bank for the groups they favor. Cookbooks, as has been noted previously, are a staple funding tool, but every once in a while, an organization comes up with a new twist that ups their sales potential. The Backers Board of the Repertory Theatre of St. Louis, which has prepared hot meals for company actors involved in back-to-back performances for many years, turned those recipes into a cookbook, *Cooking for Applause*. Within several years of its publication, the book had been distributed in all 50 states, paid back its publication costs, netted over $11,000 and was still going strong. Then, in April 1986, a new opportunity to push the cookbook arose. With four other St. Louis nonprofit organizations whose volunteer arms also had published cookbooks—several hospitals and the symphony among them—the theatre's Backers Board participated in a "What's Cooking St. Louis?" program. Underwritten by the new Adam's Mark Hotel as an opening event, the program offered a fun opportunity to see which organization's recipes were the best. With the hotel donating its chefs to cook five recipes from each cookbook and the supporters of each organization paying $10 a person to cheer their favorites on, the event not only raised money but attracted a lot of attention.

Perhaps spurred by the attention that the eating habits of its 350-pound managing director had received (see Chapter 9 in which Douglas Duncan's diet for funds campaign is cited), the Metro Opera of Des Moines opened a cooking school for two months in 1984, offering daytime and evening classes taught by local experts. Several thousand dollars from the proceeds went to the opera company. The New York Shakespeare Festival also turned the culinary interests of several of its star performers into a $5,000 profit when it loaned them to Bloomingdales for a series of food-oriented promotional appearances at the store. Theatre producer Joseph Papp lectured on Shakespeare's use of food and drink, while Estelle Parsons created a "Miss Margarida's Walnut Torte."

One of the best-publicized and most successful cooking events **185**
has been the annual "Men Who Cook" benefit for the Children's Art
Carnival in New York City. Each year since 1982, between 100 and
200 men—college presidents, publishers and well-known musicians
among them—have prepared their culinary specialties for guests who
pay up to $30 each to spend four hours sampling the dishes and ogl-
ing the celebrities who've made them. The affair has grown each year
and in 1986, its fifth year, it drew some 2,000 paying guests and raised
$30,000.

The participation of Julia Child, one of America's best-known
cooks, provided New Haven's Long Wharf Theatre with an opportunity to turn local interest in cooking into a major, multi-faceted funding event several years ago. Several weeks prior to the start of its
1981-82 season, Long Wharf presented a different kind of matinee
performance for its supporters—an onstage cooking demonstration
by Child. Not only did Saturday and Sunday "performances" sell out,
but audiences were also offered the opportunity to purchase, at an
add-on fee, tickets for a gala dinner that weekend. In all, the theatre
netted about $20,000 from the weekend, with additional income com-
ing from a recipe contest, a raffle of several of Child's dishes and an
auction of cooking items and utensils contributed by local merchants.

DINING WITH CELEBRITIES

The celebrity draw is evident in several other successful food-
oriented cultural events. The Museum of Modern Art's "An Evening
With Cary Grant" drew some 200 guests, who paid $1,000 each for
the privilege of having dinner and cocktails with the famed actor
followed by a screening of his film clips and a question-and-answer
session. The New York Public Library's annual "Dine with a Lion"
dinner, inviting donors to eat at a table presided over by one of 20
or so famed writers in attendance for a very hefty contribution, has
raised as much as $250,000 for the institution in an evening. Some
arts groups have stayed within their own houses in offering a celebrity
luncheon or dinner companion for a price. After all, how many opera
buffs could resist a "Lunch with Beverly?"

WINE AND SPIRITS

Good wine invariably accompanies good food, and arts organizations have been attentive to quenching the thirst of their audiences.
Some groups, such as the Detroit Community School of the Arts

186   whose astounding success was mentioned earlier, have built lucrative events around wine tastings, which have included dinners, lectures, wine seminars and dishes created by local chefs. Wineries, eager to reach the arts audience, have contributed a great deal of wine and volunteered other services such as the attendance of their top executives at tastings. The Des Moines Metro Opera, which has charged $35 a person for a Wine Fair, not only received donations of Cabernet Sauvignon and Chardonnay wines from Jordan Wineries of California but also had the free services of an expert to make pates and terrines—Jordan's own chef, flown in by the winery for the event. The Vancouver Playhouse has netted as much as $40,000 from its annual Vancouver Wine Festival, a four-day program featuring tastings, a special dinner and cooking demonstrations by local chefs.

Several wineries, Taylor and Paul Masson among them, have sponsored or hosted arts festivals which have benefitted performing arts groups. The giant Paul Masson summer music festival in Saratoga, Calif., first presented in 1958, donates its net proceeds to local charities, including 25 percent to arts organizations. In Reno, an annual Wine Art Competition solicits works from artists on wine themes. Winners are awarded cash prizes and have their work exhibited at Harrah's Reno Wine Adventure.

To tie in with its 1985 fund-raiser, the Operathon, the Lyric Opera of Chicago initiated a new "Wine of the Year" program, designed to be a lucrative annual event. The 1985 launching began with the selection of six wines from 50 California Chardonnays tasted by a wine-consulting firm, to be semi-finalists in the competition. In a well publicized tasting, eight prominent Chicago wine experts then selected a wine produced by Round Hill Vineyards in the Napa Valley as winner. It was this wine that was bottled and sold with a Lyric Opera label, for the benefit of the arts group.

Arts groups have pampered more plebian drinking tastes as well. In an effort to attract new young audiences to the first of its half-price "Under 40" performances, the Sarasota Opera followed the performance with a "Beer and Wurst" party. The San Luis Obispo County Symphony has taken an even deeper plunge into lager territory with its co-sponsorship, along with the Hospice of San Luis Obispo, of an annual Festival of Beers, a welcome addition to the roster of activities in the college town. The event draws some 1,000 people eager to pay $10 each to sample over 100 beers offered and listen to live music.

The Michigan Opera Theatre has gone even further and has reaped as much as $15,000 each time it has held its annual "Pub Crawl." Organized and run by the Opera Guild, the event lures hun-

dreds of people annually, a number of them middle-aged, who satisfy
their curiosity and venture into the singles bar scene for the benefit
of the opera company. For a single $5 fee, pub-hoppers are allowed
to hop on and off a group of rented buses to participate in escorted
(by opera company interns) tours of some 20 Detroit bars. The money
made from participation fees is small compared to the money the
Michigan Opera receives from the participating bars. Twenty percent
of bar sales and 10 percent of food sales—from *all* their customers
that evening, not just the opera pub-crawlers—is donated back to the
opera company by the bars.

RESTAURANT PARTNERSHIPS

Restaurant tie-ins have proved beneficial to arts groups, and
many go beyond the discounts offered to performance ticket-buyers
into such areas as membership recruitment. The Cultural Activities
Center in Temple, Tex. offers two-fer vouchers to any of eight
restaurants to new or upgraded members, while the San Diego Opera
offers new or upgraded members a bonus coupon to all five participating restaurants and a choice of three of the restaurants for those
who renew within the same membership category. The Berkeley
Repertory Theatre used 65 "Champagne and Chekhov at Chez
Panisse" dinner prizes to entice supporters into participating in a
benefit drawing for restaurant dinners for two.

Many restaurants have contributed both their facilities for funding events and a portion of their proceeds to arts organizations.
Mallards Restaurants in Rye Brook, N.Y. donated $5 to the
Westchester Arts Fund for every diner who had a Monday-to-Friday
lunch or dinner over a three-month summer period. In an unusually
supportive relationship, GianCarlo and Joan Santini, the owners of
the Chelsea Place Restaurant in New York City, have been the major
benefactors of the Children's Dance Theatre ever since the founder,
a former waitress at the restaurant, died tragically in 1978. The San-
tinis, in addition to donating an annual $6,000 to the company and
providing it with free year-round office space and office services, has
thrown an annual benefit for the arts group at the restaurant since
1978, raising over $12,000 a year.

Restaurants have also provided promotional help to the arts and
some solace to the artist. Charley's Restaurant in Louisville installed
a slide show about the Kentucky Center for the Arts on its second
floor, and allowed the center to bring groups to the restaurant regular-

188   ly to see the program. Herb's in Washington, D.C. took special recognition of the difficult economic circumstances in which performing, visual and literary artists frequently find themselves by offering special cards to qualified artists entitling them to reduced-rate happy hour bar prices at all times.

HIGH FASHION AND THE ARTS

In addition to getting fatter from their audiences' eating habits, the arts are increasingly in fashion. In fact, high fashion, including designer clothing, jewelry and perfume, is growing to be almost as familiar an arts funding tool as is food. The potential for good funding results is especially strong in this area because the purveyors of fashion, the designers, manufacturers and chic retail establishments, have discovered that arts audiences, especially those that are presumed to be affluent and fashionable, are *their* audiences. It is no wonder that the arts are a key stop on the charity show fashion circuit.

Retailers have been quick to recognize the potential that arts organizations offer to their fashion promotions, and arts groups have been just as quick to recognize the funding and promotional potential available through links with the fashion industry. Noted designers regularly use cultural institutions to introduce their new collections to a city, and boutiques and department stores include arts organizations in their marketing plans. In fact, it has become somewhat commonplace to see stores celebrate the openings of new branches with benefits for arts groups, as the examples of Pucci and Gucci in Chapter 4 so well indicate. As stores continue to open new outlets in suburban shopping malls, opportunities for the arts increase. Brettons in Ottawa benefitted the Ottawa Symphony when it opened two new stores in shopping centers, and Lord & Taylor celebrated the opening of its first store in Dade County, Fla. by hosting a benefit for the Lowe Art Museum. In Albany, N.Y. in 1985, two local arts groups benefitted from store openings at the new Crossgates Mall: The Capital Repertory Company was beneficiary of Filene's' opening, and exactly one evening later, the Albany Symphony benefitted from a fundraising opening at Jordon Marsh's new store.

An article in the May 1985 issue of *Art Facts*, the newsletter of the Rouse Company's Art in the Marketplace program, indicates the importance that the retail fashion industry places on its relationship with the arts. Titled "Hulen Mall, Fort Worth, Salutes the Arts in its Spring Fashion Show," the article begins, "On a Saturday in March,

Hulen Mall's Marketing Manager, Rhonda Pike, cleverly used a fashion show to connect the city's cultural community with the center's stores. Over 20 models, including board members of the city's major cultural institutions, were outfitted in formal fashions and the more casual clothes were modeled by arts students and professional artists." In return for winning the attention and active involvement of the arts groups, the center contributed an "Art Cart" to distribute information provided by the city's arts groups. In the well-attended fashion show, the mall included within the fashion commentary information about each arts organization and its program.

Further evidence that the arts may be *the* place to go for those introducing new fashions came from a March 1984 letter to the media soliciting national coverage for the "largest fashion show San Diego has ever seen." *Style San Diego* magazine wrote of its presentation of the fashion show at the Old Globe Theatre for the benefit of COMBO, the city's arts support organization, "We felt that Springtime at the Old Globe might be a nice time and place to unveil the hottest new local fashions, and from a cultural point of view, a benefit for COMBO speaks for itself."

Noted designers presenting their elegant new fashions prior to gala luncheons or dinners have been sure lures for audiences, who have paid anywhere from $35 for an 11 a.m. cocktail reception and showing of Adolfo's spring collection at Saks Fifth Avenue (to benefit the Museum of the City of New York) to $150 a person for a black-tie dinner and fashion showing of Geoffrey Beene's fall collection at Atlanta's Omni International Hotel. Co-sponsored by the hotel and Saks Fifth Avenue to benefit the Atlanta Ballet, the latter event raised upwards of $75,000. While daytime events are often held at department stores, the more glittering evening affairs are frequently held at hotels under the sponsorship of department stores.

Arts groups working with department stores can be creative in helping to put together the kind of fashion events that best meet their needs. When a Pittsburgh store, Kaufmann's, presented "Fashionlogue '85: An Evening of Fashion, Bill Cosby and You" for the benefit of the Pittsburgh Opera Center, the added presence of the noted comedian helped to increase the audience draw. Consequently, Fashionlogue was presented in a Broadway show setting at the Syria Mosque with ticket prices ranging from $30 to $125. To spur attendance at its annual benefit fashion show, the Friends of South Coast Repertory Guild in Costa Mesa, Calif. called its benefit a "Friendraising" party and charged only $25 a person. Held at I. Magnin, the event included a champagne and hors d'oeuvres reception along with

190   entertainment and a fashion show featuring designs by Valentino, Galanos, Blass, Beene and de la Renta.

FASHION AND PERFORMANCE

Some arts groups have integrated fashion into their artistic endeavors. With underwriting from Burberry's Ltd., Chicago's Body Politic Theatre presented a "Totally English Evening" as one of its major benefits of the 1985-86 season. Beginning at 5:30 p.m. at Burberry's with high tea and a fashion preview of Burberry's fall collection for men and women, the evening, with tickets priced at $50 and up, included transportation in double-decker buses from the store to the theatre, where guests were able to "relish the humour of England's most popular playwright, Alan Ayckbourn, at a benefit performance of *Season's Greetings*.

When the Cincinnati Opera presented a special performance of Jerome Kern's *Roberta* as a one-night fund-raising gala in September 1985, it linked the performance to a dazzling fashion show that also involved a local department store, hotel and top-name designer. Because the musical is all about high fashion, the opera company turned the finale of Act Two into a fashion show, featuring the acclaimed Bill Blass Fall/Winter 1985 Collection introduced by Mr. Blass himself. In the fashion-show-within-a-play, the collection was modeled on a contemporary set with a white cascading stairway designed especially for it by the company's resident set designer.

Along with performance tickets priced from $15 to $125, the evening included a post-performance supper dance at $50 a person with buffet, dancing and a personal appearance by Blass, who awarded a $2,000 gift certificate for his couture line as a door prize. To tie in to the fashion aspect of the performance, Gidding-Jenny, the high fashion specialty shop that underwrote the performance, introduced the well-publicized collection two days later at its downtown Cincinnati store. Adding to the special glamour of the event, which raised about $20,000 for the opera company, the Westin Hotel offered a special "Roberta Weekend" package including tickets, room, complimentary champagne and brunch.

PERFUME AND JEWELRY

Perhaps the most dramatic example of the importance that the fashion industry attaches to the arts and its audience—and an indication of the potential financial rewards coming from cultural links with high fashion—was the involvement of the famed French fashion house, Chanel, with several leading cultural institutions at the beginning of the 1985-86 season. On September 16, 1985 the Dorothy Chandler Pavilion of the Los Angeles Music Center became the setting for a black-tie "event" for the benefit of the Music Center Unified Fund. The evening began with a champagne reception outside the Pavilion doors. Guests then moved inside for a 28-minute fashion show presented along the Pavilion's Grand Staircase and an extended ramp. But this was no ordinary fashion show. This was the first showing in the United States of the Chanel couture collection, and the launching of its new scent, Coco. Guests, who paid $250 each to attend, then dined and danced for the rest of the evening.

For the privilege of having a unique launching pad for its couture collection and—even more important—for the introduction of its new perfume, Chanel donated $150,000 to the Music Center. There was still more to come, however. Exactly one week later, Chanel, collection and all, turned up at the Metropolitan Opera's glittering opening night, 3,000 miles away in New York City. Many in the audience were content to see the glamour around them and the opera itself, a star-studded performance of *Tosca* with Luciano Pavarotti and Montserrat Caballe. For the 750 guests who could afford to pay $1,000 each for their opera tickets, however, more awaited them—a lavish supper party that included a Chanel showing of its new collection and the introduction to New York society of its new perfume, Coco.

The evening turned out to be the most profitable opening in the Met's history. Not only did Chanel make a $250,000 contribution to the opera company, but ticket sales and income from the fashion show and supper raised the Met's total income from a single evening to a staggering $1.2 million. Yet, perhaps the biggest winner of all may well have been Chanel. For a relatively small expenditure (small in terms of what some businesses spend to introduce a new product), Chanel reaped the rewards of tremendous coverage and high visibility, and reached the people it most wanted to reach.

Although few other cultural organizations have been able to garner the level of support provided by Chanel, arts groups have been coming to their scents for years. Since 1983, D.H. Holmes Department Store in New Orleans has climaxed its annual Fragrance Festival with a "Scent-Sational" evening benefitting, in alternate years, the New Orleans Symphony and the New Orleans Opera. In 1985, to help the orchestra raise thousands of dollars from the benefit, Holmes transformed its Canal Street store into a medieval carnival featuring

192   palmists, astrologers, Tarot readers and handwriting analysts, and gave $50 gift fragrances to each attendee.

Diamonds, also, have been among the arts' best friends. Such events as the San Francisco Symphony's "Diamonds in the Sky" benefit, featuring a display of $15 million in diamonds as well as a champagne and seafood buffet, helped raise over $18,000 for the orchestra, thanks in part to the sponsorship of the Diamond Information Center. The Repertory Theatre of St. Louis found 21 willing firms and individuals to be patrons for its 1984 annual benefit, "An Evening with Cartier," which produced an all-time high profit of $57,000 for the theatre. Lured to the event by the year's only showing of Cartier's archival exhibition, "An Evening with Cartier," and an $11-million collection of jewels and objets d'art brought to St. Louis by Cartier, nearly 450 guests paid $150 each to attend. The kitty was sweetened considerably through the sale of Cartier jewelry, which included a 10 percent return to the company.

Happily, the fashion, jewelry and beauty fields seldom stand still. The new products introduced so frequently present arts groups with a range of new funding possibilities virtually every year. Thank heaven for little girls and—for big girls, too.

CHAPTER 12

Earned, Burned, Yearned and Spurned Income

_____

Back in the '70s, a Boston arts group undertook an unusual new activity. It became a commercial retailer. In an effort to find additional income for its arts training programs for black performers, the National Center of Afro-American Artists became the operator of the Capezio Dance Shop in Boston, as well as a partner in that venture, an activity that continues until this day.

Another organization, the Children's Museum of Denver, which has earned as much as 95 percent of its annual budget through income-producing activities, has taken such great pride in its unique achievements that it has produced a guide, *Nonprofit Piggy Goes to Market*, and sponsored conferences on the subject of how nonprofits can boost their earned income. Few groups could hope to emulate the earned income achievements of several leaders in this area, but it's interesting to see just how much money large and successful programs can produce. In 1985, the giant Smithsonian Institution took in $27 million in sales from its mail order catalogue and its 13 gift shops. The Metropolitan Museum of Art, which established its first store in 1908, grosses more than $37 million annually from its retail on-premises shop and mail order program, which together offer 15,000 different items to potential buyers.

Although, to the uninitiated, it might seem odd or perhaps even illegal for a nonprofit, tax-exempt cultural organization to become a shopkeeper or to establish a booming mail order business, these are only several of a growing number of ways that enterprising arts groups have managed to keep their ships afloat in recent years, while the churning seas around them have threatened to swamp their operations. What an arts group can and cannot do to produce extra income is a legitimate question that the organizations must ask themselves.

EARNED INCOME CAUTIONS

According to the tax codes, nonprofits are exempt from paying tax on income derived from activities that are substantially related to their primary artistic purposes. An obvious example of such activity would be a museum's sale of posters or books relating to an exhibition it has presented. But, if an arts group is judged by the IRS to be deriving income from a regularly carried-on business that is unrelated to the nonprofit purposes of the organization, then that group must pay regular corporate taxes on the unrelated business income, if the gross income exceeds $1,000 annually. Failure to do so could result in penalties including, at worst, an organization's loss of its tax-exempt status.

As arts groups have moved to find new ways to increase earned income, aside from the obvious areas of ticket sales and admissions, their activities have come under increased scrutiny. Several years ago, **197** in fact, as reported in an *American Theatre* article by Robert Holley, the U.S. Small Business Administration voiced concern that some nonprofits were competing unfairly with commercial enterprises. Perhaps that is why, in this gray-shaded area, arts groups have leaned heavily on the side of caution and on the advice of lawyers—handy people to have on their boards.

"Arts organizations should, of course, be investigating every earned-income possibility available, and should be making an attempt to select those activities that would be related to their nonprofit purposes," claims Katharine Rowe, staff attorney for Volunteer Lawyers for the Arts in New York City. "However, there is a limit to how much groups can earn from activities unrelated to their exempt purposes. If an organization's unrelated business income rises above 10 percent of its gross income, it should consult an attorney."

In spite of these cautions, "earned income" has become a key buzz-phrase in the arts. Organizations, concerned with a drop in government support at all levels and a growing competition for private funds, have been looking for ways to supplement box office and admission income, and the money they receive from grants, donations and fund-raising programs. The range of activities designed to bring in extra money has included such things as merchandise sales, licensing of artistic products, rental of space, supplementary programs, the selling of services, leasing of concessions and a growing number of real estate-oriented activities.

ENTREPRENEURIAL ACTIVITIES

Most of the non-artistic income-producing undertakings of cultural organizations are related to their overall programs, but some of their endeavors might make newly graduated Harvard M.B.A.'s green with envy. Sacramento's Metropolitan Arts Commission, for example, conceived and marketed a poster project promoting the city's image. Posters selling at $5 each netted over $20,000 in royalties for the Commission's Arts in Public Places Program in the first three years. The poster, which resulted from a county-wide competition, featured a close-up photo of a large pink camelia—a symbol of Sacramento—set against a background of deep purple. Because of the success of the undertaking—a poll of local retailers indicated that the poster was a classic, and should continue to sell for many years—the Commission then turned around and, in response to many requests from other organizations to reveal how they did it, went out and did it again. They published and sold a how-to book on the project which, along with the poster, sold for $15.

198   In San Diego, COMBO, the local arts fund-raising organization, was involved in an even more unlikely income venture. Aware that the Ford Motor Company was about to launch a new test-drive promotion, COMBO offered to do it for them instead. After COMBO identified and selected 250 target prospects, its volunteers picked up and delivered cars to them, got written evaluations from the drivers and then delivered the cars back to Ford. Paid by Ford for each test drive conducted, COMBO earned about $30,000 from its effort.

PROGRAM-RELATED INCOME ACTIVITIES

Although unusual examples still crop up from time to time, most groups have learned that the best income-producing ventures come out of activities in which they are already involved. The further they move away from their own activities, the more difficult the ventures may be to manage successfully. They have also learned that while earned-income activities can be lucrative at times, they can't be counted on to provide a panacea for all funding problems. And if groups devote so much energy to making money that their artistic efforts become secondary to the lust for funds, then that ever-alert IRS may be ready to step in from the wings to challenge their tax-exempt status.

Given these caveats, arts groups should indeed be looking at their potential for boosting earned income to supplement their other revenue sources, and they should look first at what they already do. Much of it may be saleable. An immediate and obvious income source is the selling or renting of a mailing list. Another is the sale of programs and souvenir booklets at performances. Still another is backstage tours or pre-performance lectures.

Posters related to specific productions or to the organization itself, such as the Old Globe's use of two top local baseball stars in its "Garvey, Gwynn and the Globe" 50th anniversary poster, have been good income earners for some organizations. The Toronto Symphony cashed in on its monumentally successful Luciano Pavarotti concert in 1985, which itself took in $700,000 at the box office, by selling posters of Pavarotti in various opera poses. Created by Canadian artist Harold Town, who donated his services to the orchestra, the posters were near sell-outs within months at $125 each for signed and numbered limited-editions, and $10 each for regular posters.

Art coming out of art has also been a saleable item. The Martha Graham Dance Company has sold exact reproductions of works by sculptor Isamu Noguchi, who designs sets for Graham productions. The Noguchi castings, drawn from the sets and costumes of various

Graham works, were sold in editions of six for many thousands of dollars each. The Metropolitan Opera offered patrons limited-edition bronze sculptures of *Carmen* by Paul Fairley for $2,000 each. The Children's Art Carnival in New York City has been creating and selling hand-printed fabrics and sweaters featuring African motifs from its Harlem Textile Works, an activity that grew out of the Carnival program. In a more modest undertaking, shopping bags featuring original designs by artist Frank Stella, created to salute the opening of two new galleries and a print study center at the Walker Art Gallery in Minneapolis, sold for 30 cents each at 13 Dayton's department stores in the area, and all proceeds were donated to the Gallery.

The New Music Orchestra in Washington, D.C., which focuses on the contemporary composer in its performances, has found an interesting way to emphasize the role of the composer while boosting its income. It has offered audiences the opportunity to have a text of their choice set to original music by its music director, John Webber, on a sheet of vellum suitable for framing—and all for a $100 donation. For $1,000 contributions, a composer selected by the orchestra dedicates a full-length composition to the donor.

SELLING EXPERTISE

Some everyday art activities, including the skills involved in mounting productions or exhibitions, can lead groups into providing specific income-producing services. Some theatres have had their property shops, during down periods, construct exhibit displays for local businesses. Others have used the talents available to them to introduce new training programs or seminars. The Minnesota Opera inaugurated a Wig and Make-Up Training Program in 1986, the only one of its kind in the United States, as an affiliate operation under the direction of its company wig and make-up master, Richard Stead. Held over a six-month period, the opera charged a $2,300 fee per student. New York City's American Museum of Natural History, through its Department of Mineral Sciences, has offered weekend gem seminars at $215 a person.

In a more unusual application of artistically oriented expertise, the Solaris Dance Company created and marketed a corporate exercise program consisting of videotapes and live workshops. The Warrioroebics program was based on the dance company's choreographic techniques. Equally offbeat was a service provided by the Battle Creek Symphony Orchestra during the 1983-84 season. For fees of $1,000, the orchestra sold several wedding parties of 100 guests or under an orchestra concert which featured the wedding ceremony as its finale.

LICENSING

One of the most saleable items for an established arts institution is its name. It is not an item, however, to be sold lightly or cheaply. Although few cultural institutions have been offered the opportunity to license their names or their works, those that have, have discovered that the returns can be considerable. The Metropolitan Museum of Art, for example, has realized well over $3 million in royalties since 1975 from its licensing agreement with Springs Mills. The fabric company has paid these royalties in return for the right to use objects from the museum's collections as designs for its products. In 1985, the museum concluded a licensing agreement with a manufacturer of children's clothing, Seibel & Stern, giving the company the right to adapt apparel from the museum's Costume Institute to a new line of clothing for youngsters. Performing arts groups may hold a similar attraction for designers. The American Ballet Theater, for example, in an agreement with American Theatrical Licensing Group, authorized, in return for royalties, the marketing of American Ballet Theater Action/Art Activewear, a line of leotards, sweatsuits, tights and warm-up clothes.

ITEMS FOR SALE

For the enterprising group, a performance itself can offer an unexpected opportunity for additional income aside from such obvious applications as the sale of commemorative booklets, photos or such convenience items as food and drink. When staff members of the San Antonio Performing Arts Association saw the fervor with which audiences greeted a performance by Rudolph Nureyev in April 1982, they reached an instant decision. They went out and purchased carnations at $1.75 each. During intermission, the carnations were resold at $3 each so that audiences, as a sign of their enthusiasm, could shower their favorite with the flowers.

The range of products offered for sale by arts groups to their audiences is virtually endless. Some of the more interesting items have drawn upon the arts image to entice buyers, such as chocolates designed to resemble musical instruments, mugs with such legends as "Old Musicians Never Die: They Just Go from Bar to Bar" and notepads shaped like paintbrushes, embellished with the legend, "Property of the Met Opera Scene Shop." The Baltimore Opera sold brass *Die Walküre* ticket keyrings for $5 each, while the Fort Wayne Philharmonic, for its 40th anniversary, had some success with $55 ice buckets engraved with the orchestra logo. To entice seasonal shoppers, the Indianapolis Symphony sold musical wrapping paper featuring excerpts from a work commissioned by the orchestra as its design.

Consumer items bearing arts messages or logos have also become steady income producers for arts groups, although T-shirts have become too ubiquitous, perhaps, to command much buyer attention. The Old Globe Theatre has sold watches at $30, while the Pinellas County, Fla. Arts Council, which sells calendars as many groups do, also markets bumper stickers reading "You Gotta Have Art" for only $1 each. One of the best-sellers of the Salisbury Wicomico, Md. Arts Council has been an apron, priced at $5, which reads, "The arts are cooking." While cookbooks have been the most recognized literary sales item, some groups have come up with other bookish offerings. To tie in with a seasonal production, Seattle's A Contemporary Theatre offered the *A Christmas Carol* coloring book for $1.95, while the Massachusetts Cultural Alliance sold thousands of copies of its guide to arts programs in the state, *Stepping Out*. In both of these instances, the printing costs were underwritten by local corporations, a good way to ensure that the publication will be profitable for the arts group that publishes it.

Cultural organizations with facilities that are open to the public throughout the day—museums and large performing arts centers such as Lincoln Center among them—have been able to develop their income potential through their own gift shops. The Metropolitan Museum of Art, in fact, has such a large operation that it also introduced sales outlets at Macy's in New York and Ventura, Fla., while the Brooklyn Museum has operated a gift shop at New York's Citicorp Center.

Off-site shops can do well also. For nearly 30 years, the Pittsburgh Opera's Women's Auxiliary has logged over 50,000 hours and raised over $1 million by operating an off-site "Operatunity Shop" which sells "gently used" items. A museum, Impression 5 in Lansing, Mich., has even taken its shop out of the shop. To reach potential buyers during the months prior to Christmas, the museum has had volunteers host "socials" in their homes, along the line of Tupperware parties, where museum representatives could come to display and sell items from their gift shop.

Some performing groups, however, with more limited access to traffic, have been able to create their own sales outlets through direct mail and through seasonal shops. Organizations such as the Stratford, Ontario Shakespeare Festival and the Folger Theatre in Washington, D.C. have marketed sales items through catalogues. The Cincinnati Symphony has rented hotel space to operate a Holiday Gift Shop prior to the Christmas season while among other groups, the Joffrey Ballet and San Francisco Symphony, with the very active involvement of volunteers, have operated successful sales programs during their performing seasons. The Symphony Store, located on the promenade level of Davies Symphony Hall in San Francisco, is staffed by volunteers beginning an hour before each concert and during the intermissions. It has netted over $40,000 annually for the symphony. The Joffrey Boutique has been a familiar sight to dance audiences since 1974, and has raised many thousands of dollars for the company. Staffed by volunteers in two theatre locations prior to the performance and during intermissions when the company performs in New York City, the shops feature tote bags, sweatshirts, notepads and cuddly animals. Many items bear the Joffrey logo. Interestingly, when the company goes on tour, the Joffrey Boutique, sans volunteers, is still in business, with staff or dancers acting as the sales force.

INCOME FROM FACILITIES

When cultural organizations started selling the air rights to their facilities, a lot of attention was paid to the potential of real estate as an income source. By allowing a developer to build a condominium tower using the air rights over its facility, New York's Museum of Modern Art was able to help finance a $60 million expansion that doubled its space. But even in less esoteric circumstances, property has tremendous value, if it's used. Contiguous street space belonging to an arts institution can and has been rented to commercial retail operations. Rehearsals can produce income, as they do for the New York Philharmonic, which has sold unreserved seats for $3 each at selected times. The Stanley Theater in Utica, N.Y. sold space on its marquee during unused periods. Three-line messages went for the bargain rate of $15 for two evening hours.

An institution's down time, when its facility isn't being used for performances, rehearsals or exhibitions, has good income potential. Many performing spaces provide good sites for corporate meetings as businesses increasingly seek out unusual meeting places. Washington, D.C.'s Phillips Collection has rented its facility two or three times a week at over $2,300 for six hours' use. The American Museum of Natural History earned $270,000 in 1985 alone by renting out its various spaces to such organizations as Manhattan Industries and the New York Racing Association. The Metropolitan Museum of Art limits the use of its facilities to those corporations contributing at least $25,000 for the privilege, and it has found many takers, especially businesses using parties there to introduce such new products as Deneuve and Missoni perfumes. The Milton Bradley company, appropriately, used the Met's uptown medieval art branch,

the Cloisters, to introduce its new game, Dark Tower. Similarly enter- **203**
prising was Chicago's Museum of Science and Industry, which rented
its working model of a coal mine to a mining company and its farm
exhibit area to an agricultural organization.

In an interesting and logical tie-in with its program, the Children's
Museum of Manhattan has been offering its facility for children's birthday parties—at $250 for 15 children (catered) and $175 for 15 children
(uncatered). Catered parties include cake, drinks, paper goods, party bags with souvenirs from the museum gift shop and activity
materials. Both catered and uncatered affairs, discounted for museum
members, begin with visits to the museum collection guided by
museum staff members. The parties are held in a special studio where
children create their own party favors with the aid of museum staffers.

COMMERCIAL PRODUCTIONS

Successful artistic programs have offered many performing
groups, especially professional resident theatre companies, the opportunity for a share of the income from a follow-up commercial production. Jon Jory of the Actors Theatre of Louisville, which has sent
such plays as *The Gin Game* to Broadway, has indicated that about
one-and-a-half percent of his annual budget results from Broadway
income. No arts group, however, has won anywhere near the un-
precedented success of the New York Shakespeare Festival. *A Chorus
Line* has brought in well over $15 million to the theatre's treasury,
while the rights for a pay television showing of the Festival's production of *The Pirates of Penzance* brought in $1.5 million plus 5 per-
cent of the gross the same day it opened in movie houses. On a few
occasions, arts groups have sold their artistic talents to the world of
business as an income-producing project, as when a symphony orchestra appears in a commercial. Some years ago, the Alwin Nikolais
Dance Company was featured in a film, which Nikolais choreo-
graphed, to introduce a new line of Springs Mills towels designed by
Pucci.

Other opportunities for money-making linkages with the world
of business have come from an arts involvement with the recording
industry—including royalties on albums from such musicals as *A
Chorus Line* and from television and video. Although the relationship with the latter fields has never blossomed to the degree that some
thought it would, well-established groups such as the Metropolitan
Opera have sold videocassette rights to a number of productions, while
some museums, such as the Whitney, the Peabody in Boston and
the Metropolitan Museum of Art, have marketed their own video

cassettes. By the mid '80s, several groups were looking into the possibility of making and selling music videos à la MTV.

PLAYING GAMES

Games have helped boost the earned income of arts institutions. Several manufacturers who have introduced games with arts themes—such as Aristoplay of Ann Arbor, Mich., the producers of "Artdeck" and "Music Maestro"—offer arts groups substantial financial returns to sell games to their audiences. "Box Office," a game developed by Canadian arts administrator Christopher Tyrell, was later picked up by Parker Brothers and has become an income-producer for nonprofit arts groups. Theatre Communications Group, for example, has put together a national deal in which theatres who sell the game, either through direct mail or lobby sales, receive an $8 royalty for each game sold at the $19.95 retail price.

Some arts groups, however, have gone beyond the sales outlet route to become game creators and game owners. The Museum of Scientific Discovery in Harrisburg, Pa., along with a game-developing company, introduced a scientific trivia game, "Eureka," in 1985, which it sold at $12.95. New York City's Municipal Art Society became a major investor that same year in a trivia game about a subject it was very much interested in. "Only in New York," which retailed for $29.95, included Society membership information inside, and a cover sticker reading, "Good for one donation. Each game purchased will result in a donation [20 percent] being made to your Municipal Art Society, who will use the proceeds to beautify, preserve and enhance New York life."

One of the more lucrative games offered by an arts institution within recent years was the legally authorized weekly bingo presented by the L.A. Public Theatre from 1978 to 1983. The game, which earned as much as $146,000 a year for the theatre and spawned the publication of a paperback how-to book selling at $14 a copy, was finally discontinued when too many bingo games sprang up in Los Angeles, and the theatre found that it couldn't compete with games that were giving away more money in prizes than it was.

Perhaps the institution with the most sophisticated program of developing earned income is the aforementioned Children's Museum of Denver. The museum devotes considerable staff attention to coming up with products and services that relate to its own educational goals while also interesting specific buyers, such as corporations. The result has been such projects as its annual parenting fair, a three-day exhibition of products, services and information for new and ex-

pectant parents. It elicits major participation by companies interested
in selling to the parents market, and a number of related booklets
are underwritten by corporations. *Small Change*, a booklet designed
to help children learn about money management and banking, was
used by its underwriter, Citicorp, as a giveaway to its customers.

QUESTIONS TO ASK

While entrepreneurial activity as practiced by Denver's Children's
Museum works, it works because of the great effort expended. Arts
groups that attempt to develop new enterprises for profit will discover
that there are a number of key questions they must first ask, and
answer, before they can begin to develop new profit-oriented projects.
Do they have the in-house talents to undertake new projects, or do
they have access to such talents? Do they have the time? Have they
determined, and if so, how, what markets exist for the new product
or service? Do they have the resources, or access to resources, to
finance the development of a new project? Do they have the full back-
ing of the board? Is the contemplated activity related to the program
of the organization? Most important, does the organization have a
product or service to sell that someone will want to buy?

Cultural organizations have failed in the commercial marketplace
and at some expense. New York City's public television station, Channel 13, used over $500,00 in contributions from its supporters to
become an "angel" for the $2 million Broadway production of *Alice
in Wonderland*. Thirteen, unfortunately, suffered the same fate that
befalls many Broadway investors: The play got bad reviews, closed,
and the station suffered a considerable loss. A Channel 13 investment
in publishing its own magazine, *The Dial*, also suffered tough financial sledding before the television station linked up with a commercial publisher.

In spite of the cautions, new opportunities for increasing earned
income will be available to the arts in the coming years. Edward
Skloot, a specialist in developing income-producing projects in the
nonprofit area, suggests that special attention be paid to joint ventures with the private sector, and he strongly urges that arts groups
closely examine the fees they normally charge for services with the
thought of increasing them.

As the funding crunch in the arts continues, groups will and
should persist in exploring realistic opportunities for increasing their
income base. But they should be aware that while earned is desirable,
yearned is more likely, spurned will be frequent, and burned, unfortunately, is a distinct possibility.

EPILOGUE

If the Sky's the Limit,
Then Funding Can
Be Heavenly

———————————————————

208   If imagination alone were money, then many arts groups could dismantle their development offices, shoo away all the fund-raising consultants camped on their doorstep and retire their boards. Imagination helps a great deal, and often in competitive situations it separates the haves from the have-nots. But imagination without professional execution, flair without follow-up and inspiration without long-range planning won't deliver the funds and audiences consistently.

Funding is the end result of a great many activities, beginning with an organization's artistic program and its clearly articulated aesthetic goals. If funding has any real importance to the funder, it is to help the organization realize those goals. Yet, at times, those goals are not sufficiently clear to the organization's inner family, and they are not addressed and reassessed frequently enough.

Having had the opportunity to work with hundreds of arts organizations in every discipline, and write about many hundreds more over the last quarter-century, I have been pleased and often pleasantly surprised by the professionalism and high artistic standards demonstrated by so many groups. Yet, at times, I have been chagrined by the pell-mell rush forward by others seeking instant solutions to complex, ongoing problems or turning to outside experts to give them answers to questions that they themselves haven't really taken the time to study.

Although it has not been my intention that this book be a primer for professional long-range planning, it would be remiss to offer the many examples of creative efforts by arts groups cited in these pages without some caution about their application. Nothing, no activity, event or promotion, should ever be undertaken if it is not studied first and then adapted to fit the needs and goals of the organization. Few things work "as is." If there is any slogan I would leave with you, it would be *adapt don't adopt.*

The ability to adapt has been evidenced many times in the arts. Many tiny organizations have taken concepts originated by giant groups and scaled them down to fit their own special needs. Where many groups have used car washes to raise money, arts fund-raisers in the wide open spaces of Fort Smith, Mont., relied on a local adaptation to raise money for a poetry residence. They held a horse wash. When the Feld Ballet came up with the idea of using baseball-style cards to promote their performers, sell subscriptions and make a little extra income, they tossed an interesting idea into the public arena. Yet although it had instant adaptability for many performing groups with resident company members to promote—and the Cleveland Ballet *adapted* the idea to its 37-member company months later, upping the pack price to $5.50 and selling individual cards for 15 cents each—it didn't seem, on the surface at least, to have much appeal to visual arts institutions. Yet when a small visual arts institution, the University of Chicago's Renaissance Society, decided to utilize baseball cards (perhaps without awareness of the Feld project), it developed a project unmistakably suited to its identity.

To produce its baseball cards, the Society, a nonprofit organization involved in promoting contemporary art, went directly to the ballpark. Several of its leaders won permission from the Chicago White Sox baseball team to have a group of talented local artists draw pictures of every member of the Sox and make up 450 sets of baseball cards from the drawings, signed by both artists and players. Aroused by the unique concept, the artists contributed their services in return for a signed set of cards, an invitation to the benefit event in the project's behalf and an opportunity to meet a player. The original drawings for each card, auctioned off under the scoreboard prior to a summer 1985 Sox game, brought in $19,800. When sets of cards, both signed and unsigned, and posters made from the cards were sold and added to the total, the Society had netted close to $25,000 and attracted tremendous publicity for itself and for the project.

In addition to professionalism, planning and adaptability, other factors demonstrated by the experience of arts groups, can be useful in helping an organization realize its funding potential. Getting the most from the immediate family would be one. Many groups turn to others for help without first calling on their members, donors and volunteers. When groups tap their internal resources, however, they frequently find that help is available. The Bloomingdale House of Music in New York City compiled a list of more than 100 businesses with either a record of arts support or employee matching grant programs, and sent them to donors and friends asking for their help in opening the doors to companies where they had contacts. Other groups have adapted a funding tactic used successfully by many religious organizations—getting a member of their board or a volunteer skilled in the taxation field to conduct tax seminars at which potential donors learn how to make donations through trusts or bequests while getting tax benefits at the same time. When Sarah Caldwell's Boston Opera canceled the 1984-85 season due to her illness, many company supporters responded to her plea to turn their ticket payments for that season into donations and to pay again to resubscribe to the following season.

Cooperation has become an essential ingredient of arts success; cooperation between arts groups in the same discipline, in different disciplines, in the same city, in different cities and cooperation be-

210 tween arts groups and non-arts groups. Years ago, when a cultural organization received a major grant from a first-time donor, it would often keep that grant a secret as long as possible, for fear that other groups might "steal" the funding source away. Happily, those days are long gone and groups have learned to join forces in their quest for grants—and even share donors when a major program becomes too costly for a single funding source to support.

Although it would be impossible to catalogue the many significant cooperative programs that have developed within recent years, a sampling might indicate the kind of positive opportunities they represent. It would include the National Performance Network linking alternative spaces in 14 cities for over 100 artist/company residencies; an Eastside Theatre Festival joining nine New York City theatres in a 10-day program enabling audiences to visit all of the theatres for a single price; the merger of eight contemporary chamber music groups in a pooled organizational, funding and audience effort; the joining of three upstate New York theatres to present a cooperative production at each of the theatres consecutively, with funding from a single corporate source; the coming together of 11 science museums to jointly develop a film production program; and the linking of eight top Canadian dance companies in a weekend Canadian Dance Spectacular to promote the nation's dance achievements. United arts funds within communities, and united disciplinary fund campaigns in both theatre and dance, have also proved the value of a united approach.

Arts organizations must be extremely sensitive to the needs and feelings of the audiences they serve. The uproar some years ago when the Metropolitan Museum of Art presented an exhibition focusing on the black experience, "Harlem on My Mind," and neglected, according to many black leaders, to consult them on the material included, left bruises at the museum that took a long time to heal. Yet, unfortunately, new examples still crop up. In 1986, when the need for arts real estate was a major concern of the field, a *cause célèbre* of several months earlier was still on the minds of many art leaders—the eviction of the New York School of Ballet from its space by its landlord, Zabar's, a noted New York gourmet food shop. Yet, when New York City's Department of Cultural Affairs hosted a meeting of the United States Urban Arts Federation in January 1986, its first morning panel discussion was preceded by a somewhat ironic coffee break. The panel topic was "Is There a National Crisis in Space and Real Estate for the Arts?" The coffee break, as noted in the program credit, was "Courtesy of Zabar's."

Arts institutions must learn to find new ways to reach their audiences and look for the "quid pro quo" in their relationships with a range of publics. The Athens-Clarke County, Ga. Office of Cultural

Affairs helped local advertising agencies in their campaign to convince potential business customers that good advertising was an art, by giving them a showcase—an ad billboard campaign which, not incidentally, also promoted the arts of the area. To make it easier for businesses that might support the arts to learn which arts groups offered what programs, groups such as New York's Arts & Business Council, the Greater Columbus Arts Council and the Massachusetts Cultural Alliance have put together publications listing programs in need of support and what those programs would cost businesses to sponsor.

While broadening their artistic horizons, cultural organizations must also broaden their administrative horizons by expanding their reach each year for audiences and support. Depending on the same satisfied audience to renew subscriptions year after year without going after new audiences is a sure path to disaster. Similarly, for a group to be satisfied with current funding sources because they have been supportive over a period of years is to lose sight of change and development. Even the most supportive business source can lose interest, change leadership, suffer financial reverses or, as has happened often during the '80s, be taken over by another company with little or no interest in honoring past commitments.

During the coming years, arts groups will also be subjected to technological changes whose effects can be monumental. Perhaps the worst thing an arts group can do is to stand aside, reasoning that the technology won't affect them because they're too small or too limited in their programs. Technology will affect everyone, as computerization already has, and for a group to bury its head in the sand is to chance losing the opportunity that new technology might offer. Who knows? Perhaps the day isn't far off when a home viewer will be able to press a button on his television set and make an instant donation to his favorite charity.

In preparing for the future, a range of tools and resources should be available and utilized by every arts organization, from materials that they themselves produce—mission statements, planning data, annual reports and audits—to those that they gather from other sources. Over the past few decades, an unrivaled number of resources in virtually every area of activity have been made available to arts groups. Service organizations representing access to virtually every public from the elderly to the hospitalized to schoolchildren to the corporate community have been established. Although we are resource rich, we are usage poor. To be truly effective, the resources must be used more than they are now, and the proverbial wheel must be seen and recognized instead of being invented anew.

Although there is very little that is totally new in funding and

212   promoting the arts, every once in a while an adaptation of something that has been done before finds new expression. Over a period of years, I've been quietly nursing some adaptive concepts of my own, in the hopes that I would find some group ready to undertake them. I now leave the undertaking to any readers who have progressed this far in the book. In the interest of sparking some new activity and leaving the reader not only with something to think about but something to try, the following list of **"Reiss's Outrageous Suggestions"** is offered with tongue firmly rooted in cheek:

Concept: Retitling an Organization to Win Business Support. Some programs have won funding because their names or themes had special interest to a particular company. For example, a children's play called *Sneakers* was once sponsored by Kinney Shoes. At the end of a performance of *Albert Herring*, the Bronx Opera Company treated audiences to free herring snacks, courtesy of the Vita Company.

Suggestion: Why doesn't some enterprising musical ensemble name itself the Treo Trio? Might not funding, or at the least "support," be available from a girdle manufacturer interested in the name? Couldn't one of America's leading arts centers win major support from a leading automotive firm by adding one word to its name and thus becoming the Lincoln Continental Center? Couldn't a production of Wagner's *Ring* cycle win funding from the local phone company? And might it be possible for a symphony orchestra that shares its music director with another orchestra—as is not uncommon—to find funding from an electronics firm for its "semi-conductor"?

Concept: Naming the Series.
Arts series usually bear predictable names although some changes have come about with the advent of corporate marketing programs. For example, the San Francisco Symphony's Great Performers Series became the Merrill Lynch Great Performers Series. But might not some enterprising arts organization win attention if it named a series like it really was, especially if the talent wasn't quite up to the original name?

Suggestion: The titles for three proposed, attention-getting series follow—The Mediocre Artists Series, the Hopefully Artists Series and the Catch Them Before They Give Up Their Careers Series.

Concept: An Anniversary When One Isn't Available.   **213**
Anniversaries are wonderful vehicles for organizational fund-raising.
Yet, in order to be viable, anniversaries traditionally must be rooted
to certain seemingly magical numbered years such as 5th, 10th, 25th,
50th or even 100th. This can be a great nuisance to the organization
in desperate need of celebrating an anniversary but rooted hopeless-
ly to 17 or 43 years of existence with seven or eight years ahead before
they can see daylight.

Suggestion: Why can't several organizations with awkward anniversary years get together and jointly celebrate a meaningful anniversary? Couldn't a group with a 62-year history join forces with
a 38-year-old organization and celebrate a combined 100th anniversary? Any funds raised through such a joint venture could be split
on a 62-38 basis. In those rare instances where the stakes are especially high, three or four groups might even get together to celebrate
something significant, such as a bicentennial. Think of it. It really
adds up.

Concept: Indulging Audiences.
Many arts organizations have closet artists among their supporters
who might be willing to increase their donations significantly if they
could sing with the opera greats or act with the threatre giants. Sports
promoters indulge the fancies of the dreamers in their audience for
a price, $3,000 or thereabouts, for fantasy camps where overaged
armchair athletes can play ball for a week with their heroes of old.

Suggestion: Why doesn't some enterprising theatre, dance
company, opera group or symphony orchestra establish its own fantasy camp? It can bring back its former artists, for pay, to spend a
week with those members of the audience willing to pay for the opportunity to perform with them. Just envision a "Symphony Fan-
tastique" with amateur cellists, violists and clarinetists performing
with former first-chair players in a new symphony orchestra created
for the occasion. The fantasizers could come home with orchestra
group pictures, a recording in which they're featured, a host of
backstage stories about celebrated conductors, a printed orchestra
program listing their name and the memory of a culminating Saturday night concert before their friends. Perhaps it might even be possible to find a few "make believe" critics (a term that some audiences
might apply to some professionals) who would pay for the privilege
of writing a review of the performance.

214   *Concept:*   Suppressing the Cough.
A continuing problem for many arts groups is finding ways to suppress the coughers in their audiences who disturb performers and other audience members. The cough is so disruptive that Marilyn Horne, during a concert at Colden Center for the Performing Arts at Queens College, held her hand up following a cycle of songs and told the audience to "all cough at once."

Suggestion: Find a cough drop manufacturer to sponsor a "Cough Off" contest. Promise that, with the company's support, an audience will vie for a listing in the *Guiness Book of World Records* for the performance with the longest interval between coughs, thus reaping worldwide publicity for the sponsor. Because audiences love to be a part of history-making events, not only will they strive to suppress themselves throughout the concert, but they will gladly pay well, or more aptly "cough up" the money to be in the audience on such a momentous occasion.

Concept: Restaurant Tie-In.
It's been standard fare for arts organizations to arrange discounts at nearby restaurants for audiences attending their programs. With escalating costs in the arts, however, perhaps it's time for the arts groups to give themselves, rather than their audiences, an extra benefit.

Suggestion: Let the restaurants turn over the discount that normally goes to the diners to the arts group instead, and let this be noted on the check. Most audience members would be happy to patronize restaurants that support performances they'll be seeing, and besides, when you're spending $40 or $50 for dinner, a 10 percent discount doesn't mean very much. But, added up from a number of restaurant diners, it could mean significant dollars for the arts group. And might not restaurateurs be happy not only to attract arts audiences as diners but to be identified as donors instead of just discounters?

Concept: A Sound Idea.
Many young people use portable stereo boxes and stereo car radios to inflict an auditory bombardment of hard rock on pedestrians and motorists.

Suggestion: If several hundred supporters of good music marched downtown with stereo boxes all tuned in to the same good music station, or, better yet, tuned in to the same recording of something shattering such as the "1812 Overture," and were backed up by car stereos playing the same music, the resulting crescendo would strike a chord for good music. It might even be newsworthy.

Concept: Boxed In.
Many professional sports teams reap a giant bonanza from the sale of special corporate "sky boxes" at thousands of dollars each, which include, in addition to comfortable seating for 12 or more, bars, stereos, drop-leaf buffet tables, giant television screens and other amenities. Although boxes are traditional in the arts, they lack the accommodations that "sky boxes" routinely offer, for a price.

Suggestion: Remodel older theatres and build new theatres to include special corporate suites or sky boxes, which can be offered to businesses at reasonable prices, perhaps $10,000 a year. Since many users of the suites won't be watching the action on the stage anyway, good sightlines aren't a concern, and the boxes can be set in areas where they are least expensive to place. With suites equipped with closed-circuit television screens, guests can catch part of a play if they wish. As a special concession to boxholders, and included as a selling lure, their television screens can permit them to "visit" the stars' dressing rooms prior to a performance, and can electronically whisk them backstage afterwards to personally congratulate the performers.

Concept: Reaching New Audiences Through No-Cost
Telemarketing.
As radio's late-night phone-in talk shows attest, there are many lonely people who enjoy speaking to someone about subjects that interest them. Many of them enjoy talking about theatre or music or dance.

Suggestion: Why doesn't some enterprising theatre place ads to recruit insomniacs who enjoy talking to strangers? Operating from their homes and without any pay (although they would receive complimentary tickets to performances), these people would be listed in all the theatre's materials as available for conversation with other insomniacs late at night. Those selected would be free to discuss any

216   subjects that might arise, but they would be asked, because of their love of theatre, to orient the discussion to the programs and performances of the participating theatre and suggest, where possible, that their partners in the dialogue consider subscriptions and donations.

While a list of fanciful suggestions could continue ad infinitum, obviously, suggestions alone won't solve arts funding needs. Ultimately it is the execution that is more important than the idea. As the previous chapters indicate, there is no shortage of good ideas to be gleaned from the experience of hundreds of arts groups over the years. If effective execution accompanies the good ideas, then good funding will follow, and all for the good of the arts.

Over the past two decades America's cultural institutions have broken new ground constantly, and it has never been easy. With limited funding support, low prices despite high quality offerings, and adventurous programming when the familiar and the tried might have continued to attract audiences, the arts have never rested on their laurels. They can't affford to now. They must move ahead and break new ground. In the process, mistakes will be made, certainly, but mistakes are far preferable to inertia. After all, as my old philosopher friend Mae West is reported to have said, "To err is human. But it feels divine."

BIBLIOGRAPHY

Books and Periodicals Worth Reading

Many important books dealing with various aspects of funding and promoting the arts and other nonprofit areas have been published within recent years. While it would be impossible to list all of these, there are certain key works that every arts institution should at least be aware of, if not actually own. I have included in this listing some of those works that I have found essential to my library. Books should be supplemented with regular reading of key periodicals, several of which are also included within the following listing.

BOOKS

Arts Management Reader, The, by Alvin H. Reiss, Marcel Dekker, Inc., 270 Madison Ave., New York, NY 10016, 1979. 704 pp, $32.50. A compendium of articles, case histories and news reports dealing with virtually every aspect of running an arts institution, drawn from material originally published in *Arts Management Newsletter* over a 17-year period.

Arts Money, Raising It, Saving It and Earning It, by Joan Jeffri, Neal-Schuman Publishers, 23 Leonard Street, New York, NY 10013, 1983. 240 pp, $24.95. A look at the financial concerns of arts organizations and suggested ways to meet them.

Auction Book, The, revised edition by Betsy Beatty and Libby Kirpatrick, Auction Press, 96 South Clermont, Denver, CO 80222, 1984. 160 pp, $25. A guide to running charity auctions.

218   *Audience Development: An Examination of Selected Analysis and Prediction Techniques Applied to Symphony and Theatre Attendance in Four Southern Cities*, National Endowment for the Arts Research Division Report, Publishing Center for Cultural Resources, 624 Broadway, New York, NY 10012, 1981. 48 pp, $6. A tool to help groups with audience-building programs.

Board Member's Book, The, by Brian O'Connell, The Foundation Center, 79 Fifth Ave., New York, NY 10003, 1985. 208 pp, $16.95. Advice to boards members, current and potential, on their involvement in nonprofit boards.

Buck Starts Here, The, ed. Robert Karl Monoff. Volunteer Lawyers for the Arts, 1560 Broadway, New York, NY 10036, 1984. 165 pp, $9.95. Transcript of a Volunteer Lawyers for the Arts 1983 conference on profit-making ventures for nonprofit groups.

Community Arts Council Movement: History, Opinions, Issues, by Nina Gibans, Praeger Publishers, 521 Fifth Ave., New York, NY 10175, 1982. 341 pp, $26.95. A detailed examination of a key force in arts funding and promotion, the community arts agency.

Confessions of a Fund Raiser, by Maurice G. Gurin, The Taft Group, 5130 MacArthur Boulevard, NW, Washington DC 20016, 1985. 162 pp, $23.95. A top fund-raiser looks at many of the campaigns on which he's worked, including major drives in the arts.

Culture & Company: A Critical Study of an Improbable Alliance, by Alvin H. Reiss. Twayne Publishers, Division of G.K. Hall & Co. (out of print). A social and economic study of the changing relationship between the arts and business in America.

Directory of Matching Gift Programs for the Arts,, Business Committee for the Arts, 1775 Broadway, New York, NY 10019, 1985. 152 pp, $5. A listing of 255 corporate matching gift programs.

Effective Corporate Fundraising, by W. Grant Brownrigg, American Council for the Arts, 1285 Ave. of the Americas, New York, NY 10019, 1982. 162 pp, $12.95. Strategies for tapping corporate support; includes tables and exhibits.

Emerging Arts, The, by Joan Jeffri, Praeger Publishers, 383 Madison Ave., New York, NY 10017, 1980. 301 pp, $21.95. A close look at the development of smaller, less-established arts organizations.

Enterprise in the Nonprofit Sector, by James C. Crimmins and Mary Kell, Partners for Livable Places, 1429 21st St., NW, Washington, DC 20036, 1983. 141 pp, $7. An exploration of some untapped money sources available to nonprofits.

Finances of the Performing Arts, The, The Ford Foundation, 320 E. 43rd St., New York, NY 10017, 1974. Vol. 1, 259 pp, $5. Vol II, 117 pp, $5. A major survey of the economics of the arts, along with a companion volume surveying arts audiences in 12 cities.

Books and Periodicals Worth Reading

Fund Raising for Museums, by Hedy H. Hartman, Hartman Planning and Development Group, 14645 N.E. 34th St., Bellevue, WA 98007, 1985. 530 pp, $85. A looseleaf workbook on museum fund-raising, with appendices on funding sources for museums.

Grants for Arts & Cultural Programs, Comsearch printout from The Foundation Center, 79 Fifth Ave., New York, NY 10003, 1985. 158 pp, $32. Detailed listings of some 4,500 grants of $5,000 or more made to cultural institutions.

Grants for the Arts, by Virginia White, Plenum Press, 227 W. 17th St., New York, NY 10011, 1980. 360 pp, $19.50. Detailed study of fund-raising and grantsmanship for the arts in the public and private sectors with detailed appendices.

Guide to Corporate Giving, ed. Robert Porter, American Council for the Arts, 570 Seventh Ave., New York, NY 10018, 1983. 592 pp, $30. Key data on the giving policies of more than 700 corporations.

In Art We Trust: Boards of Trustees in the Performing Arts, ed. Robert W. Crawford, Foundation for the Extension and Development of the American Professional Theatre, 165 W. 46th St., New York, NY 10036, 1981. 72 pp, $12.95. A close look at the effective organization and operation of an arts board.

In Search of an Audience, by Bradley G. Morison and Kay Fliehr, Pitman Publishing Corp., 1968 (out of print). 230 pp. Developing an audience for the then-new Tyrone Guthrie Theater.

Market the Arts!, ed. Joseph V. Melillo, Foundation for the Extension and Development of the American Professional Theatre, 165 W. 46th St., New York, NY 10036, 1983. 287 pp, $19.95. An anthology with contributions by arts professionals on devloping effective marketing techniques.

Marketing the Arts, ed. Michael Mokwa, William M. Dawson and E. Arthur Prieve, Praeger Publishers, 521 Fifth Ave., New York, NY 10075, 1980. 286 pp, $23.80. A book based on papers presented at a conference on arts marketing.

Membership Mystique, The, by Richard P. Trenbeth, Fund-Raising Institute, Box 365, Ambler, PA 19002, 1986. 292 pp, $34.95. A detailed examination of virtually every aspect of launching and maintaining a successful membership program.

More Dialing, More Dollars: 12 Steps to Successful Telemarketing, by Michael E. Blimes and Ron Sproat, American Council for the Arts, 1285 Ave. of the Americas, New York, NY 10019, 1985. 93 pp, $7.95. A step-by-step guide to telemarketing.

No Quick Fix (Planning), ed. Frederic B. Vogel, Foundation for the Extension and Development of the American Professional Theatre, 165 W. 46th St., New York, NY 10036, 1985. 96 pp, $9.95. Four contributing arts professionals discuss efficient planning for the arts.

220 *Orpheus in the New World*, by Philip Hart, W.W. Norton & Co., 500 Fifth Ave., New York, NY 10036, 1973. 562 pp, $20. A detailed study of the growth of the symphony orchestra in America, with case studies of specific orchestras.

Partners: A Practical Guide to Corporate Support of the Arts, Alliance for the Arts (formerly Cultural Assistance Center), 330 W. 42nd St., New York, NY 10036, 1982. 112 pp, $8.95. A report, using New York City corporations as examples, that looks at different areas of business support for the arts.

Performing Arts: The Economic Dilemma, by William J. Baumol and William G. Bowen, Twentieth Century Fund, 41 E. 70th St., New York, NY 10021, 1966. 581 pp, $35. A pioneering economic study analyzing the financial concerns of America's performing arts organizations.

Performing Arts: Problems and Prospects, The, Rockefeller Panel Report, McGraw-Hill (out of print). The first major study, with recommendations for action, to focus on the problems of performing arts groups in every discipline.

Professional Performing Arts: Attendance Patterns, Preferences and Motives, Two Volumes, by Arnold Mitchell, Association of College, University and Community Arts Administrators, 6225 University Ave., Madison, WI 53705, Vol. 1, 1984, 134 pp, $40. Vol II, 1985, 156 pp, $40. Both volumes, $65. A key study relating lifestyles and values to arts attendance.

Regional Theatre: The Revolutionary Stage, by Joseph W. Ziegler, Da Capo Press, 227 W. 17th St., New York, NY 10011, 1973. 227 pp, $5.95. A history of the development of the nonprofit regional theatre.

Sold Out: A Publicity and Marketing Guide, by Kate MacIntyre, Theatre Development Fund, 1501 Broadway, New York, NY 10036, 1980. 48 pp, $5. A reference guide to publicity and promotion in the arts.

Subscribe Now! Building Arts Audiences Through Dynamic Subscription Promotion, by Danny Newman, Theatre Communications Group, 355 Lexington Ave., New York, NY 10017, 1977. 304 pp, $10.95. The key step-by-step guide to developing successful subscription campaigns.

Surveying Your Arts Audiences, a National Endowment for the Arts Research Division report, Publishing Center for Cultural Resources, 625 Broadway, New York, NY 10012, 1985. 77 pp, $9. A guide to planning, conducting and interpreting audience surveys.

Theatre Profiles 7, ed. Laura Ross with John Istel, Theatre Communications Group, 355 Lexington Ave., New York, NY 10017, 1986. 327 pp, $18.95. A detailed reference guide to America's nonprofit professional theatres, with a special 25-year retrospective view of theatre by leading artists and commentators.

United Arts Fundraising: 1984 Campaign Analysis, ed. Robert Porter, **221** American Council for the Arts, 1285 Ave. of the Americas, New York, NY 10019, 1985. 80 pp, $20. A detailed statistical study of over 50 united arts fund campaigns in America in 1984.

PERIODICALS

ACA Update, American Council for the Arts, 1285 Ave. of the Americas, New York, NY 10019. Monthly.

ACUCAA Bulletin, Association of College, University and Community Arts Administrators, 6225 University Ave., Madison, WI 53705. Eleven times a year.

American Craft, American Craft Council, 401 Park Ave. South, New York, NY 10016. Bi-monthly.

American Theatre, Theatre Communications Group, 355 Lexington Ave., New York, NY 10017. Monthly.

Art and Artists, Foundation for the Community of Artists, 280 Broadway, New York, NY 10007. Bi-monthly.

Arts Management, 408 W. 57th St., New York, NY 10019. Five times a year.

Arts Reporting Service, 8404 Carderock Drive, Bethesda, MD 20817. Bi-weekly.

ASTC Newsletter, Association of Science-Technology Centers, 1413 K St., N.W., Washington, DC 20005. Bi-monthly.

Aviso, American Association of Museums, 1055 Thomas Jefferson St., NW Washington, DC 20007. Monthly.

BCA News, Business Committee for the Arts, 1775 Broadway, New York, NY 10019. Bi-monthly.

Chamber Music, Chamber Music America, 545 Eighth Ave., New York, NY 10018. Quarterly.

Connections, National Assembly of Local Arts Agencies, 1785 Massachusetts Ave., NW, Washington, DC 20036. Monthly.

Crafts Report, 700 Orange St., Wilmington, DE 19801. Monthly.

Dance Magazine, 33 West 60th St., New York, NY 10023. Monthly.

Fund Raising Management, 224 Seventh St., Garden City, NY 11530. Monthly.

Grantsmanship Center News, 1031 South Grand Ave., Los Angeles, CA 90015. Bi-monthly.

Horizon, 1305 Greensboro Ave., Tuscaloosa, AL 35401. Ten times a year.

Museum News, American Association of Museums, 1055 Thomas Jefferson St. NW, Washington, DC 20007. Six times a year.

222   *Museums' Management & Marketing*, 66 Old Farm Road, Sturbridge, MA 01566-1221. Eight times a year.

NASAA News, National Assembly of State Arts Agencies, 1010 Vermont Ave., NW, Washington, DC 20005. Bi-monthly.

Nonprofit Marketing Insider, P.O. Box 5311, Evanston, IL 60204. Bi-weekly.

Northwest Arts, 538 N.E. 98th St., Seattle, WA 98115. Bi-weekly.

Opera America Bulletin, Opera America, 633 E St., N.W., Washington, DC 20004. Monthly.

Opera News, Metropolitan Opera Guild, 1865 Broadway, New York, NY 10023. Seventeen issues per year.

Special Events Report, 213 W. Institute Place, Chicago, IL 60610. Bi-weekly.

Symphony Magazine, American Symphony Orchestra League, 633 E St., NW, Washington, DC 20004. Bi-monthly.

Theatre Crafts, PO Box 630, Holmes, PA 19043-0630. Ten times a year.

Update, Dance/USA, 633 E St., NW, Washington, DC 20004. Monthly.

Vantage Point, American Council for the Arts, 1285 Ave. of the Americas, New York, NY 10019. Five issues per year (bound into *Horizon* magazine).

INDEX

Index

Index

Index

Printed in the United States
85742LV00004B/287-308/A